Random Notes, Random Lines

D. Sidney-Fryer has written or edited the following books:

Poems in Prose, by Clark Ashton Smith (1965)

Etchings in Ivory, poems in prose by Robert E. Howard (1968)

Other Dimensions, short stories by Clark Ashton Smith (1970)

Songs and Sonnets Atlantean: The First Series (1971)

Selected Poems, omnibus by Clark Ashton Smith (1971)

The Last of the Great Romantic Poets, i.e., Clark Ashton Smith (1973)

Emperor of Dreams: A Clark Ashton Smith Bibliography (1978)

The Black Book of Clark Ashton Smith, his commonplace book (1979)

A Vision of Doom, poems by Ambrose Bierce (1980)

The City of the Singing Flame, tales by Clark Ashton Smith (1981)

The Last Incantation, tales by Clark Ashton Smith (1982)

The Monster of the Prophecy, tales by Clark Ashton Smith (1983)

Strange Shadows: The Uncollected Fiction and Essays of Clark Ashton Smith, edited by Steve Behrends with Donald Sidney-Fryer and Rah Hoffman (1989)

The Hashish-Eater; or, The Apocalypse of Evil, 1922 version, by Clark Ashton Smith (1990; with CD 2008 performed by D. Sidney-Fryer)

As Green as Emeraude: The Collected Poems of Margo Skinner (1990)

The Devil's Notebook (complete epigrams and apothegms) by Clark Ashton Smith, edited with Don Herron (1990)

Songs and Sonnets Atlantean: The Second Series (2003)

Gaspard de la Nuit, by Aloysius Bertrand, translation (2004)

Songs and Sonnets Atlantean: The Third Series (2005)

The Atlantis Fragments: The trilogy of "Songs and Sonnets Atlantean," omnibus (2008, 2009)

The Outer Gate: The Collected Poems of Nora May French (2009)

The Golden State Phastasticks: The California Romantics and Related Subjects: Collected Essays and Reviews, edited with Leo Grin and Alan Gullette (2011)

The Atlantis Fragments, The Novel: The Existing Chronicle: A Vision of the Final Days (2011)

Hobgoblin Apollo: The Autobiography of Donald Sidney-Fryer (2016)

Odds & Ends (poetry, 2016)

The Averoigne Chronicles, by Clark Ashton Smith, edited by Ron Hilger with Donald Sidney-Fryer (2016; rpt. 2021)

West of Wherevermore and Other Travel Writings (2016)

Aesthetics Ho! Essays on Art, Literature, and Theatre (2017)

Ends and Odds (poetry, 2017)

The Case of the Light Fantastic Toe: The Romantic Ballet and Signor Maestro Cesare Pugni—A Chronicle and Source Book (magnum opus, 2018)

West of Wherevermore and Other Essays (second version, 2019) / *The Miscellaneon* (poetry, 2019)

A King Called Arthor and Other Morceaux (2020)

Random Notes, Random Lines

Essays and Miscellanea

Donald Sidney-Fryer

Hippocampus Press

New York

Grateful acknowledgment is extended to the periodicals for first publishing the following items: "A Report from Clark Ashton Smith Country," *Nyctalops* No. 8 (April 1973); Cosmic Troubadours," "The Spenser Experiment," and "An Interview with DSF" by Frederick J. Mayer, *Nyctalops* Nos. 11/12 (April 1976); "An Interview with Donald Sidney-Fryer" by Rick Kleffel, *World Fantasy Convention 2009;* "An Interview with Donald Sidney-Fryer" by Darrell Schweitzer, *New York Review of Science Fiction* (August 2010); "*Dreams and Damnations:* A Review," *Diversifier* No. 14 (May 1976); "Klarkash-Ton and 'Greek'" and "Brave World Old and New: The Atlantis Theme in the Poetry and Fiction of Clark Ashton Smith," from *The Freedom of Fantastic Things,* ed. Scott Connors (Hippocampus Press, 2006); "Continuity via *Songs and Sonnets Atlantean*" and "Gaspard de la Nuit and the Poem in Prose," *Continuity,* ed. Scott Connors (mailing 136 of the Esoteric Order of Dagon Amateur Press Association, Hallowmas 2006); "Letter to the Editor," *Crypt of Cthulhu* No. 110 (Roodmas 2018); "A Poetic Original," *Spectral Realms* (Winter 2019); "A Guidebook for Witches and Warlocks," *Spectral Realms* (Summer 2019). "Providentially Speaking Again," *Dead Reckonings* (Spring 2020).

All other essays and poems appear here for the first time.

Published by Hippocampus Press
P.O. Box 641, New York, NY 10156
www.hippocampuspress.com

Cover artwork and design by Daniel V Sauer, dansauerdesign.com
Hippocampus Press logo designed by Anastasia Damianakos.

First Edition
1 3 5 7 9 8 6 4 2

ISBN 978-1-61498-338-5

To Kathryn Hohlwein with love and gratitude.

Contents

RANDOM NOTES

O Brave New Sphere!

Fantasy and Science Fiction in the ballet theatre of the 1800s.

Ever since his adolescence, when he first experienced in performance the "full-length, evening-long ballets," the Tchaikovsky masterpieces *The Sleeping Beauty* and *Swan Lake* (via the then Sadler's Wells Ballet, and now the Royal Ballet if England), Donald Sidney-Fryer as the author of *The Case of the Light Fantastic Toe*—or for short, *The Big Toe*—has remained profoundly impressed by the strong weird or fantastic elements in the ballet theatre of the 1800s and earliest 1900s, especially as found in *La Sylphide* (1832) on through *Le Miroir magique* (1903). These weird or fantastic elements persisted on through Diaghilev's Ballets Russes (1909-1929).

Before Adolphe Nourrit began a new mythology with his libretto for *La Sylphide*, the ballet-masters regularly relied for their narratives on the older Graeco-Roman mythology, always a rich and varied corpus of myth and legend, of all types of stories. Now a new kind of dance drama evolved, implicating a supernatural being (usually a woman) falling in love with a human mortal (usually a man), and then the conflict engendered between mortality and immortality, with love as the dynamo.

(We should state parenthetically that, while chronicling the early life and career of the composer Cesare Pugni at Genoa, Milan, and Paris—the last-cited in the course of the 1830s—Part One also gives an account of the pre-Romantic Ballet as developed in Italy, above all at Milan.)

During the Romantic Ballet that spanned the nineteenth century on into the early twentieth, the folklore of Northern Europe, no less than the Gothic element per se, came to enrich the dramatic mixture of this new mythology, both in opera and ballet, but in ballet most of all. The innovative productions of ballet at Her Majesty's Theatre in London under ballet-masters Jules Perrot and Paul Taglioni reflect this novel and intoxicating dance drama, even more so than at the then Paris Opéra.

Part Two of *The Big Toe* fully explores both the old and the new mythologies, as exemplified in one big ballet after another: *Alma, Giselle, Ondine, Esmeralda, Eoline, Rosida, Catarina, Lalla Rookh, Coralia (Undine), Fiorita, Electra,* not to mention *La Jolie fille de Gand, La Péri, Le Diable à quatre, La Filleule des fées, Le Corsaire,* and many others. Thus Part Two covers the period from 1841 through 1850 in Western Europe.

In Part Three, under the aegis of the Tsars, Jules Perrot and the composer Cesare Pugni, his chief musical collaborator, move to St. Petersburg in Russia during the mid-century. There they continue in the same rich mythological vein, reproducing and enlarging their productions from Western Europe, creating new big ballets, and founding the traditions that have led to the modern dance drama kept alive in modern, largely Soviet Russia, now the Russian Commonwealth, all of this following in the wake of the Tsarist Empire.

In Part Four *The Big Toe* explores the many long and elaborate productions innovated by Marius Petipa during his long tenure as ballet-master at St. Petersburg from *Pharaoh's Daughter* (1862) through *Le Miroir magique* (1903–1904), but it also deals with other productions on the international (European) ballet scene. The scientific romances by Jules Verne and other authors (the earliest science fiction *en masse*) now came into existence, and flourished across Europe and the Americas, no less than in much of the world overall. This yet new source of mythology apparently lies behind the expansive trilogy or trinity of big balletic extravaganzas engineered by Luigi Manzotti at La Scala in Milan and elsewhere: *Excelsior* (1881), *Amor* (1886), and *Sport* (1897). We place emphasis on the word trinity.

In fact, *Excelsior* has undergone revival in recent years, and not so long ago: a phenomenon as remarkable in its fashion as the retrieval and rebirth of something outlandish and antediluvian, comparable to finding somewhere a live dinosaur, and bringing it back for public exhibition. The revival of *Amor* and *Sport* could not prove any the less extraordinary.

Not only did Marius Petipa uniquely keep alive many masterpieces of the earlier Romantic Ballet but added to this repertoire with one big production after another for almost half a century, not to mention many exemplary miniature ballets in one act, an almost unbelievable catalogue of labor. Because of the literary sources which the dance dramas of the nineteenth century levied for their narrative inspiration, *The Big Toe* is as much a study of literature as it is of ballet, including both fiction and poetry. Let us not forget how literate and patently literary educated people were before movies and television.

D. Sidney-Fryer in the tradition of the pioneer ballet historians Cyril Beaumont and Ivor Guest brings to life the many aspects of the ballet theatre extant in the 1800s, then spilling over into the early 1900s by a decade or more. A greater knowledge of these highly stylized dance dramas, or story ballets, might now become a rich and unique sourcebook of narrative material for readers and fictioneers of the weird and fantastic today, no less than of science fiction or science fantasy. (It is often difficult to draw a line between the last two genres.)

*   *   *

The preceding statement has been prepared by its author, Donald Sidney-Fryer, on behalf of his magnum opus, for dissemination (along with other materials) by Alan Gullette via his website (alan-gullette.com). The said opus has been finally published as of this past summer of 2018 after some twenty-five years of preparation.

The title in full of this opus is *The Case of the Light Fantastic Toe, The Romantic Ballet and Signor Maestro Cesare Pugni, and their survival by means of Tsarist Russia, A chronicle and sourcebook*. The set of the five consecutive books, or volumes, totalling some 3000 (densely printed) pages, is available for purchase from Amazon Books.

The big question after the preceding (the statement and then the note just above) becomes why did we create this opus in the first place, and how did we engineer it into existence. At least with great care and precaution! Like a good general embarking on a major campaign, the author marshals his forces and secures the practical support behind them.

It all goes back to the late 1940's and early 1950s in New Bedford, Massachusetts, during our four years of high school when we took a college-preparatory curriculum, rather than a business or commercial one. The British-born conductor Leopold Stokowski (1882–1977), having assembled a special symphonic ensemble for the recording, conducted these particular forces in what became a pioneering selection of excerpts from Tchaikovsky's music for *The Sleeping Beauty*, as released by RCA Victor on 78 rpm discs. Sometime soon after this, but through Columbia Records on a 33 rpm long-playing disc, André Kostelanetz directing his own long-since established (symphony) orchestra released a major selection of excerpts from that other landmark Tchaikovsky ballet *Swan Lake* in a marvellously electric and exciting performance that caught the attention of Tchaikovsky fans.

We had already become one fan of that composer's music in general, starting in grammar school during a music-appreciation class with the celebrated *Marche slave*, the size or length of a concert or operatic overture. The revelation of this eminent Russian musician as a composer of music for ballet, other than a sequence in disparate excerpts and rather in a more or less continuous sequence or flow, stopped us dead in our tracks, and made us a balletomane even before we had seen any ballet or other professional dance company, except in the form of dance recitals mounted by local dance studios in southeast Massachusetts. At least those were fun and entertaining as the student dancers took their various turns on the stage of some local movie theatre.

Thus energized, if not electrified, by these pioneer recordings, we went to the downtown public library, looked through the card catalogue under the heading of ballet, and found the *Complete Book of Ballets* by Cyril W. Beaumont (Putnam, London, 1937), a big pioneering tome (as we discovered later). At over 1000 pages, recounting the plots of the principal ballets of the 19th and 20th centuries, it seemed the ideal source for someone who had become seriously interested in the subject of the *danse d'école*.

We had communicated some of this basic data about Tchaikovsky and his music for ballet to one of my two Latin teachers in high school who had turned into a firm friend and ally to us. Lo and behold, the then Sadler's Wells Ballet, as promulgated by Sol Hurok and his classical-culture agency, announced a series of performances at the old Boston Opera House in the heart of that old city. Miss Loftus kindly offered to buy us tickets for their performances of the "full-length, evening-long" ballets with Tchaikovsky's music, The *Sleeping Beauty* with Moira Shearer on a Tuesday evening, and *Swan*

Lake with Margot Fonteyn on a Saturday evening.

Taking the train or bus between Boston and New Bedford, we attended both performances, and we became a fervid balletophile from that time onward. Our having witnessed the film *The Red Shoes* sometime before attending these live performances, had surely primed us for a deeper appreciation of them, above all the stellar performances of Shearer and Fonteyn, but not to leave unmentioned the superb choreography by Marius Petipa and Lev Ivanov. Beaumont's enormous tome had already alerted us to the long development in the ballet theatre of the 1800s that preceded and made possible the productions with music by Tchaikovsky and Delibes, when the balletmasters, not the composers of the music, dominated the ballet theatre of their time, as they had for several centuries.

Although somewhat disdained here and there in other books on ballet, Cesare Pugni's name seemed to crop up almost anywhere in Beaumont's tome. This disdain piqued my curiosity, especially as mixed-in with considerable praise from the period of the Romantic Ballet, which confused the entire issue. How could a composer praised at one time, then later become nothing less than scorned?! Tastes changed, I guessed.

We slowly began our research in books and periodicals during the 1950s, and when by the late 1970s, we had amassed enough materials, we began the organization and writing of our monograph in 1980, and more or less completed it by 2000. Much additional research continued behind the scenes as conducted both in person at various libraries or by professional researchers both here and abroad.

Subsequently, starting around the midpoint of the second decade of the 21st century, Alan Gullette—as my skilled computer-specialist collaborator (who had already scanned some ten or twelve of my manuscripts, that is, into E-documents)—now scanned the entire 5000-page typescript into an E-text, which then reduced to the 3000 pages of the printed book, or rather set of five books. We the author also proofed the sheets or pages before their eventual book publication.

Such is the saga behind our own balletic saga, and how it came into print. How many layers or phases of preparation had to precede the eventual book appearance! Also as part of the creative saga we should give a little of the practical background of how the author had to arrange his life and livelihood so he could spend the time needed in organizing and writing the magnum opus.

Once he moved back to the Auburn-Sacramento area, the author maintained his part-time cleaning business (he was both the boss and the only worker) between two sets of clients in San Francisco and Sacramento. He gradually phased out the customers in San Francisco, and increased those in Sacramento; and by 1980 or so, he and a housemate had established themselves in an unique attic flat above a two-story Victorian. There he resided while working part-time at cleaning for some lovely customers. The Victorian house stood in a vicinage of the same vintage in downtown Sacramento.

And there he lived while he completed most of his magnum opus until his dear friend Rah Hoffman asked the author to live with him in Westchester north of LAX, the main L.A. airport, LAX by the sea. In this new residence, to which he was no stranger, the author Donaldo completed the oversized typescript of *The Case of the Light Fantastic Toe*, alias *The Big Toe*. It had resulted in a much bigger and more extended project than at first anticipated, an understatement.

In mixed extenuation and endorsement of his own work the author not only acknowledges his paramount indebtedness to certain chief books by Cyril Beaumont and Ivor Guest for much material but much more for their direct inspiration to create his own history. He soon discovered why no one else had attempted an overall historical account of the ballet from the 1820s to the 1920s. He decided to use the life and career of Cesare Pugni as the chief key to and catalyst for the author's investigation and then correlation of the balletic activities in Western Europe with those in Tsarist Russia. But he also added much from his own research or from that which he himself sponsored by means of other people, hired researchers or people working in libraries here and abroad.

Letter to the Editor, *Crypt of Cthulhu*

Noble Hierophant of the Horde, Avé

I recently had the pleasure of a visit from Scott Connors, among other guests, who kindly gave me a copy of issue number 108, for Hallowmas 2017. Congratulations on starting *Crypt of Cthulhu* in 1981, and continuing it into late 2017! That is 36 years, a long time for a specialist magazine.

I recall Rah Hoffman's collection of the magazine piled up neatly in a corner of the hallway between the two bedrooms, leading to the bathroom between them.

I know that you sometimes feature news of Ashton Smith and his publications, even if not all books are offered for review, for obvious reasons of expense. The publisher does not need the reviews, having his own special public who buys the books on general repute of the given press.

Such seems to be the case of Jerad Walters and the Centipede Press, who brought out *The Averoigne Chronicles* in a stunning *édition de luxe* during 2016 (with remarkable art by David Ho), ably edited by Ronald S. Hilger. Donald M. Grant originally accepted it c. 1990, but after his demise his partner Robert Wiener delayed its publication for years for no apparent reason. Ron finally took the MS. back, and within a few years Jerad Walters brought it out at long last.

More recently, this past summer (2017), Mnémos in Paris published a massive 3-volume set of Ashton Smith's fiction (in a handsome and sturdy slipcase). Volume I contains the Zothique and Averoigne stories; Volume II, Hyperborea and Poseidonis; Volume III, Autres Mondes (Other Worlds). All these volumes have maps of those realms, and all of them feature some quite original art by Santiago Caruso. This edition is even more deluxe than Jerad's Averoigne book; it is the fanciest ever done for Ashton Smith.

Stéphanie Chabert shepherded the whole project through to publication, an enormous task, with contributions from many people, over 3000! It evidently represented an ideal project for her. She achieved it magnificently.

Especially noteworthy are the translations done by a different translator for each volume. Each one did it not only as a commission but out of love for the project. Amazingly, they not only managed to preserve the sense and the characteristic tone, but even the complex prose rhythms in an equivalence of French, something much harder to do, given the different accentuation between French and English. No pun, but French remains the lingua franca of many cultivated people, especially in Europe, which bodes well for the dissemination of these volumes and of Ashton Smith's name.

Bard of the Hyborian Age

Robert E. Howard: A Literary Biography, by David C. Smith. Pulp Hero Press, 280 pp. (including index). Foreword by Rusty Burke. Afterword by Fred C. Adams, Jr., Ph.D.

In saluting the publication of David C. Smith's literary biography, we can do no better than to quote the piece of poetry artfully cited by the biographer himself before the final chapter, sic:

> The pulse of war and passion of wonder,
>> The heavens that murmur, the sounds that shine,
> The stars that sing and the loves that thunder,
>> The music burning at heart like wine,
> An armed archangel whose hands raise up
>> All senses mixed in the spirit's cup
> Till flesh and spirit are molten in sunder—
>> These things are over, and no more mine.
>>> Swinburne, from "The Triumph of Time."

Although other biographies or biographical accounts of R.E.H. exist, the need and importance of a literary biography become at once apparent, particularly to counter the negative assessment of him as a writer by such an eminent and qualified critic like S. T. Joshi as highlighted in the final chapter by David Smith, and we cite the latter's quotation:

> Although many of Howard's stories were written purely for the sake of cash, his own views do emerge from them. The simple fact is, however, that those views are not of any great substance or profundity, and that Howard's style is crude, slipshod, and unwieldy. It is all just pulp—although, perhaps, a superior grade of pulp than the average.

As David ably points out, "Howard's own stories were often written with a sophisticated appreciation of poetic diction as well as the elevated use of language. And to say that Howard's views are not of any great substance or profundity is to mischaracterize his work, demonstrably so."

We cite as our own best Bible of the weird and fantastic anent R.E.H. a text that we bought during our military service in the middle 1950s: *Skull-Face and Others* as edited by August Derleth, owner-editor of Arkham House. It was published as an omnibus volume during 1946. For some reason we did not read it then and there but waited to do so during the early to mid-1960s.

Thus in D. C. Smith's monograph we have yet another serious re-counting of the life and career of R.E.H., the third of the so-called Three Musketeers of *Weird Tales* (per L. Sprague de Camp) as well as of other pulp-paper magazines. It is an odd coincidence, but worthy to be mentioned overtly (even if seldom done so in print), that Howard Phillips Lovecraft and Robert Ervin Howard share one of their triple-decker names, H.P.L. as his first name and R.E.H. as his last name. (Spiritual consanguinity?!) They had much more in common, but their historic and family backgrounds could not have turned out more differently.

The biographer lays out Howard's life and career, his immediate family background, in a clear and elegant manner from the Preface and then through all the other chapters: 1. Beginnings / 2. *Weird Tales* / 3. The Poet / 4. God's Angry Man / 5. Worlds within Worlds / 6. Outremer / 7. Certain Compensations / 8. The Hyborian Age / 9. Splashing the Field / 10. "All fled—all done" / 11. Legacy. As the narrative unfolds, David pinpoints Howard's creativity as it evolves relative to certain events in that evolving life and career.

Even if we have read other accounts of R.E.H., it has proven an invigorating and enlightening experience to refresh our memory and general cognizance of Howard and his literary output by means of David's astute biography, but with the extra depth and range conferred by a specifically literary approach. It reminds us that R.E.H. was an instinctive artist in words. That his *oeuvre* has now touched the lives of so many people outside the world of fantasy and science fiction, or science fantasy, has become a convincing and adequate proof of his genius.

That Howard very much lives in the here and now proper to his own historic period, we find undisputed evidence in his bodybuilding, in his system of personal hygiene. He worked hard at his boxing, at which he became fairly proficient, never mind growing up in the midst of the Texas oil boom of the 1920s and 1930s: that dangerous, violent, and organized chaos! What a contrast to poor H.P.L., living amid and reared by his mother and his two aunts, rarely coming into contact with nature and the outside world, or with pure physicality!

The biographer brilliantly registers the differences and similarities between Lovecraft and Howard in Chapter 7, "Certain Compensations." The great thing that they had in common inheres in their love and intimate knowledge of poetry (particularly in British and American English). R.E.H. remained the poet from the start of his creative life until the end; not only in his poetry, but in his stories long and short. As part of his experimentation, he created the outstanding sequence of prose-poems "Etchings in Ivory" (written around 1928, per Glenn Lord). They run parallel with certain of his tales, especially "The Mirrors of Tuzun Thune," but many of his stories take rank as extended poems in prose. This poetic power, so hard to define objectively, adds immeasurably to most of his fiction. Howard is always in dead earnest, and like Bierce or Ashton Smith, takes no prisoners, or but rarely.

Another false impression that we had, which the biographer adroitly dispels, is that, even if he had some college, he turned out as much of an autodidact as Lovecraft and Ashton Smith. Wherever he lived or went, whether at home or at college, R.E.H. gathered a circle of like-minded friends around him.

Before we close, we must make a direct mention of something that has bothered us and other sensitive readers, and for some extended time, who admire Howard's work—that major and essential component of his writing, the violence in his fiction. R.E.H. discusses this ingredient or component in his letter of August 1932 to H.P.L.

> One problem in writing bloody literature is to present it in such a manner as to avoid a suggestion of cheap blood-and-thunder melodramatics— which is what some people will always call action, regardless of how realistic or true it is. So many people never have any in their placid lives, and therefore, can't believe that it exists anywhere or in any age. A huge mistake on their part. [Amen!]

But, alas, violence does exist and always will, whether we like it or not, that it should be so. The human race carefully shields its eyes from directly looking at it. Apart from the arts and sciences, its recorded history is often a catalogue of horrors and atrocities. Howard's poetry and prose remind us of the violence that we perpetrate or have perpetrated. David Smith does us much good by reminding us of this via his judicious and balanced literary biography. As an especially lovely touch David has dedicated his monograph to the pioneer R.E.H. scholar, sic: "In Memory of Glenn Lord."

The Emperor of Dreams
Comes into His Own

The Emperor of Dreams. A Clark Ashton Smith documentary creat-
ed by Darin Coelho, Placerville, California, recently premiered in the
Northwest and the Northeast, U.S., during October 2018, both under
the sponsorship of Derrick Hussey.

Lovecraft Film Festival, Portland, Oregon, 5–7 October 2018, the
showing of the C.A.S. film, 1:30–3:30 PM, Sunday afternoon, 7 Octo-
ber 2018.

Cinemonde film series at the Roger Smith Hotel, mid-Manhattan,
New York City, the showing of the same film, Thursday evening, 8:00
to 10:00 p.m., 25 October 2018.

(For Darinho.)

During the last three or four years Darin Coelho, bookseller online
and at the Bookery (a wonderful bookstore by the way), Placerville,
has worked with much skill, assiduity, and love on what has turned
into a remarkable film on the poet and fictioneer, one C. Ashton
Smith of Auburn, California. Darin achieved this just in time in terms
of the CAS-informed people interviewed (some dozen or half-dozen
individuals). I cite some of their names at random, and as an old
man's memory permits: Ronald Scott Hilger, Scott Connors, Bill
Dorman (one of Smith's three stepchildren), the Auburn artist who
goes by the simple, or single, name of Skinner, Harlan Ellison, etc.
(including the author of this report).

   Thanks to Darin I had witnessed a DVD that he sent me, but sans
music and sans titles, somewhat earlier. The film like the DVD runs
not quite two hours. Instead of running one interview following an-
other *en bloc*, Darin interweaves the interviews as the subject changes,
or aspects of the topic change. Those interviewed who seem to make
quite a good showing include Bill Dorman, Ron Hilger, Scott Con-
nors, Skinner, and above all the late Harlan Ellison, who did not live
long enough to see the film, or its release, alas!

We know from his letter-memoir included in the CAS bibliography *Emperor of Dreams* (Donald M. Grant, 1978) that Smith exercised a profound influence on Ellison at his then age of fifteen. He discovered in August Derleth's science-fiction anthology *The Other Side of the Moon* the echt-Smithian story "The City of the Singing Flame" (coupled with "Beyond the Singing Flame"). Ellison read the novella more than a hundred times, and as he confesses in his letter-memoir, the story uniquely decided him to become a science fiction author. This he did, and quite successfully, enriching himself and his many readers.

However, in the CAS film, Ellison really goes to bat for him and his *oeuvre*, even more so than in the letter-memoir. As the patient chronicler of Smith's life and career (per my CAS bibliography) from 1893/1910 up to his death and its aftermath following that through 2016 with *The Averoigne Chronicles;* even I, one Donald Sidney-Fryer, remain amazed at what Harlan has opined and formulated about one C. Ashton Smith. Inspired by his initial immersion in CAS at the age of fifteen, Harlan came to know very well the meaning and value of words, even if as a writer he is very different from Smith in style and perspective.

For me personally the CAS phenomenon has now come full circle. My involvement in things Smithian began in the middle 1950s and has extended into the middle 2010s, c. 1956–c. 2016. When I began my serious interest in his work, Smith had become relatively little known apart from the early (Northern) Californian poetry circles and the connoisseurs of the fiction published in the early fantasy and science-fiction magazines of the 1920s and 1930s. Wherever he was known, however, he was highly regarded. By now he has at least achieved serious cult status, and possibly even more than that.

Smith has now gained outstanding aficionados in Britain and throughout the English-speaking world, that is, the extensive linguistic territory dominated by the British Commonwealth (in one sense still the British Empire) and by the U.S. The English at any rate seem to have claimed him and his writings as one of their own, which in one sense he is, and widely translated, has admirers in many other languages. Since about 2000, with the founding and prospering of Hippocampus Press under Derrick Hussey (New York City), Smith appears to have discovered, and/or to have founded, a veritable school of poets throughout the English-speaking world, or poets who have felt profoundly the influence of his poetry and his poetic vision (not to mention his poetic fiction), strongly cosmic-astronomic in its inspiration, but different in kind and in style from that of the established fantasy and science fiction of today.

His many and often distinctive stories continue in publication and republication as included in anthologies and no less than in fiction collections uniquely devoted to his work. His unique poems in prose continue to attract readers and serious students to his overall *oeuvre*. Thanks above all to S. T. Joshi and Derrick Hussey, Smith's complete poetry and translations of poetry (mostly from French and Spanish) have seen ideal hardcover publication, as have the poetry and poetic dramas of Smith's mentor George Sterling. Among poets in English not otherwise universally recognized or acknowledged, this complete republication must be signalized as an unique and paramount accomplishment.

When I began my serious investigation of Smith and his output back in the middle to latter 1950s, I had very little companionship in my particular endeavor. My situation was parallel to that of Glenn Lord, who also was starting about the same time as myself his own serious investigation and promulgation of the prose and poetry of the Texan author, Robert Ervin Howard. Glenn and I could at least give each other help and encouragement as fellow scholars and aficionados, even if dedicated to the separate cause of two different writers. Now new scholars have come along to take over these labors and endeavors.

For me personally the Smith documentary, creatively and adroitly put together by Darin Coelho, caps the climax (as it were) of things related to this great poet. I remain profoundly grateful to him for what he has managed to do for Smith via this unique film. On an even more personal note I wish to express my gratitude to Darin for dedicating the film "For Donaldo," something I did not discover until I saw the completed documentary in Manhattan on Thursday, 25 October 2018, something that took me completely by surprise, and deeply moved me, at the end credits.

With the sponsorship and sale of this CAS film in DVD form, and with the publication of his complete poetry and poetry translations (not to mention that of the complete poetry and poetic dramas of his mentor, George Sterling)—quite apart from his espousal of Lovecraft and his output, especially the ongoing series of his voluminous letters—Derrick Hussey has probably done more than not only anyone else for the cause of Smith's writings but just as much for the cause of modern imaginative literature, at least in the last two decades or so. We can say the same for the modern, even if largely tradition-styled, poetry that Derrick publishes by other and much younger poets.

N.B./P.S. We wish to thank the people in charge of the film series at the Roger Smith Hotel in mid-Manhattan for accepting on behalf of its East Coast première Darin Coelho's CAS film, and as part of their ongoing film series. The people in charge did the hosting in exceptional style with very good *hors d'oeuvres* (a meal in itself) and an open bar; the event took place on the hotel's topmost (enclosed) floor. The fifty or so people who showed up (by invite, it would seem) came from all over greater New York City, and appeared to be both moved and impressed by the documentary. A social hour preceded and then succeeded the official showing. Everyone in attendance appeared to have a grand and edifying time of it. We should mention that Donald Sidney-Fryer as the senior CASophile spoke briefly after the film, and moreover by request.

Dreams and Damnations: A Review

RICHARD L. TIERNEY. *Dreams and Damnations.* The Strange Company, Madison, WI, 1975, [30] pp.

Anyone familiar with fanzines devoted to fantasy and science fiction will appreciate what a neat and quite imitable poetic formula H. P. Lovecraft bequeathed in his sonnet-sequence *Fungi from Yuggoth.* Considering that he was at best a "minor poet" (if that former distinction between "major " and "minor " still possesses any validity), old H. P. L. has exerted a far greater influence on other poets and versifiers especially in the field of fantasy and science fiction than what would seem warranted by the rather small quantity of poetry that he left behind him at his death. We deliberately ignore here for the most part that huge mass of verse he indited largely in imitation of eighteenth-century poetic forms and styles. August Derleth undoubtedly gathered together the best of Lovecraft 's poetry in the slender but still substantial volume *Collected Poems* (1963), And as he perceptively points out in his Foreword to that collection, this Lovecraftian imitation of eighteenth-century verse when experienced in small doses may seem attractive enough in its own way (surely always gracious and polished) but when experienced all in a mass, it does indeed become deadly dull, as dull as most of the tremendous amount of satirical verse once assiduously penned by Ambrose Bierce.

Fungi from Yuggoth, however, is altogether a different and a better order of things. These sonnets are distinctly Lovecraftian, as much so as the best of his prose fictions. There is the same atmosphere of mingled wonder and horror, the same strong narrative sense, the same documentary-like detail, and the same apocalyptic ending. In addition there is the same potent aesthetic sense, and that same curious mixture of nostalgia and continuity. Since their first publication in part and in whole, these sonnets have inspired a host of imitations, some quite good, some indifferent, and some nothing less than wretched and inept, but always demonstrating the undeniable vitality of the poetic formula crystallized in Lovecraft's original sequence,

But some of the poems done in the Yuggothian tradition have at their best risen above mere competent imitation, and have become original work in their own right. Certainly this is true of the present volume, to wit, Richard L. Tierney's first collection of sonnets and other imaginative poems . Manifestly he writes in the Yuggothian tradition but he uses it for his own ends and continues it in his own way. In fact, until the publication of this book, Mr. Tierney had only one serious competitor. Now he has none.

The one serious competitor was none other than the chief editorial consultant for Ballantine Books' Adult Fantasy Series, to wit, Lin Carter. This reviewer has heard and seen some harsh criticism of Carter, and candor compels him to admit that some of it at best seems justified. However, to be perfectly fair, various acknowledgments must be made on Carter's behalf. First and foremost, he has rendered invaluable service to the cause of contemporary fantasy by his editorship for Ballantine Books, whereby meritorious older works have been republished and meritorious newer works have been published for the first time; the scope of such popular distribution is much greater than what one might otherwise reckon, since Ballantine paperbacks appear in all manner of places: bookstores, drugstores, pool halls, etc. Secondly, he has pioneered a number of important surveys—e.g., *Imaginary Worlds, A Look Behind the Cthulhu Mythos*, etc.—These which must rank as useful and sometimes unique syntheses, whatever their faults or deficiencies: superficial scholarship, something considerably less than 100% accuracy, over-facile and often erroneous assumptions, etc. Thirdly, as a poet of undoubted gifts and considerable technical expertise, he has found his own true creative métier. Fourthly, he is a writer of prose fantasies, some of which must surely be accounted as amusing and entertaining, especially the shorter works. (We pass in silence over his Robert E Howard and Clark Ashton Smith pastiches.—These last are particularly misguided as well as such longer works as his *Thongor of Lemuria* series which reflect little credit on the fantasy field over-all, and even less credit on Mr. Carter as the author.) The preceding is by no means a complete catalog of Carter's abilities and achievements.

But it is as a poet that Lin Carter has made his greatest mark in terms of his own creativity, and his finest work to date has plainly proven to be in the Yuggothian tradition, to wit, his collection of *Dreams from R'lyeh*, an obvious imitation—in the best sense of that word of Lovecraft's original sonnet-sequence.

However, to judge by these poems and similar ones in the Yuggothian tradition published elsewhere, Mr. Carter is clearly no match for Mr. Tierney, despite his obvious talents and gifts. What then precisely does make the difference between these two contenders for the Yuggothian crown of bay-leaves commingled with fungi? Technically they appear to be more or less on a par, and we are sure they both have spent equal time in polishing and repolishing their respective verses.

Anyone who has attempted the forms and techniques of the traditional prosody will appreciate from first-hand experience the dedication, the study and the often unremitting labor necessary to turn a decent piece of verse. And it is manifest to anyone who has made the effort to follow Mr. Carter 's career from his beginnings in fanzines, and such early collections of verse, as *Sandalwood and Jade*, that in terms of his over-all output he has lavished the most thought, the most care, the most serious intentions on his poetry. That which then does make all the difference in the world, and gives the edge to Mr. Tierney, is the difference discernible in their respective attitudes (as far as may be gleaned from a close consideration of their published work).

In Mr. Carter 's earliest work one could perceive a genuine sense of wonder, and a clear-cut respect for the ideal of wonder, as well as a definite commitment to the cause of fantasy that is, imaginative literature as its own most serious end. As his work has matured in technique and gained in sheer professionalism, there has unfortunately been revealed a concomitant decline in Mr. Carter's aforesaid sense of wonder and in his *respect* for wonder. For a professional writer of fantasy, such a decline forms a tragic loss. If such a writer cannot himself be inspired by an exalted sense of wonder and marvel, how can he expect to stir the reader's emotions, and to liberate his imagination?

On the other hand we can sense in *Dreams and Damnations*— beyond mere intellection and sophistication, beyond mere sterile reason, beyond all "reasonable" bounds—a vast and profound sense of wonder, an intuitive "primitiveness" and intensity, a completely original and exalted quality of liberation. There is evident in this collection an absolute sincerity, almost to the point of desperation or insanity. We turn from the book at hand with the conviction that creating this poetry was a matter of life or death—a matter of dead-earnest seriousness—for Mr. Tierney. We do not feel such a sense of dedication in Mr. Carter's work, no matter how good it may appear in purely technical aspects. In sheer imaginative power, therefore, Mr. Tierney surpasses Mr. Carter.

Richard L. Tierney in his first book has provided a rich and relevant feast for the lovers of imaginative literature, and easily deserves his Yuggothian crown of bay-leaves commingled with fungi. We have now no hesitation in conceding him this unique honor, and we urge all, sincere collectors to obtain this book for their libraries. This is some of the finest original work done in the tradition of Lovecraft's own cosmic lyricism since the death of the master himself, and we can give no better recommendations.

The Shadow of the Unattained

The Shadow of the Unattained: The Letters of George Sterling and Clark Ashton Smith, edited by David E. Schultz and S. T. Joshi. Hippocampus Press, New York City, 2005, 342 pp., $20.00.

The publication of the complete extant correspondence between Sterling and his chief protégé Ashton Smith, a correspondence covering the long span of the sixteen significant years from January of 1911 on into November of 1926—an exchange of letters with other papers as extant in the Berg Collection of the New York Public Library (facing east onto Fifth Avenue in Manhattan) since c. 1957–1958, certainly the prime factor in the fact of its existence, or survival, and in its accessibility, rather than in the hands of some private guardian or collector—marks an epoch in the annals of the California Romantics, that stalwart group of independently minded poets and writers including Ambrose Bierce at its head, no less than Sterling and Ashton Smith, as well as Nora May French, among other less eminent figures. This volume makes a worthy companion-piece to the *Selected Letters of Clark Ashton Smith,* edited by the same David E. Schultz in collaboration with Scott Connors (and in a completely worthy way), published by Arkham House in 2003. Just as that volume gives us an excellent over-all perspective on Smith's career from 1911 until his death in 1961, so then does this compilation grant us a detailed account of Smith's early life and career as a poet above all else.

The task of preparing such a volume (with all that such implies in terms of information-gathering and annotation of persons, places, etc.) represents a colossal piece of work in its own right, a task assumed only in the long term. In this as in their other collaborations of a similar nature Schultz and Joshi have covered themselves with glory. They deserve every praise for making this material available in such an exemplary manner. So does Derrick Hussey, the owner and editor of Hippocampus Press, for bringing the volume out. Doubtlessly, reasons of economy dictated the necessity to print this book as laid out on 342 pages and at 50 lines per page more or less. For those readers who have problems perceiving small type, we recommend a pair of reading spectacles.

However, at six inches in width by nine inches in height by three quarters of an inch in thickness, it remains a big book—as realized in the trade paperback format that has now become the norm—and what is more, a handsome book, the cover over-all designed by Barbara Briggs Silbert. The cover art itself, painted by Philip Fuller after photographs, shows the two poets on the beach at Carmel against a somewhat cloudy firmament at sunset (extreme center right) not far from the ocean lying just beyond. Sterling, looking rather big and burly with slouch hat, sits in a rustic arm chair of wood (center right), and the much younger Smith, bare-headed, sits on some piece of rock (center left) just next to Sterling's right. As both a realistic and a symbolic depiction of these two very close friends, observed here dramatically at the very edge of the western littoral of North America, and likewise at seemingly the very end of a great tradition in romantic poetry, Mr. Fuller's painting carries a heavy cargo of emotional weight.

Furthermore, it underlines with considerable poignancy Joshi and Schultz's own statement that appears almost at the very end of their intelligent and very well informed introduction, a statement that deserves emphatic quotation: "Smith has many devotees [. . .] but most fair-minded readers would judge his poetry to be his supreme aesthetic accomplishment; and in this body of work he gained so much from his mentor of fifteen years that, however much he surpassed his teacher, the two forever will be linked as a pair of writers who carried imaginative poetry to its outermost limits of expression." To this forthright statement we can only add a strong and ever-echoing *Amen!*

For anyone already familiar with these letters exchanged between the two poets, and cognizant of their value, such a pleasure is it to be able to peruse and study the correspondence in the privacy of one's own home, rather than in the Berg Collection itself with all the bother and expense of needing to travel to New York City to do so. But first a few caveats are in order. Smith negotiated the sale of these papers with the New York Public Library in the mid-1950s, but only after the Bancroft Library had expressed its lack of interest in buying and/or preserving this great pile of letters and related materials.

And thereby hangs a little tale as related to me by Clark and Carol Smith during my first visit to their home in Pacific Grove during August of 1958. The 1950s doubtlessly represented the nadir of Smith's career in an outward sense. Fantasy and science fiction had not yet claimed the larger audience that it would somewhat later in the latter

1900s; and Smith's earlier fame as an extraordinary poet, as well as Sterling's own favorite protégé, roughly for the period 1910–1930, had become almost forgotten except perhaps to California literary specialists. The Bancroft Library at the University of California in Berkeley was not the same institution that it has become today. Whether conducted through letters or in person or both, the Bancroft granted Smith quite an insulting interview or audience. They not only refused the sale, but they did so in an especially insulting fashion, implying to Smith's face that such a correspondence could have little or no value if it involved a second-rate or little-known, merely California, poet like Smith. Although he could encompass the refusal and the snub, the further insult that the refusal represented profoundly hurt Smith's feelings after the initial shock and anger.

The New York Public Library purchased the letters and other papers for the sum of more than $2,000 (not such a small one for that period of the Cold War), and thus California as his native state lost the chance of keeping this valuable correspondence within its own borders. However, before he had the box of materials shipped east to the Berg Collection from his then home that he shared in Pacific Grove with his wife, the former Carol Jones Dorman, Smith went through the letters and papers, resolutely removing certain poems and letters of a particularly sensitive (biographical) nature, as connected to certain events and individuals, that he did not wish just anyone to see, statistically only a small fraction of what we have in the present volume. Presumably these items as carefully deleted from the correspondence by Smith himself, he may have destroyed, or they may still exist somewhere among the effects preserved by CASiana Enterprises, Inc., the literary estate of Clark Ashton Smith.

Another and more important caveat. Although published collections of personal epistles, especially as deriving from writers themselves, have been appearing now for hundreds of years, the epistolarians themselves rarely, or never, had any intention of publishing them, or of their being published. Made available posthumously, such collections presumably justify their existence because of the light, the understanding, that they bring in elucidating the private lives and struggles of the individuals involved. However much they may seem validated or self-validating on that level, strictly speaking, such collections at their worst represent, of course, an unethical invasion of the private lives under scrutiny, and do not lend themselves to the

common methods of literary criticism, since they came into being as
something other than finished creative work intended for public as-
similation, a distinction increasingly obscured in our day and age of
autobiographically based or debased art and of personal gossip-
mongering of the most intimate or trivial nature. Therefore, although
we may prepare or peruse such collections of letters, we have no gen-
uine right to complain that one or both of the letter-writers under dis-
cussion may seem on occasion less than sympathetic. Letters are
private communication, and in them the epistolarians have every right
to express themselves however they wish, to rant and to rave, and to
let off steam in general. On one level they represent a private steam-
valve, and one that deserves every respect.

One final caveat. We learn, just after Joshi and Schultz's introduc-
tion, that sometime after their acquisition by the Berg Collection
many letters and related papers became separated from each other,
thereby making the mutual interrelationship among them sometimes
or often conjectural, and much less easy to understand. It is a shame
that the separation had to happen. However, for anyone familiar with
the poems of Sterling and Smith in depth, this disjunction should
cause no serious problem, and it does not really impede the general
understanding of the ongoing lives and creativity of the two poets,
among many other people mentioned in these letters as covered by
the years 1911–1926.

Having made these strategic caveats, what then exactly do we learn
from these letters? We learn a great amount in detail about the state
of poetry and other literature, together with much else, that was taking
place in the wide-ranging Anglophone world whether British or
American, but above all how they related to Smith and Sterling in
their private and not so private lives. That "along with much else," of
course, soon develops into the rather more interesting part. Unlike
the letters exchanged between Sterling and Mencken, say, where the
constant mention of drinking and womanizing by both men rapidly
becomes an outright bore, this correspondence plainly shows the el-
der poet at his best, as the serious artist that in fact he was, not less
than the fascinating personality and indeed the life of the party, a role
that he often played so well that many friends of his often forgot that
Sterling always remained quite the serious artist from the latter 1890s
until his death. He also had in general a hell of a good time, both be-
fore and after the great San Francisco earthquake and fire of 1906.

Socially Smith and Sterling make quite a congruent as well as contrasting pair, and not just because of the quarter century in age between them, albeit an important factor. Sterling was born in 1869, thus at the very heart of the Victorian Age (1837–1901), whereas the younger Smith was born in 1893, thus towards its tail's-end, even if in a sense the Victorian Age continued on into the Edwardian period following it (1901–1910). However neither Sterling nor Smith qualify as typical Victorians in any way, just the opposite! Whether on the east coast or the west coast, there was hardly an eminent person or personality that Sterling did not know, and whose company he did not enjoy. What a contrast to Smith! Unaccustomed to cities or to having other people around him (apart from his older than average parents), Smith led a very quiet life with his nuclear family just outside Old Auburn, a life just above survival; but somehow they managed to exist thanks to both their own efforts and the assistance given them by friends and neighbors. Sterling on the other hand often led quite a flamboyant life whether in Carmel or San Francisco, whose antics found regular chronicling in the local newspapers and magazines. Charismatic and handsome, the elder poet almost always made colorful and interesting news.

When they began writing to each other, Sterling thanks to his first two collections (no less than to the controversy that swirled around him after the magazine publication in 1907 of "A Wine of Wizardry" as trumpeted by Sterling's mentor Bierce) had established himself as the unofficial poet laureate not only of San Francisco but of the entire west coast of the U.S.A. Albeit immensely gifted, Smith was just beginning as a poet of quite an unusual kind, somewhat like Sterling, but which would eventually elect him to the Brotherhood of the Unearthly Imagination—in the not inconsiderable and influential opinion of critic and connoisseur Benjamin De Casseres, as published in a special flyer in late 1937 by the Futile Press under the title "Clark Ashton Smith, Emperor of Shadows." In the short term, or at least no later than late 1926, it would also elect Smith to the eminence of "Emperor of Dreams" per the young Donald Wandrei, an early convert to the cause of Smith's poetry.

By the time of his death, in late 1926, Sterling had published some dozen and a half volumes of poetry, including a dozen or more collections or separate poems done up as little books, four poetic dramas, and a bad imitation of the early narratives in verse by Robinson Jeffers. (Incidentally, Sterling became the first major champion of Jeffers' first characteristic work, as testified by the last book of Sterling's in production while he still was alive: *Robinson Jeffers: The Man and the Artist.*) Sterling had become profoundly dissatisfied with the kind of lyric and other poetry that he could best create. He had not yet found a new mode or a new subject, although we must applaud him for trying something radically different, even if he had to borrow the modus operandi from another, superficially more modern poet. As the achievement for the period of 1903–1926, representing some dozen or more years of more or less uninterrupted work, Sterling's output remains distinctive and impressive. One would not mistake it for anyone else's literary product (as pointed out by Jeffers himself in the mid-1930s). In depth and range, in imaginative brilliance, as well as in mythopoeical quality, Sterling's output stands almost alone. If we had no Clark Ashton Smith, George Sterling would stand in his place.

With few lapses the elder poet remained faithful to the classico-romantic legacy that he had inherited, to the high technical standards of the 1800s, but far more important, to the highest and noblest ideal-ism of the same century, and fortunately not to the spurious gentility of the Gilded Age. But we must not fail to state: Sterling had added something that had not existed before him, not only deriving from the California world extant from the 1890s on into the 1920s, but just as much from the scientific thought of his time, which certainly did not move in the same channels as the genteelism of the late 1800s and early 1900s. This new poetic element or quantity took the shape of a startling and implicitly revolutionary cosmic-astronomic-mindedness, together with a certain cosmic pessimism, and this in an immediate sense became the chief artistic legacy that Sterling bequeathed to the young Ashton Smith, along with the fantastic imagination displayed in "A Wine of Wizardry."

By the time that he died, the elder poet had obviously become less than the Late Romantic that one can too easily categorize him, and much more the Modern Romantic into which he had subtly meta-morphosed. This trend would probably have continued had not his alcoholism killed him, or at least hastened his death. (Doubtlessly he committed suicide, if that is what it was, for health reasons immediate-ly connected with the godawful booze illegally available during Prohi-bition, 1918–1933.) In a productive sense the elder poet had about ten years (c. 1900–1910) of mature poeticizing before Smith began creating his own first mature poetry (1911–1912). But when we compare Sterling's output of poetry for 1911 through 1926 to that of Smith's for the same period, we have some dozen or so books by Sterling as compared to only three or four by the younger poet. This bears out Sterling's own self-confessed assertion that he made in his preface to the *Ebony and Crystal* of late 1922, Smith's single greatest collection: "Because he has lent himself the more innocently to the whispers of his subconscious daemon, and because he has set those murmurs to purer and harder crystal than we others, by so much the longer will the poems of Clark Ashton Smith endure."

Three prime poetic phenomena marked the young Smith before Sterling and he first met through letters during January of 1911 and in person during July of 1912. First, at the age of thirteen, Smith discovered, and saturated himself in, the highly individual poetry of Edgar Allan Poe (as well as the latter's prose fictions). Second, at the age of fourteen, Smith discovered, and absorbed, Sterling's fantastic masterpiece "A Wine of Wizardry" (via the *Cosmopolitan* Magazine for September of 1907). Third, at some point somewhat later than this when Smith was fourteen or fifteen, Smith obtained Sterling's first published collection *The Testimony of the Suns,* which featured its astonishing and ground-breaking title poem, the most significant product of the elder poet's first mature poeticizing. The young Smith not only read and re-read these two poetic monuments by Sterling, but he pored over them, virtually memorizing them. Echoes from them re-appear and resonate throughout Smith's output from *The Star-Treader* and his other early poetry collections through his highly imaginative short stories of the 1930s, as well as through his final poetic cycles of the late 1930s on into the 1940s.

All this reading and study supplemented Smith's earlier absorption of the standard fairy tales and *The Arabian Nights* around the age of eleven, which in turn prompted his earliest attempts at prose fiction. Equally significant, and concomitant with his assimilation of Sterling's two greatest poems, Smith at the age of fifteen discovered William Beckford's unique Arabian-Nights fantasy *The History of the Caliph Vathek.* This all made up quite a heady brew for an adolescent evidently starved for genuinely imaginative literature whether in verse or in prose. Even more than "A Wine of Wizardry," Smith did not just absorb *The Testimony of the Suns* but he subjected its divers and multiple quatrains to close and exacting examination in the crucible of his intellect, or as we might express it more accurately, but also perhaps more fancifully, via the alchemistical testing and proving in the arcane laboratory of his own unique imagination. Therein, following the notable experiments of Sterling as his immediate poet-magister thus alive at the same time as his disciple, the young Smith discovered and created his own cosmic-astronomic-mindedness, which then manifested in *The Star-Treader* as the product of his own first mature poeticizing during 1911–1912.

At the same time that he was absorbing the poetry of Poe and Sterling, Smith was also conducting his own high-school education by much other reading in depth, reportedly one or more unabridged dictionaries and/or encyclopaedias, including the etymologies of words and phrases. After finishing with grammar school, he and his parents decided that he could conduct his own education better than by attending the local Placer Union High School in Auburn. As recalled by Dr. William Farmer, after the local Auburn Library opened in 1908 (as one of many funded by millionaire-philanthropist Andrew Carnegie throughout the U.S.A.), Smith spent much time there, studying as well as checking books out in the usual fashion. Whatever shape the contents of the little library may have taken, Smith made full use of them, evidently reading almost all the books that the facility possessed. This further education apparently took place during 1906–1910 from the age of fourteen through eighteen.

During this adolescence he not only wrote his next fiction, long adventure novels of Oriental life, reflecting *The Arabian Nights* and Rudyard Kipling's tales of India, but also conducted his first experiments in poetry, slowly gaining a feeling for meter and rhythm. By the time that Sterling and Smith first met during 1911–1912 (through the auspices of a mutual friend, Edith J. Hamilton, who taught English language and literature at the local high school), the younger poet had already obtained an extraordinary grounding in language and literature, as thorough a self-education as possible in terms of his chosen calling of poet and scrivener. Evidently just prior to, or about the same time as, his first contact with Sterling, Smith had acquired or discovered a book that almost marked him as powerfully as the works of Poe and Sterling. This was *Pastels in Prose* (published by Harper and Brother in 1890), a remarkable and yet little known volume containing quite a quantity and variety of poems in prose translated masterfully by Stuart Merrill from the French of thirty-two (French) poets. Between Poe's examples in this genre and those afforded by Stuart

Merrill's pivotal volume, Smith acquired his understanding and mastery of this rare and rather difficult form.

To his first mature poetry Smith brought something that went far beyond Sterling's cosmic-astronomic-mindedness, as well as his cosmic pessimism. The young poet and his parents resided just outside a small city and its duly constituted society, and thus in a literal sense rather outside ordinary civilization. They survived or existed in a condition still actually like that of the old frontier in the wilderness, in their case on some forty acres of their own land in the forested reaches of Placer County amid Northern California. Auburn still remained a relatively small city, and the Smith family lived some real distance from town, in a three-room or four-room cabin, and in a rather primitive but still adequate fashion. This involved a kitchen sink, a wood-burning stove, candles and kerosene lamps for illumination, well water stored in pails and buckets, and at a little distance from the cabin, an underground cooler-cellar built around their well, and at a greater distance, an outhouse. The Smiths had few close neighbors, but apparently goodhearted people. At the time the family resided where they did, it remained a place of great natural beauty.

In this locale of comparative isolation, little or no town or other illumination interfered with the perception of the heavens when the weather was clear. Smith in fact knew the stars and constellations especially well from early childhood, and he would have recognized the names and references in Sterling's long cosmic-astronomic poem from long-term familiarity with them. This would have greatly heightened the depth of his appreciation for this extraordinary opus, and might even have prompted him to further study. With the aid of star maps and without interference from any city lights—he might even have had a small but adequate telescope—he could have conned the immensitudes of the nocturnal heavens, now perceiving them with even greater interest thanks to Sterling's greatest poem, as he continued to read and study those highly imaginative quatrains. Smith's genius had already enabled him to look deep into life and the cosmos, and so now he added something in his own work that went far beyond Sterling's cosmic pessimism, in order to attain a more profound and rather frightening vision of things that perceived the cosmos at best as either impassible or indifferent.

If, in writing about Smith, we deal yet once again with the same sources and influences as we have done many times before, it is only

to demonstrate and emphasize both how like and unlike, how differ-
ent, his work has emerged from what preceded him. In one sense it is
the deliberate avoidance of the sentimental fat that saturated so much
of the ordinary Victorian American literature current in the late 1800s
and early 1900s, as well as the forthright promulgation of his cosmic
pessimism, along with the stoic acceptance of the universe's lack of
special concern for humanity per se, that can still redeem Sterling and
his poetic output for us today, quite apart from technique, music,
magic, etc. In the same fashion it is at least the same things that earn
our continuing respect for the poetry and fiction of his protégé. Smith
not only takes these even much further than Bierce or Sterling, but in
addition explores boldly and bravely the dark side of everything
whether human or cosmic, never flinching in the face of the worst
emotional consequences of such a stance. To offset these, we have in
Smith's own scheme of things an unending abundance of beauty, no
less than the special oasis of love, even if there is no hope.

Unlike Sterling who had many distractions in his life that often took
him away from his professed art, Smith had few or none, and so he
had no choice but to concentrate on creating his extraordinary poetry
to the best of his ability, even if it did not often bring him any particular
satisfaction or consolation. Here Sterling helped Smith enormously.
Just as Bierce had advised Sterling in minute detail in regard to his po-
etry from about 1897 until about 1907, so did Sterling do the same for
Smith in regard to his own poetry from 1911-1912 until 1922-1923.
At that latter time Sterling conceded to Smith that he no longer need-
ed to counsel him in this way, because the pupil or disciple had sur-
passed the master. Here as well, in his need to concentrate on his
poetic art, Smith's atrabilious nature, amazingly so strong in such a
young person, stood him in excellent stead, and helped him to reach
those uncompromisingly stern conclusions that in fact he did. In this,
in his desire or need to speak the truth as he perceived it no matter
the consequences, he resembles Bierce the closest of all. Bierce like-
wise knew no fear in this regard, philosophically or otherwise.

The letters exchanged between Smith and Sterling chronicle in
considerable detail the lives of both poets, usually on a weekly or
monthly basis, but sometimes almost from day to day. They let us
know not only what they are writing, but what they are reading—what
books impress them, and what books do not. They comment on the
news and trends of the day, the weather, their hopes and aspirations,

their disappointments—what poems of theirs have sold, what might sell and to what market, and what might not sell in terms of the prejudices and predilections of their times. In a sense the letters form a personal and a literary biography for both poets. Some of the revelations prove inspiring, e.g., Smith's very positive response to the book of poems by Nora May French that Sterling had helped to edit and publish after her death, and that he had sent to his pupil. Some of the revelations prove rather disappointing.

On one occasion Smith had sent Sterling two recent sonnets cast in alexandrines (a somewhat rare metre in English, and which Smith handles magnificently), the standard medium of French classical poetry in the same way that iambic pentameter is the standard medium of much English-language poetry. Sterling had a definite prejudice against this metre, as his response indicates.

> There's any amount of poetry in the two sonnets ["Mirrors" and "Inferno"] you enclose. The metre sets all my poetic nerves a-howl, as I've already said. And yet the French love it. Well, poetry was never their strong point.

This amazing statement makes us wonder if Sterling read or spoke any French, or knew French literature in any depth, and not in translation. Anyone who has conned French literature in depth and in detail, especially the poetry, from *La Chanson de Roland* up through Guillaume Apollinaire, Jean Cocteau, and St. John-Perse—that is, from about 900 A.D. into the 1900s—could never come up with such a dismissive reaction to over 1,000 years of French poetry; a body of literature, moreover, that exercised a profound impact on the literature conceived in the English language, particularly during the Middle Ages and the Renaissance, not to mention during the 1800s!

At least on much literature written in English, Sterling's opinions appear comparatively sound and reliable! Not only did the elder poet advise the young Smith on his first major collection, on the poems chosen for it, and especially on the poems that went into *Ebony and Crystal,* but all through that period of 1911–1922 he actively campaigned among the wealthiest persons whom he counted among his friends (and he counted a goodly number), to give Smith and his parents a monthly or quarterly stipend. In this he succeeded, and the stipends helped quite a bit, however small they might seem today, even if some of the wealthy people seemed not to have liked the hypersensitively shy Smith, and found his poetry with its austere conclusions less than appealing. Sterling had much nobility of character, and helped as many people as he could, poets particularly, and—above all—those poets who produced notable work in traditional forms, rather than in free verse, including Samuel Loveman and Ashton Smith. (Loveman became such an admirer of Smith's poetry, and helped his education by sending him so many books—whole shelfloads, it would seem—that Smith dedicated *Ebony and Crystal* to him in gratitude.) But Sterling regarded his assistance to the young Smith almost as a sacred calling, and one which he never shirked.

If at times the young Smith seems less than sympathetic in these letters, we must remind ourselves that genius or greatness of any kind often proves difficult on the individual so blessed, or so cursed, and on those around him. For those who have never essayed it on a sustained basis, writing and especially the thinking behind it can emerge as very hard labor, indeed, requiring considerable discipline to stay chained to desk and chair while cogitating and redacting. In addition to the stipends obtained by Sterling for the Smith family, the young Smith in his turn supplemented their income by doing odd jobs when available: cutting and preparing cords of wood (hard physical work that the young man relished to the point that he became expert at it), and picking and packing fruit (also hard *and hot* physical work), among other kinds of season-dictated labor. However, he refused to become a regular wage-slave working at a regular job with regular hours. He considered such labor soul-destroying, and in his case he was probably right.

An added factor loomed increasingly important as the years passed. In regard to those parents of his who gave him every encouragement, Smith found himself in an awkward position, had he gone to work at a regular job. He had been born to much older parents, the father in his latter 30s, and the mother in her early 40s. During the poet's greatest period of production, 1911–1925, the parents reached old age. The mother Fanny appeared to be a healthy little dynamo full of irrepressible good cheer, but the father Timeus endured years of poor health, possibly from diseases contracted in the tropics while he was traveling around the world and squandering a large patrimony through gambling as a young man. Thus the son found himself in a kind of "Catch-22" situation: damned if he did, damned if he didn't. Increasingly he had to stay home to help his parents, even if serious illness or decline on their part did not demand yet his constant or near-constant attention and care. That would not happen until the mid-1930s as the parents approached their death, the mother in latter 1935, and the father in very late 1937.

Although no reflection of it appears directly in these letters, the family lived very close to each other whether physically or affectionately, and in considerable harmony. From the recollections of E. Hoffman Price, Rah Hoffman, and others we can form some idea of the Smith cabin, their home, erected on a slight rise of land, and facing west. One entered the main entrance through a kind of porch, and found oneself in the spacious main room that ran the width of the cabin, the kitchen and dining area to the right, with sink, wood-burning stove, dining table, and work table, and the son's combined study and workshop on the left, where he would read and write, and also create his pictorial art and sculptures, and where he kept his art and writing supplies. The two bedrooms lay beyond the main room, the son's bedroom off his studio-workshop, and the parents' bedroom off the kitchen. Some forty or fifty feet further up the gentle slope and to the south of where the cabin stood, lay the underground cooler-cellar with their well, an abandoned mine shaft.

Smith's direct cultural inheritance from his father Timeus while both were alive has received little attention, but its essence inheres throughout the son's output, what we might call the actual or historical exoticism of everyday life. It even extends at times, even if intermittently, to such minutiae as British orthographical and other preferences. The first impression that we might get from *Ebony and Crystal* might possibly stem from its arch-exotic or otherworldly qualities, from its unusual imaginativeness, but somehow rendered concrete in palpable or literary terms. Possibly one half of *Ebony and Crystal* reflects the travels around the world undertaken by Smith's father, especially the locales with a general Oriental or Asiatic background whether in the tropics or in the desert wherever found. The father had enjoyed some notable adventures that included a meeting with Dom Pedro II, the last Emperor of Brazil, before the revolution of 1888 exiled him back to Portugal. The stories and other recollections from his extensive travels as a young man, as told by the otherwise reserved or non-committal father to the son, would have nourished Clark's imagination from his early childhood almost until the father's death.

This is what lies behind the "merely" mundane exoticism that we find in *Ebony and Crystal:* real adventure, real experience, direct observation. Despite all that Smith owed his parents, and although they receive occasional mention, they make their appearance in these letters at best but as half-shadowy figures. However, as solid and sustaining entities in Smith's own life, we feel or sense their presence even without their being limned immediately. Otherwise, if you wish to discover the trials and tribulations of two genius poets, one patiently and nobly tutoring the other, moreover at the end of a great romantic tradition during the first quarter of the twentieth century, you will find this volume of their complete extant correspondence a fascinating and richly rewarding look behind the scenes. Thanks to the hard and painstaking labor of Messieurs Joshi and Schultz, we are enabled at long last to read, peruse, and savor Sterling and Ashton Smith's exchange of letters, and we extend to the editors our deepest gratitude.

Afterword

A statement from the blurb on the back cover, presumably written by Schultz and Joshi, arrests and holds our attention, prompting further meditation and recollection. "We come to see why Smith took over the mantle of poetic greatness from Sterling, whose suicide in 1926 left Smith shocked and bereft." An interesting phrase and an interesting concept: "The mantle of poetic greatness." We recall and quote from *Footloose in Arcadia, A Personal Record of Jack London, George Sterling, Ambrose Bierce,* by Joseph Noel—a substantial volume published by Carrick and Evans of New York City sometime during 1940—from Chapter 32, "George Sterling: Requiescat in Pace," included in the last major section, "Book Three: The Cavalcade of Death," the following pertinent passage:

> One outstanding characteristic of Sterling's that developed during the last half dozen years of his life into something tender and holy was his devotion to young poets. No matter who they were or where they came from, if their singing were free of the prevailing sentimentalities, he did what he could to get them an audience. Clark Ashton Smith, the inspired youth from Auburn, was helped to early articulation by him. [Op. cit., p. 314.]

Among those other then young poets, Robinson Jeffers (1887–1962) looms the largest, and here, soon after the mention of the then still young Smith (born only six years after Jeffers), Noel in his valuable personal record first raises the issue of a metaphoric mantle passed from one generation to another.

> It was apparent to those concerned with such matters that he had chosen Robinson Jeffers for the mantle of Elijah which Bierce had entrusted to his keeping.
>
> "Jeffers will go far," Sterling said. "He does not waste his heart on life as I did. He sits in his ivory tower down at Carmel, keeping casual visitors away and living as austerely as a medieval monk. I never did that enough. I always loved life too well." [Op. cit., pp. 314–315.]

Noel speaks here of Bierce's metaphorical Cloak of Elijah, the great and fiery Hebrew prophet of the 9th century B.C., who spoke the truth to king and commoner alike with no concern for the personal risk to his life that such truth-telling might entail, a mode of behavior espoused by Bierce in his fearless and forthright journalism. All four writers—Bierce, Sterling, Smith, and Jeffers—had the habit of speaking the truth straightforwardly whether in verse or in prose, but why Jeffers per se, rather than Smith, should rank as more worthy to receive Bierce's Cloak of Elijah, is not clear, at least in this context. Smith lived even more simply than Jeffers, devoting himself no less to his art. It is a curious fact or coincidence, which might bear serious pondering, that all four writers, especially the three major poets involved, Sterling, Smith, and Jeffers, found themselves equally obsessed with the cosmos, but expressed this obsession in their poetry each in his own unique way, although Sterling and Smith tend to converge, not surprisingly.

However, as it turns out, it was not Noel in 1940 who first publicly raised this issue of a metaphoric mantle, as related somehow to Smith immediately or not, but David Warren Ryder in late 1934 reporting on something said by Sterling about Smith shortly before the elder poet died. It is obvious that Ryder was in contact with Smith, who must have informed him concerning statements made by other writers about Smith's own considerable stature as a poet. Only the year before, during the spring, the *Auburn Journal* for Thursday, April 27, 1933, had published an article "Local Poet Praised by Noted Author. Clark Ashton Smith Declared Greatest American Poet." It is worth quoting this article in full, given its brevity.

> George Work, author of "White Man's Harvest," and one of the best known writers in the country, paid high tribute to Clark Ashton Smith, Auburn poet, in a press interview which he granted on a recent visit to

his former home in Bakersfield. Work with the late George Sterling and David Starr Jordan, considers Smith the greatest American poet of today.

In speaking of Smith's poems, Work recommended all the volumes published since 1913 [i.e., 1912], "Star-Treader," "Ebony and Crystal," and "Sandalwood." Mr. Work said that the poems do not compare unfavorably with those of Byron, Shelley, Keats or Swinburne. He does not think the poet has been given proper recognition in his own state.

(Where did the high regard for Smith as expressed by David Starr Jordan (1851–1931), make its public appearance? Or, as voiced by Dr. Jordan, perhaps to him privately, did Sterling communicate this directly to Smith? Such an opinion is worth quite a bit coming as it does from this well-known and respected biologist, educator, and man of letters, a former president of the University of Indiana, as well as the first president and hence "the builder" of Stanford University, the Harvard of America's west coast. Dr. Jordan presumably would have known Sterling socially at divers locales in the San Francisco Bay Area, and would have rubbed shoulders with him as a neighbor in Carmel not far from Sterling's bungalow there.)

Whatever exactly must have impelled Ryder now to pen his article on Smith—was it the press interview by George Work possibly published in some Bakersfield newspaper and then possibly picked up and reported in other California newspapers including the *Auburn Journal?*—the piece by Ryder presently made its appearance in the periodical *Controversy* for December 7, 1934 as "The Price of Poetry." It is in this article that Ryder apparently first raises the issue of a metaphoric mantle of some kind of greatness when he declares that "While versifiers and poetasters without number were gaining the public's accolade, this man who, in our generation, in all probability is the fittest to wear the mantle of Shakespeare and Keats, has remained unheralded and almost unheard—more proof, it seems, that we have eyes to see and ears to hear only the lurid and the sensational."

In the middle of the article Ryder vouchsafes us a statement from George Sterling otherwise unrecorded, embodying an opinion that the elder poet never makes to Smith himself directly in their exchange of letters, especially towards the end of that exchange. Did he fear that such an amazing opinion would have made the otherwise humble protégé boundlessly vain?

And only a few weeks before he died, Sterling said to me:

"Clark Ashton Smith is undoubtedly our finest living poet. He is in the great tradition of Shakespeare, Keats and Shelley; and yet, to our everlasting shame, he is entirely neglected and almost unknown."

When Benjamin De Casseres reviewed Smith's first major prose collection *Out of Space and Time* (Arkham House, 1942)—in his column "The March of Events" featured on the editorial page of the *San Francisco Examiner* for Wednesday, September 23, 1942—he hailed the author as "a great prose writer," and concluded his brief but favorable notice as follows:

> Ashton-Smith [*sic*], George Sterling and Robinson Jeffers are a trinity of California poets no other State in the Union can touch—for great poets and story-tellers seldom come in threes in one place.

Was it the cosmic-mindedness common to all three major poets that prompted De Casseres to group then together? It is tempting to think so. If Sterling thought so highly of Smith, and said so to David Warren Ryder, it might seem odd that the elder poet never expressed this opinion to Smith, although the younger poet certainly knew that his mentor did in fact rate him quite highly. Such an opinion, stated forthrightly in some last letter by Sterling to Smith, would have greatly heartened him during the decades to come. And so this brings us back full circle, via Bierce's Cloak of Elijah, to Smith taking over "the mantle of poetic greatness from Sterling," in Schultz and Joshi's memorable phraseology, prompting yet a further line of thought, and perhaps a little more daring. We must proceed with unusual care here because we find ourselves in the midst of Sacred Cows or Sacred Monsters, however otherwise validated as great poets.

That George Work and David Warren Ryder, no less than Jordan and Sterling, considered Smith the greatest American poet of the first third of the twentieth century; that Work stated that Smith's poems compare favorably with those of Byron, Keats, Shelley, and Swinburne; that Sterling considered his own protégé to belong to the great tradition of Shakespeare, Keats, and Shelley; and that Ryder considered Smith the worthiest modern poet to wear the mantle of Shakespeare and Keats:—all this should give us a big collective pause to ponder the fact. All this represents without a doubt rather heady and heavy-duty stuff, indeed. None of these individuals, all genuine men of letters, to whom literature meant something of great value, would have stated opinions like these unless obviously they held them in all sincerity and seriousness. Given their dates of death and birth, Sterling—not quite sixty when he died—and Jordan—around eighty when he deceased—did not exactly figure as impetuous youngsters without judgment or considerable experience of life when they pronounced these rather elevated opinions.

Although new poetic divinities have made their sacred appearance among us since the 1920s, we cannot exaggerate the prestige and even reverence that certain poets of the 1800s, the romantic century above all, such as Byron, Coleridge, Keats, Shelley, Wordsworth, Tennyson, and Swinburne, among other poets in the Anglophone world, enjoyed at least in the early 1900s among serious poetry lovers—to say nothing of the elder giants of English literature such as Chaucer, Spenser, and Milton, or for that matter, of the adulation lavished on the sainted Shakespeare in perpetual apotheosis from the time of Dryden and Pope onward. Judging from his highly rhythmical and image-laden blank verse with its exuberant metre, particularly the examples in *Ebony and Crystal,* Smith had made a profound and extended study not only of Milton's great epics in blank verse hut especially of the poetic dramas attributed to Shakespeare, in which the poet pushes cadence and language to extreme developments. Thus the Auburn poet had assimilated these greatest examples through and through, and this profound assimilation certainly shows.

If the analogy with Milton and Shakespeare can stand up, it cannot hold by virtue of Smith's mere deliberate imitation of their own poetry. Smith's blank verse and the other examples of the traditional prosody that he mastered and practised so well in a technical sense—he made very much his own as a conscious vehicle for his own original thought and his own original subject matter despite all the influences thematically and stylistically derived from Sterling and his own considerable output. Smith achieved this with great verve and originality, and moreover for his own philosophical or metaphysical purposes. In that larger sense his output justifies his placement by his own mentor "in the great tradition of Shakespeare, Keats and Shelley," and hence the worthiest to wear the mantle of poetic greatness inherited from them by means of Bierce and Sterling. Ashton Smith did indeed venture forth with extreme daring into poetic regions hitherto undiscovered and unexplored. The lack of recognition from the literary mainstream does not invalidate the inherent greatness of his poetry.

A Poetic Original

G. SUTTON BREIDING. *Ill Desperado, 2013/2014.* A collection
of ten free-verse and/or free form poems. A booklet 8½ × 11 inches,
12 pages, glossy black cover (some kind of card material), poems
photocopied from elegantly hand printed sheets. An edition de luxe
as a privately printed or published book or booklet. Issued only to
friends and fellow poets. August 2018.

In its own way *Ill Desperado*—the title is a clever take on Gérard de
Nerval's melancholic sonnet "El Desdichado"—is almost as excep-
tional (although much smaller and with different proportions) as
Frank Coffman's tome *The Coven's Handbook* (2018/2019).
   On the dedication page of his *Selected Poems,* Clark Ashton
Smith quotes what seems his own translation of the first four lines of
Nerval's lyrical poem "El Desdichado." Nerval is that unique precur-
sor as a great poet to Baudelaire with *Les Fleurs du mal,* just as Aloys-
ius Bertrand with his *Gaspard de la Nuit* is the unique precursor to
Baudelaire with his *Poèmes en prose.*

> I am that dark, that disinherited,
> That all-dishonored prince of Aquitaine.
> The star upon my scutcheon long hath fled,
> A black sun on my lute doth yet remain.

This translation might also be from the pen of Arthur Symons. Wheth-
er in English or in French, it has very strong affinities with the final po-
em in Sutton Breiding's most recent collection. We quote this final
poem in full to demonstrate him as a full-fledged legatee of Nerval,
Baudelaire, and Rimbaud, albeit an original and considerable figure
in his own right, and one who mines his own vein of melancholy and
the beautiful, no less his disaffection or discontent with his own era.

> I am that wasted
> that dysfunctional troubadour
> hanging in a noose of silk stockings
> from the overburdened lamp post of hopes

above the Stygian gutters
where my diamond sonnets putrefy
I snap my lute strings one by one
disconsolate as a neutron sun
in the toxic void of that birth canal where Death was waiting
with the charred escutcheon of my inheritance
smeared all over in the blackest of lipsticks
of all the kisses I dishonored with a poem

I have long followed the life and career of Sutton Breiding, proba-
bly since the later 1960s in San Francisco, where I lived during 1965–
75, in fact through the whole hippie period. We most likely met
through the auspices of Don Herron, himself a recent arrival from
Tennessee, just as Sutton and his family, mother and siblings, hailed
from Morgantown, West Virginia. They resided at that time in a sev-
eral-storied family house in the Haight-Ashbury district. I myself re-
sided in a big flat in a similar but larger building not far from where
Haight and Ashbury intersect.

Soon Sutton began issuing the notable series of his handmade and
homemade booklets containing his poetry, at once free verse and free
form, remarkable for its depth and the great variety of its wide-ranging
imagery. We often visited back and forth between our respective
domiciles, and I even stayed overnight at the Breiding abode several
times, in addition to sharing their regular meals. They made a lively
and enjoyable household. We passed many pleasant evenings togeth-
er, and I cherish the memories that I still have of those happy times.

Of course, we had all become united through our fervid interest in
modern imaginative literature as purveyed not only by Lovecraft,
Smith, Robert E. Howard, etc., but also by *Weird Tales* and Arkham
House, i.e., August Derleth. And here we wish to pay tribute, a big
tribute, to a veteran and fellow poet, one G. Sutton Breiding, on the
basis of his last booklet, in case we have not so done before.

Sutton has assuredly stayed the course, whether receiving lauda-
tion or brickbats. He has followed his own star, his own Muse, forth-
rightly. That says a lot for a poet in America who does not receive
mainstream recognition. At his age Sutton should have a volume of
his collected poems published in his honor by some acolyte in con-

junction with a small press other than the poet's own. Let us quote some random lines from his latest booklet to give the reader an idea of Sutton's range and characteristic imagery. Let us grant the poet himself the last significant word or phrase.

chewing on air
I chase my manias in shrinking circles
hypnotized by the psychedelic monitors
in the hospital of words

it's the tragedy of the mystic impulse
bejeweled staircases going nowhere
magical toys that broke long ago

I medicate
with words and walks
gaze at the river in supernatural dawns

what is all this starry-eyed nonsense
the smeared snot of dreams all over the place

I ride my skeleton horse to Death
the beggar king of fog and off ramps
out among the powerlines and derelict toilets

the past was once a Goth chanteuse
crooning in the dead city of my heart

I am haunted unto madness
by the strangeness of this world

from the slimy troughs of verse
I dig my way to another unrequited day

I croak and stutter over stacks of paper
my hands hardening into the luminous mud of language

I'm on my way there down that dark lane
with my solid gold jetpack strapped on tightly

　　in the meantime my rotting head
　　screams out its erotic dirges

　　and terminally ill chimaeras lick at me
　　with the barbed and merciless piercings
　　of their long and golden tongues

No doubt about it, G. Sutton Breiding remains one of the great poetic originals of our time and still abides with us!

[N.B. The translation of Nerval's sonnet "El Desdichado" is the work of Andrew Lang.]

A Guidebook for Witches and Warlocks

FRANK COFFMAN. *The Coven's Hornbook and Other Poems: Weird, Horrific, Supernatural, Fantastic, Science Fictional, Broadly Speculative, and Traditional.* Preface by Donald Sidney-Fryer. Foreword by Frederick J. Mayer. Illustrations by Yves Tourigny. Bold Venture Press, 2019. 254 pp. $14.95 tpb.

This volume has fifteen separate sections, as well as a Glossary of Forms and an Alphabetical Index of Titles. The section titles are as evocative as the well-honed verses of the poems themselves. Let us list them:

Witchcraft and Warlockry
Ghosts and Hauntings
Sorcery and Summonings
The Lycanthopicon: Werewolves and Their Ilk
Lovecraftiana
Halloween/Samhain: A Chronographia of All Saints Eve
Vampires: The Undead
Ghoulies, Beasties, and Things that Go Bump in the Night
Arch Weirdness: The Inexplicable and Abnatural
Horribilis Mundus: Physical Fear and "the Mundanely Gruesome"
Fantasy and Myth: The Realms of Gold
Ekphrasis and Hommage: Poems on the Other Arts and for Some of my Fellow Poets
Other Genres of the Imagination
Ars Poetica and Wyrdskaldskaparmal
Metapoesis: Poetry about Poetry
Some Traditional Verses

This amazing "handbook"—a kind of collected (but not complete collected) poems—announces a major voice (in a single published volume) in American poetry of the fantastic and supernatural. The voice belongs to Frank Coffman, or (in full) Dean Franklin Coffman II.

I say forthrightly that this is one humdinger of a book. Although I would not suggest that you read it all at once from cover to cover—as I have only now done, rather at a gallop, in one fell swoop, even if over a period of days—I can certainly recommend that you somehow acquire a copy. It is a delectation of a poetic feast. Frank Coffman must rank as one of the most erudite poets whose work we have ever encountered so far. He is not just a master craftsman, above all as a sonneteer, and of the sonnet form in its innumerable variations (and there are many); he is also a master of many little-known metres, often of recondite provenance. What is more, he demonstrates mastery of them all, whether sonnets or metres or other forms.

It is best to read such a book as this by dipping into it here and there (perhaps one whole section per sitting) from time to time, and savoring several items on occasion. Do not do as I have done, rushing through the book from one end to the other. That procedure might turn out as exhilarating but also (alas!) exhausting. Do not imitate our example, a flagrant one of poor reading practice, especially of poetry.

I claim a certain fraternity with Coffman because he is not only a traditionalist as a poet but a damn good one. I have never presented myself as anything other than a traditionalist, thanks to the "ensample" of Edmund Spenser and his idiosyncratic forms and practices. I say this even if I admire good or great non-traditional poetry as much as the practitioners of it admire it themselves. Hence, as traditionalists, the bond of fraternity between Coffman and myself! We traditionalists must stand together, to counteract the disdain toward the traditionalists sometimes emanating from the non-traditionalists!

Proceeding from front to back, let me quote in whole or in part certain poems by a fellow practitioner that have struck and captured my fancy. Professor Coffman proffers a great many adventures to the lover of traditional poetry not just in arch-imaginative endeavor but in language and linguistics as well.

But before engaging with the main text, the "Dear Reader" should read, nay, *must* read the professor's introduction (a solid piece of work at five full pages). In this he lays out his credentials as a traditional, but innovative, Formalist practitioner, yes, of poetic forms and norms. For people no longer accustomed to reading poetry in formalist verse (particularly aloud) it is essential reading. For those acclimatized in traditional versification, even those readers might discover some surprises. As Clark Ashton Smith has observed, the forms and themes of poetry do not become outmoded or exhausted. The exhaustion inheres in the poets themselves. The good professor certainly demonstrates that the older forms and themes (that is, of love and fear) have not exhausted themselves.

As we proceed into the first poems presented here, we come up against a real problem: which poems to cite in whole or in part. Coffman has much to say, to relate, to narrate, but his uniformity of craft, with everything well honed, makes it almost impossible to choose which poems to highlight by quoting them. I might refer the reader, if of Keltic derivation, to the sections listed at the head of this review. The poems in "Witches and Warlocks," for example, abound in Keltic lore of all types, which the poet beautifully defines: Beltane, Lughnasadh, and Samhain, and so forth similarly.

One thing the reader gains is an admonition: treat older people with respect and circumspection, especially older women. Some "old crone" might turn into a sorceress, a necromancer, of great power. Show respect: dire things might otherwise occur!

To keep this notice within reasonable bounds, I shall quote only a handful or less of poems, among Coffman's unique shape-shifting art. But first and foremost, we cite in full the poet's own adumbrated poetic credo in "Prelude." It also serves as a fine example of a villanelle.

Prelude

They wind through Realms where what is "Real" is gone,
These verses meant to urge the chill of Fear,
These lines I've penned to show a different Zone.

Perhaps best not read when you are alone,
Some outline shapes—we hope not really here!
Seeking Lost Lands whereof the "Real" is none.

These visions, ragged, rough, I've sought to hone:
Fantastic Worlds that sharpened from the blear.
These scrawls outline a wholly different Zone.

They ring quite loud, or muffle with odd tone,
Born from the Dreams and Nightmares of a Seer
Who's traveled where no stuff of "Real" is known.

Turning this leaf, your Journey has begun.
This page is but a gateway! You are near!—
Traveler, most welcome to this different Zone.

Open the gate! There is much to be shown.
Look! Up ahead! Now hazy, but soon clear!—
Strange Visions never met, Weird Places never gone.
Come, Reader, and explore this different Zone.

Again, it is near impossible to give in this limited space any coherent idea of the wealth and variety in this collection of the author-poet's power of invention and imagination. A strong narrative drive manifests itself in virtually every morceau. These poems are much more than mere celebrations of isolated or static images. Coffman pays notable tribute to fellow poets, whether traditional or not. What might appear at first as mere cleverness usually leads to some deep and often ominous discovery.

Not all the selections are grim and ghastly. Several purposely fabricated "for Sir Arthur Conan Doyle" possess much urbanity and charm. The following may serve as an apt example.

The Repetitious Client

Many's the time I've climbed these stairs before
(I know the count: precisely seventeen);
Paused but a moment, knocked, then welcomed in
Where two friends wait, beyond that magic door.
I scan the room for old, familiar things:
The mail jack-knifed in mantelpiece is seen,
Cigars coal-scuttled, Persian slipper pouch,
Papers in disarray upon the couch.
The bullet pocks that praise Victoria, Queen.

*   *   *

I'm greeted warmly, asked to come along.
"The game's afoot!" you see, and we must go—
"No time to lose!" And once again I know
A case awaits us. And I hear the song
That beckons! And whither we shall see.
Adventure calls again to them—and me.

The poems commenting on other poems and poets appear particularly well done and memorable. Ditto for "an irregular Italian sonnet" evidently commenting on himself, the author-poet. We cannot resist quoting it in full.

Meta-Poesis

I, meta-man, who searches his own soul
And hyper-pens on keyboard ultra-thought,
Who hopes in his faux-quilling, will be caught
Some bits of mega-Truths as seasons roll.
    Such meta-tedium will take its toll:
To contemplate the difficulties fraught
With not-so-micro-dangers as we plot
The demi-lines that sum some hoped-for whole.

This meta-man too often semi-seeks
To peek behind the ink upon the page.
Why not just let each sentence max-engage
The proto-reader? Hope some meaning leaks
Through letters in this daring alpha-Bet?
Send forth the veri-thing without regret.

Ending our notice, we can do no better than to quote in full the good professor's final selection, his profoundly manifested and embraced belief in poetry, and almost in the fervent sense of religion.

Credo

Sweet summer solstice sun sets my blood surging;
Wild winter blizzards blast my bleaching bones;
The dew of the new dawn down is my sweat urging
Damp of the dusk that seeps deep under stones,

Cleansing the old roots and the new seeds purging.
Bright burning leaves in autumn's ancient hues,
Fall as do all that hopeful poets pen,
Blown by the Winds of Time, waste and confuse

Themselves in heaps. Most single leaves unseen—Then
To return to Earth, leaving behind no clues.
But starting buds of so-sweet greeny spring
Will come again after the Winter's blight.

Some herded words might be heard—That's the thing
That keeps the poet's quill aflight at night,
Hoping that some will savor, clutch, and cling.
Praying that some might hear and sing along

To the tune, in tune with Nature's native verse;
Touch some things human; delay—for brief or long—
The prancing worms that haul the poet's hearse:
For it is my fierce need to sing that song.

We should add that the art chosen for the cover is intriguing, and that for the frontispiece is gruesome and repulsive. In addition, the collection boasts six adroit and artful illustrations by Messire Yves Tourigny, seemingly perceived "Through a Glass Darkly."

House-Guarding for Friends

The first night that he went over to the neighbors' house to make sure that all was going okay, he could not help but feel a little bit like a burglar or a thief in the night. He, Keith Allen, lived only a few houses away somewhere in East Sandwich, and in a somewhat smaller house with two relatives, his cousin and her husband that Keith liked to call his cousin-in-law. The house owned by his friends, the Turners, loomed large above him, a typical Cape Cod family home, a big block of a house, with two stories, a full cellar, and a finished attic. A smaller, one-story wing connected at the back with the original saltbox abode that stood with its immense central chimney, and with all the fireplaces and rooms opening up from that central feature.

How quiet it was on this night in early summer! The sun had set in a clear sky, and the twilight was yielding to the night. No scream of gull nor chirp of cricket broke the silence. Keith did not enter by the front door but by the less imposing door in the one-story wing as he walked around to the back. The Turners would be travelling in Europe for a month, the parents and their two young adult children. Although Keith did not need to reside in the dwelling, he would probably end up doing so, but he had not planned to do so this first night of some thirty days during the family's absence.

He inserted the key, it went in smoothly almost without a sound and unlocked the door. Keith entered into the main big room with kitchen. It was even more quiet inside, the air remaining fresh from the central heat and air. Everything functioned almost automatically, and the Turners had the house checked out in advance of their departure. The lights in parts of the house went on by themselves, mechanically set on timers. He did not need to deal with the new dog or the old cat. The Turners were boarding them out at an animal hotel owned by some friends of theirs.

Keith would have little to do. He locked the usual entrance door behind him, just in case of unwanted intruders. He had house-guarded for many friends sometimes for payment, sometimes not, but he had learned to take no chances with trespassers. He went at once to the front door that opened into the large staircase hall that dominated the main block of the house. The floor boards did not creak, he noted. There he picked up the mail that the postal carrier had inserted through the large letter slot in the big front door consisting of only one big panel of wood. He put the mail to one side in a neat pile next to the grand wide staircase that went upstairs. The architect had arranged the rooms in traditional order, symmetrically, three to each side off the staircase hall, whether downstairs or up.

Keith decided to make a tour of inspection, clicking lights on and then off as he went from room to room. He also carried a long flashlight with him, in case he needed it for extra lighting in darkened corners. Made of hard black plastic, he could also use it as a weapon, as a club, if an intruder attacked him. First he checked on the rooms on the first floor, where everything seemed in apple-pie order. Then he went upstairs to the four bedrooms, two to each side, with the big bathrooms between them. All appeared in good order, the same as downstairs. He even ascended to the attic, and checked on the extra bedrooms up there. Again everything appeared okay. He descended back to the first floor, and even went down to the basement, the full cellar, where everything also seemed in order.

Some of the automatic equipment and appliances, like the refrigerator, gave off a low-key hum that Keith found reassuring. He returned to the surprisingly good-sized room, including the modern kitchen constructed on one side of the big space. This chamber constituted the one-story wing between the massive block of the main house and the original saltbox abode just beyond.

With the big old-fashioned key that the Turners had left on the kitchen table along with a typed list of instructions, Keith went up to what had once served as the main portal, but now enclosed. He inserted the key, and after a little struggle he managed to pull the door open. In this old abode the floor creaked often as he slowly promenaded, using liberally the flashlight that he held firmly. He did not switch on any lights, even if the family had rewired the old place for electricity.

Here the warm stale air hit his nostrils hard, and he opened a screened window on the first floor as wide as he could. After circling through the rooms downstairs, Keith ascended via the narrow cramped staircase. His big feet could scarcely negotiate the individual steps. Then he circled through the rooms upstairs. Here the stale air, now still hot, hit his nostrils even harder. Here he opened another screened window as wide as he could, to get the fresh outside air circulating through the two open windows downstairs and up.

Keith did not need to check the attic: there was none but he did check on the cramped, old-fashioned cellar, which smelled of the earth. Here the massive central chimney had its foundation firmly planted on the ground. As he ascended out of the musty-smelling cellar, he thought that he heard a floor board creaking right above him. Was there somebody else in the house? He felt a mild shiver, and flashed the light from his electric torch as he circled again the rooms downstairs.

He called out, "Is anybody there?" Nobody or nothing answered him. Then he realized that a loose floor board had responded to the cool air circulating from the open windows. He laughed with relief, and went out through the ancient front door, locking it behind him. Keith sighed, he had made his tour of inspection, and all seemed okay. He phoned home, and let his relatives know that he had decided to sleep over in the Turner mansion for at least that night. The Turners had stocked the kitchen with plenty of food, fresh, frozen, or canned, and had stocked the liquor cabinet with plenty of spirits and other liquor. He would return home in the morning.

Before he went to sleep in an upstairs bedroom, he retired to the family's well-stocked library to select an old-fashioned novel that he had noticed when inspecting the book-jammed shelves. Keith retrieved it from where he had slightly pulled it out: *The Veil: A Fantasy* by Mary Harriott Norris published in Boston by the Badger Press in 1907. It began with a haunted house in Pennsylvania somewhere. Perfect for him to savor in his bedroom after locking the door from the inside.

A Mistress of Major Spells

The long and mostly unrewarded period had gone by. Circumstances and her then waning powers had condemned her to largely minor spells. Once more had Atalantossa the enchantress—actually a sorceress for hire—returned by some outré miracle beyond her ken or understanding onward into the full endowment of her major spells, of her epic and epoch-making spells.

Once again people of rank, whether of nobility or merchantry, sought her out for her enchantments and philtres, and not just the young people in love, with their variable disaffections, frustrations, and other problems. Such a relief to be able to handle these problems again!

The enchantress was enjoying a day off, a day of quiet and solitude. She sighed a big sigh of satisfaction. However, she remained accessible to clients, if any showed up, on that sunny, but clement, late afternoon. She still resided in her semitropical abode that stood within a small woodland, really a tiny wilderness, that grew between the western shore proper to the island kingdom of Atatemthessys and the western end of the low, verdure-clad Issvess Mountains that dominated the island's interior, and that ran more or less east to west.

Atalantossa had purchased the unpretentious but sturdy structure, a simple rustic cottage, from the former owner, an old woman. The enchantress remained with her, and cared for her until her death, not so long after the sale of the cottage.

Perhaps this good deed had created the karma that had brought back the full resurgence of her sorcerous powers. This in turn had thus restored her command of major spells, beyond the merely and less rewarded minor ones. Clients once more had begun seeking her out, and they often came from far away in the other parts of the island kingdom that lay in the southern expanse of the great Ocean Sea of Atlantis.

People coming from afar, particularly those by foot, often found themselves amazed when they first met her. Hearing of her often miraculous powers, they usually expected to meet some poor but dear old crone. Instead, they found a beautiful older woman with long and silver-tinged hair, causing them not just amazement but unexpected pleasure.

As he came up the well-worn path leading to her unpretentious cottage, what did the young painter Dlanod Yendis observe? A rustic dwelling with a tiled A-framed roof, and with gardens all around it. The enchantress like many people in remote regions apparently grew her own food, her fruits, vegetables, and flowers, All the many doors and unglazed windows (whose shutters could be closed in case of any tempest), Atalantossa had flung wide open.

What did Dlanod notice most of all, and what rivetted his gaze? The enchantress herself, where she sat near the open front door, erect on a big bench with a back in the shade from the wide-spreading fronds of an old, short, and thick-trunked palm tree. Of course, the painter noted her great beauty, dressed as she was in a flowing robe of gauze-like fabric.

At once he began to wonder and plot how he could capture her beauty with sketches and with paints on some suitable surface, paper, wood, or parchment. She rose from her seat, and smiled him a welcome. He bowed, and kissed with a suave gallantry the right hand that she proffered him.

Smiling in turn, he spoke. "I am the painter Dlanod Yendis, and I seek your help or at least advice with a problem that I have endured for a long time now, for several years. I pray that you can and will help me." He bowed again. She pointed to the bench. They both sat down, and when she proffered him some refreshment, he merely said, "Thank you, not right now."

Atalantossa could not help but note in her turn how handsome and well-built he seemed, garbed in a simple, dark gray tunic and kilt that did not quite hang down to his knees. She also noted his well-turned and muscular legs like those of a runner or a dancer. She spoke, continuing to smile. "Please tell me your problem!" He frowned as he thought for a moment before speaking.

"Well, it does involve love and lovers. Given my age, that should not come as a surprise." (She nodded.) "I entertain several paramours on an ongoing basis, both male and female. They all complain about the same thing. It seems that I have too much passion for them, and that I wear them all out. Yes, too much passion." He looked at her enquiringly.

She became thoughtful, and paused before she spoke. Keeping it to herself, she thought ironically but grimly, "Too much passion? And I haven't had a lover in a long time. That was why I retired from the field of love! My lovers never seemed to have enough passion for me. I wore them all out!"

Presently she spoke after due reflection. "Too much passion," she repeated back to him. Then she questioned him, "You have of course tried out other lovers? To find a matching level of desire?" Rather ruefully he smiled. "Yes, of course, but almost never to any avail. I'm thinking of giving up making love to my own kind, and returning to the farm animals. I began with them when I was in my beginning teens, and just discovering sex or love, whatever term is best."

She: "Yes, that is one solution, and a practical one, even if awkward, depending on the quadruped and her size or height. Either that, or you must learn how to restrain your natural ardor. Would that be possible? Could you not manage to do so?—that is, unless you would rather not continue your search?"

He: "Yes, I suppose that I could learn to harness my passion, however frustrating. Could you perhaps not give me some philtre that could incline me that way toward some kind of continence? How does one not think about making love?!"

She: "Yes, I could give you a philtre, and also the recipe for it. It is made from simple but efficacious herbs that you can find in your own or any garden, and so you need not come all the way on foot from where you live. I understand that your home lies inland of our island's australian shore, and west of the capital Meirion. Of course, you are always welcome to visit me here, and to consult me about this problem, or any other you might have, particularly of an amorous nature."

Atalantossa smiled warmly, looking deeply into his eyes. Dlanod warmly smiled back, and said, "Yes, I would like to try this philtre. But I hope that it won't snuff out the flames of love completely." He said this last more as a question than a statement.

She: "Have no fear. Given your passionate nature, the philtre will probably reduce your passion only to moderate levels. Your playmates would probably welcome the change. Let me go prepare it, and meanwhile I'll give you a cup, a big cup, of pomegranate wine. You can promenade among my gardens. Is that alright?"

He: "Yes, thank you." He smiled at her gratefully. They parted after she brought him an enormous cup of pomegranate wine, his favorite. He wandered off into the gardens around the house while she prepared the philtre in her studio, her alchemical laboratory.

The late afternoon shadows were lengthening when Dlanod wandered back to the bench, still nursing his wine—it was an especially capacious cup—and sat himself back down. Presently the enchantress returned with a small box. They greeted each other.

She: "This little box contains enough powder, made of dried herbs, that should last, say, for fourteen days. I have also enclosed on a scrap of vellum the recipe on how you or someone else can make the powder. You can also make it from fresh herbs, which will last for several days in liquid form, and in particular when combined with wine or some heavier alcohol.

She paused, and smiled at him. "Early in the day, take a spoonful with your first cup of wine, and early in the evening, take another spoonful in another cup of wine. Is that clear?"

He: "Yes, thank you very much. And what pray do I owe you?"

She: "You are a wealthy and successful artist. I charge you one big coin, the biggest in our Empire of Atlantis, one crown and trident of orichalch. Can you afford it?"

He smiled back, while he reached inside the coin purse, the pouch, hanging from the girdle of his kilt. After fishing for a few moments he brought out not one but two big coins of the desired metal. He handed them to her with a question, "Is that alright? I appreciate your help."

She: "That is very generous."

He: "I must be going. I must find accommodation in that little village nearby through I passed to reach you here."

She: "Might I invite you to stay overnight in my cottage? I always have accommodations for guests. You can share my evening meal, and go to bed whenever it suits your fancy."

He: "I gladly accept, and thank you for your kind invite!"

Enchantress and painter passed a beautiful but very quiet evening together, as they talked and ate and imbibed more of her seemingly unending store of pomegranate wine, no less than of wine made from grapes, imported from Atlantigades, the island kingdom that lay between Atlantis and Gades.

When he felt ready to retire, even if somewhat reluctantly, his hostess lighted his way to one of the bedrooms that she kept ready for her clients. They said goodnight, and lightly bowed to each other. He felt very tired and sleepy all of a sudden. He had imbibed so much wine that he fell asleep almost immediately.

Dlanod woke an hour or so after midnight, and at once noted his hostess in another gauzy gown, walking in his room, but she seemed to be sleepwalking. However, she did not stumble against anything. Her eyes were closed, as much as he could tell by the light coming in from the main room where a few candles were still burning, however faintly.

He got up off his couch, pushing the light coverlet to one side. In the eternal springtime that formed the regular climate peculiar to Atatemthessys, no one but rarely needed orthodox blankets or almost any covers of any type. Still he always felt more comfortable even if with nothing but a sheet.

Dlanod went over to Atalantossa, and gently put his arm around her lovely shoulders. She did not open her eyes. He brushed his lips against an upper arm. Still no response. Silently she put her arms around him, and he did the same to her. She opened her eyes, and they gently kissed, but said nothing. Nothing needed to be said, as in a dream.

The few candles that still burned in the main room easily lighted them, as she guided him to her bedroom in the not quite utter darkness.

* * * * * *

Dlanod did not leave now for several days, and when he did return home, he did not linger there. By mutual agreement with Atalantossa he would now reside alternately in her cottage as well as in his own. He could sketch and paint, and accomplish his art anywhere. Henceforth he would use his own place chiefly for those interludes when he would be painting the portrait of some wealthy merchant or official.

The painter used the special powder only when he stayed in his own cottage. The powder worked very well indeed, and he managed to moderate his passion when away from Lady Atalantossa. By mutual consent he never needed to use it when he was living with his enchantress, who had become his enchantress in more ways than one. His other lovers had no cause to complain about his insatiable passion anymore.

Cosmic Troubadours

A new romanticism is definitely alive and well in these the present 1970s, a romanticism that was born in the early-to-middle 1960s, and above all with the triumphant emergence of the popular rock group the Beatles. However, the role of the great poet Bob Dylan, amongst others, in preparing the way for—and then later contributing to—this new romanticism (at the time of its most splendiferous birth), should not be underestimated.

Such phenomena as the various "renaissance fairs" (the Oregon fair in Elmira, the Minnesota fair just outside Minneapolis and St. Paul, the fairs held every May and September in the Los Angeles and San Francisco areas, respectively, as well as others on the east coast and elsewhere), together with the various American medieval societies (such as the Society for Creative Anachronism), indicate that we are living at a time of Renaissance or Neo-Renaissance. We have now witnessed the birth of a new romantic age. Poetry in our time has re-turned to the popular singers and music groups. The olden troubadours and trouvères have re-emerged in the new poets: the folk musicians, the rock musicians, etc., of the new-style popular music.

Such singers and rock groups as Bob Dylan, Jim Morrison, Jimi Hendrix, Donovan, Judy Collins, Joni Mitchell, the Beatles, Pink Floyd, Neil Young, Tim Buckley, etc. fulfill the same function in our "global village" as the troubadour-poets did in the Western European world of the 12th and 13th centuries; indeed, they *are* the new troubadour-poets, along with a legion of others.

To a sensitive observer of the late 'sixties music scene, it was apparent that much of the new-style popular music had obvious "cosmic" or "cosmic-astronomic" elements and affinities. "Echoes"—the entire second side of the Pink Floyd's album *Meddle*—is replete with cosmic feeling, as are numerous other selections by the same group. Much of the work by the then Jefferson Airplane is likewise informed with a rather similar feeling, as well as with a distinctive poetic animus. Such lines as "Life is change" / "How it differs from the rocks"(from the title song in their album, *Crown of Creation*)—while refreshingly clear—can attain their full "zen" or "cosmic" meaning only through the corroborating music; together, the words and music project a depth and resonance and general power of evocation impossible to mere lifeless words on a page.

The first moon landing (that is, by men) in 1969—an event of interest and magnitude for the entire modern world—but, even more, the masterful motion picture *2001: A Space Odyssey* (1968) helped to define a cosmic-astronomic awareness to a mass audience all over the world, especially amongst the new generations. Indeed, the young perceived the apparent point and thrust of this unique film far more readily than most mainstream film critics, many of whom have remained singularly opaque to its excellence and monumental achievement. Despite any hostile or unsympathetic critics, *2001* has by now passed into the common culture of our times, and willy-nilly will continue to provide a general background and point-of-reference for cosmic-astronomic elements and achievements in the other arts.

It is not surprising that *2001* should have found a ready audience among the younger generation, since quite a few had been primed for such a major film breakthrough by the profound cosmic-astronomic feeling in the works of H. P. Lovecraft, especially in those tales of his that belong to the Cthulhu Mythos (although the cosmic-astronomic perspective is apparent in most of his *oeuvre*—stories and letters alike). The quondam rock group called H. P. Lovecraft certainly helped to popularize his name with audiences that might not have otherwise come into contact with it. However, since then, although Lovecraft the rock group has disbanded, Lovecraft the writer has become internationally known, and still capable of arousing the most intense enthusiasm amongst young readers, despite any and all critical put-downs, whether they emanate from Avram Davidson on the one hand or Jorge Luis Borges on the other.

Although the cosmic-astronomic ambiance was thus evident in the rock-music scene of the late 'sixties and early 'seventies, relatively few groups or singers devoted an entire (more-or-less unified) long-playing album to such subject matter. The Rolling Stones' album *Their Satanic Majesties Request*—with such songs as "2000 Man" and "2000 Light-Years from Home"—is one of these rare exceptions. Donovan's more recent album *Cosmic Wheels* is another. However, late in 1974 (in October, to be precise), the Jefferson Starship—with an outstanding album entitled *Dragon Fly*–arose phoenix-like from the ashes of their former group, the Jefferson Airplane.

From the opening number "Ride the Tiger" to the final selection "Hyperdrive," Jefferson Starship masterfully synthesizes, articulates, and projects a cosmic-astronomic ambiance with an excitement and exuberance that we have not heard from this group since their earlier albums *Surrealistic Pillow* and *Crown of Creation.* Most of the songs they use are their own, but one or two others have been carefully culled from the works of other musicians. And such is the case with "All Fly Away" (the penultimate cut on side two) by singer-guitarist and song-writer Tom Pacheco.

However, the excellence of "All Fly Away" is not unique in the midst of Pacheco's over-all output of songs to date. (Incidentally, this particular song has received good critical reaction.) Neither is the cosmic-astronomic element unique in his output, nor is it a mere gimmick. Although he describes his style as that of a "New England country singer"–this descriptive phrase only becomes fully intelligible as one comes to know Tom Pacheco's work in depth. The fantasy and science-fiction elements are abundant and inventive, displaying a considerable reading in the modern literatures of the genres in question.

Born some 29 years agone in southeastern Massachusetts not far from New Bedford, the one-time whaling capital of the world, Tom Pacheco is the son of the eminent guitarist and guitar teacher Tony Pacheco (and featured soloist of the long-playing album *I'll Remember Reinhardt*). Like his father, Tom is a thorough-going musician and the master of various guitar styles (classical, flamenco, country, rock, etc.) as well as an excellent guitar teacher. Of Portuguese-American descent he shares completely in the Latin lyric flair and rhythmical animation. To some extent this does explain his style and artistic preoccupations. But, not far to the west of New Bedford, there lies the capital and principal city of Rhode Island, the one-time home for that outstanding writer of supernatural fiction, the Edgar Allan Poe of New England par excellence, to wit, H. P. Lovecraft.

None too surprisingly, Tom Pacheco is a keen student of Lovecraft. He understands and appreciates Lovecraft's poetic imagination as possibly only a fellow New Englander can. But he is no less a student and admirer of the cosmic lyricism uniquely purveyed in the works of Clark Ashton Smith. Other modern masters of the weird and phantastick whom Tom highly regards are Arthur Machen, William Hope Hodgson, and Robert E. Howard. But at the same time he has read widely and profoundly in the science-fiction output published in the last 20 years or so, and possesses an enviable private library which is rich in both fantasy and science-fiction. Growing up in the beautiful New England countryside, he has become a connoisseur of Nature in her varying moods and seasons, and like many others of his generation he partakes of the newly awakened ecological conscience and consciousness.

In addition to his musical talents Tom paints various canvases as well as large (Californian) Almaden wine bottles for the delight of an intimate circle of musicians and friends—in a style that might be described as American country primitive à la Grandma Moses of Maine—with scenes ranging from bucolic springtime landscapes to apocalyptic visions of Atlantis, or such milieux as only H. P. Lovecraft could invoke for a "colour out of space" or a "shadow out of time." Tom is an instinctive folk artist who improvises and executes his canvases and wine-bottle frescoes with considerable speed and undeniable flair.

Indeed, there exists at times a close correlation—in theme and mood—between subjects of Tom's paintings and those he chooses to delineate in his "country-flavored tunes" and "mini-epics"; as perceptively phrased by Charles Crespo writing in *The Aquarian* (New York City) for December 4-18-74: "Generally simple and sensitive, the songs are tales that could not be made more interesting than by Pacheco's tunes. . . ." The narrative skill within the strict confines of the American country folk-song structure makes possible the retelling of supernatural, interplanetary, or plain down-home adventures, all with their own unique effects of poetic refrain and skillful melodic repetition.

As Tom points out, "The basic human feelings are very simple. A good woman. Home. Work. Love. Death. And maybe it's time to get back to the basics." And as reported sympathetically by Jan Hödenfield in his column POP SCENE in the NEW YORK POST for Wednesday, November 20. 1974. "To get there himself . . . he paid his 'sixties dues." Tom's own song style is a fusion of elements from rock, folk, and country; and bears witness to a long-term practice and expertise. Some of the more outstanding of his "cosmic ballads" cover a wide range of setting, mood, and emotion.

His next album (recorded for and produced by RCA Victor) will be released either mid-November 1975 or early February 1976, and is fairly typical of his present spectrum of theme and mood. Entitled *Swallowed Up in the Great American Heartland* and carefully structured as an over-all concept album, it features these songs: "The Tree Song"; "Jesse Tucker"; "Song for Marylyn"; "Willie Nelson"; "Dancing Closer to the Bedroom Door"; "Jimmie the Fiddler"; "Last Bike in Town"; "The Land Will Roll On"; "All He Ever Wanted Was to Sing a Country Song"; "The Beer Song"; "Swallowed Up in the Great American Heart-Land." "The Beer Song" for one example is distinguished by a delightful country-music feeling but yet owes its main narrative animus to a rather modest but all-important "scientifictional" element. "The Tree Song," remarkable for its ecological sensitivity, tells in compact form the life-story of an old tree and some of the main events it has witnessed. It is a touching ballad without being sentimental, not that there is anything the matter with a modicum of frank, old-fashioned sentimentality. "Song for Marylyn" is an especially lovely tune that recounts the singer's meeting up with an old girlfriend. Make no doubt about it: Tom Pacheco writes excellent melodies and excellent songs, but their true artistic value is only revealed by a careful consideration of their lyrics every line of which is important to telling a story or detailing a scene or setting a mood.

Because of these lyric productions, as well as others, the present writer dedicated his monograph *Clark Ashton Smith—The Last of the Great Romantic Poets* (Silver Scarab Press, Albuquerque, NM, 1973) to Tom Pacheco (then under the professional name of "Tom Hawkins") as a "Cosmic Troubadour of the 1970s / whose remarkable folk-ballads / of fantasy and science-fiction/ continue with signal originality / the pioneering tradition / of Clark Ashton Smith's / as well as H. P. Lovecraft's / cosmic lyricism."

While the above explains more fully Tom Pacheco's native and artistic backgrounds, his experience as a rank-and-file performing musician is no less extended and impressive. He first appeared as a singer-guitarist in his native southeastern Massachusetts and then on the

Cambridge/Boston folk scene with a psychedelic-acid-rock group called the Ragamuffins: according to Tom's own chronology, "after the Byrds and before Jefferson Airplane." He subsequently formed a second group, Euphoria, with which he toured extensively and with which he recorded an album for MGM. His girlfriend at that time, by name of Sharon Alexander, and he were then signed to Columbia by Clive Davis.

Their joint album *Pacheco and Alexander*—released in 1970—received generally good reviews but did not sell outstandingly (only around 15,000 copies). However, Tom continued to write and sell songs, and it was particularly during the early seventies (outwardly a quiet period in his own career) that he experienced the first major flowering of his cosmic-astronomic muse, and created a whole new repertoire with his remarkable folk-ballads of fantasy and science-fiction. Recently Tom has once again surfaced as a performing artist, and this time with a new group, the Posse. With this new group he has now appeared at various music spots in Manhattan—performing his imaginative adventures in rime and song—and among other places, upstairs at Max's Kansas City in Greenwich Village, whereat for two weeks in late 1974 he very definitely created a "music biz interest."

It is then altogether reassuring to know that the cosmic lyricism of Clark Ashton Smith, H.P. Lovecraft, and others did not die with their passing but has found instead a continuation of their themes and their particular kind of cosmic-astronomic imagination in the same as well as other but related fields of artistic endeavor. And it is equally reassuring that the often-ignored but always-indwelling sense of wonder and marvel still finds poets and singers of distinction to hymn its praises. As the refrain in one of Tom Pacheco's folk-ballads puts it:

> "Come on through,
> Come on through,
> All the stars are waiting there for you."

To which we can only add in chorus: Amen, amen, amen!

However, it is important to note that the particular Californian tradition of cosmic lyricism peculiar to Clark Ashton Smith and George Sterling has found a direct continuation in the same general area of the state once frequented by Smith, Sterling, Ambrose Bierce, Nora May French, and other figures.

The present writer has before him a complete (or almost complete) set of the personal magazine *Black Wolf*—in addition to two issues of *Phantom Poet* and the one-shot *Stolen Fire*—all edited and published by the poet and prose-poet G. Sutton Breiding, Esq., and presently of San Francisco.

Whereas Tom Pacheco on the east coast is around 29, Sutton Breiding on the west coast is 27, and continues in his own original fashion the particular Californian lyric tradition of cosmic-mindedness mentioned immediately above. *Black Wolf, Phantom Poet, Stolen Fire,* and an occasional appearance in *Starfire* (the personal magazine edited and published by Sutton's brother William Breiding, and with each new issue gaining in distinction, it might be added), all chronicle the development and enduring presence of an exciting new fantasy poet.

But rather than damn him with such really unnecessary "genre" distinctions, let us call him instead an exciting new *imaginative* poet; a poet, moreover, notable for his honesty. Thus, *Black Wolf* has become at times not only a vehicle for the publication of Sutton Breiding's poetry but also at other times a forum of reaction to that poetry on the part of his readers. This can be irritating, this can be embarrassing, this can be fascinating, but it is not boring, and it does guarantee a kind of interest and intensity denied to more overtly "professional" but surely far less *personal* publications.

Such an editorial policy also guarantees our young poet a variety of reaction, and a reaction immediately forthcoming, whether good, bad, indifferent, or ecstatic; but reaction of some kind and that is far preferable to creating in a vacuum. It is also important to note that Sutton Breiding's poetry has constantly improved in quality, and he has a large enough backlog of material now from which to put together an impressive and valuable collection in book form. And we hear good rumors to the effect that such a collection is indeed in the offing and possibly from the Mid-West. We devoutly hope so.

The present writer certainly would not do without Sutton's remarkably compact but infinitely evocative *Dancer from Atlantis,* to say nothing of his magisterial and poignant lyric *San Francisco,* one of the single best poems created about the City by the Golden Gate without striving to be just that alone.

This latter poem captures in definitive form a certain elusive but very real mood emanating from the City and from her multifarious Victorian structures (particularly on fog-bound evenings), a mood otherwise difficult to delineate, but one of fantasy, mystery, and strangely beckoning beauty. In the recent issue of *Starfire,* Number Six, Sutton has an especially fine memorial poem to Dave Mason, the outstanding late fantasy writer, in addition to the curious and enigmatic effusion "What the Outlaw Sang to the Mirror," which features such passages as "I dream my dreams alone. No man or woman shares them. I am a solitude of echoes, a wilderness of mirrors." Later, this disquieting but appealing rhapsody closes with "Whiskey phantom. One last song in a ghost town saloon." Brave young poet, sing on into the death of old worlds and the birth of new primordial planets!

Speaking of collections in the offing, when shall we see at last—in actual book or booklet form—the singularly disturbing and haunted sonnets of "the outer dark" by Richard L. Tierney? Presently living in St. Paul, Minnesota, this excellent essayist and fictioneer is also a supernatural bard extraordinary as well as a sculptor of no mean talent who specializes in fantastic figurines whether in stone or ceramics. Mr. Tierney must rank at the very least as the finest living poet who is earnestly continuing (in his own completely original way) the not inconsiderable tradition of H. P. Lovecraft's greatest poetry, *Fungi from Yuggoth.*

Forthcoming from Arkham House at some future date, *As Green as Emeraude* by Margo Skinner forms one of the single best compilations of non-horrific fantasy poems to emerge since *A Hornbook for Witches* by Leah Bodine Drake (Arkham House, 1950). One of the San Francisco Bay Area's best professional film critics, and a general writer of unusual ability, Margo Skinner is no less talented than the late Leah Bodine Drake, moreover commands an unique style which is a skillful amalgam of traditional prosody with modern technique. Born and raised in the City by the Golden Gate, and a true San Franciscan to the core of her being, Margo has travelled nonetheless far and wide, and has lived for extended periods of time in countries as diverse as England, India, and the Philippines. Her modern romantic poetry, endued with a signally rich (but strictly disciplined) vein of brilliant imagery, reflects her experience of life in foreign lands and climates. Furthermore, it is remarkable for the warmth of feeling and the tone of compassion which predominate throughout her collection. Typical of the cosmic-mindedness or cosmic-astronomic-mindedness which permeates her best work (a cosmic-astronomic-mindedness equal to that of George Sterling or Clark Ashton Smith), the following lyric indicates (in token form) something of her scope and sympathies. (This poem is quoted in full by special permission, and is copyright 1975 by Margo Skinner.)

New Frontiers

"When the last frontier is a delicate jest
"And death is a laughable fable,
"When the islands that reel down the rim of the west
"Must yield up their bounty and give of their best
"To furnish a potentate's table . . ."

(From the incomplete poem
"The City of Trolls" by Charles Hopkins.)

Frontiers do not end; the stars are there,
Secret, mysterious, luminous, far away—
Though astronauts become buffoons today,
Red Mars glows ruby-like in the secret light,
Translucent Venus rises from the space sea's waves,
Far Centaurus beacons, and distant Altair
And a hundred thousand worlds more fair
Call "Come." Once conquered, colonized, made tame,
There lie beyond more magic realms;
The cosmos stretches infinite.

[N.B. Arkham House did not publish this collection, but Don Herron did in 1990 under the imprint of the Dawn Heron Press.]

The Spenser Experiment

Since March 1970, the author of this paper has been testing an unique concept within the improvisatory theatre of (primarily) the traditional academic lecture-hall: the viability of performing sundry cantoes (in whole or in part)—from the epic poetry of Edmund Spenser—as a dramatic, one-man, storyteller's kind of show, complete with mime and mimic gestures, with asides and glosses, with props fancy and ridiculous, with forays into and around the audience, and above all, with a sense of fun and good will, with a sense of enthusiasm and wonder.

Thus, this is the essence of the author's unique romantic poetry-act built around Spenser's epic *The Faerie Queene* as the classic or cornerstone. This is, however, but one half of the Spenser Experiment, the overt or "spectacular" half. The other half is the "quiet" or "introspective" part, to wit, the author's own first book *Songs And Sonnets Atlantean*, a deliberate artistic mythos created in the Spenserian tradition. Conceived in the style of a Renaissance "conceit" or *concetto,* it demonstrates in a singularly original way the author's grasp of his own epic-lyric-romantic tradition, both in theory and by creative example. (The book took the author ten years of careful work to complete.) The myth is presented, very much in the modern manner, as a presumably random series of "fragments in verse and fragments in prose"—together with copious notes and introduction by "Dr. Ibid Massachusetts Andor, the premier Atlantologist in the world of today." Carefully extrapolated and elaborated from Plato's Atlantis Mythos, the book is thus designed as a large-scale metaphor—a deliberate intellectual "puzzle"—on various levels and with various applications, resulting in a truly novel aesthetic construct.

Note: This is one of two papers that formed part of the materials of an application (made in late September 1973) for a grant from the Renaissance Centre in San Francisco, the sponsors of the California-based Renaissance Pleasure Faire. The Renaissance Centre will on occasion give grants to qualified Renaissance scholars. Whilst they did not challenge the authority or validity of the applicant's Renaissance scholarship and achievements, the Centre could not afford at that time to give him the (rather large) grant he had requested. Despite this lack of support, the poet-author has persevered, and continues to find his own way through his own efforts as well as with the help and advice of numerous friends both in the U.S.A. and abroad.

A further feature of the book is the author's own innovation of a special sonnet-form, and thus an original contribution to the older (traditional) prosody,—to wit, the Spenserian stanza-sonnet, based upon a fusion of both the Spenserian stanza and the Spenserian sonnet. This innovation of form incidentally demonstrates that the traditional prosody (descended from the troubadours, trouvères, and minnesingers of the High Middle Ages) is by no means exhausted, as divers authorities have previously maintained.

Although published by a small house in the American Midwest, and although unable to command any major publicity, the book has met a largely distinguished reception in the general field of fantasy and science fiction, as well as in selected sectors of Academe. A "gallery of written reactions" is hereby appended as evidence of this distinguished reception.

The poetry-performances themselves—that is, the first half of the Spenser Experiment—have likewise met a generally friendly reception. A small selection of reviews and "recommendations" is likewise hereby appended as evidence of these kind and good-natured reactions.

The poetry-act itself was originally conceived—and has been performed since—with certain considerations always to the forefront. What is the particular beauty or validity of *live* poetry or *live* literature? Never before—evidently—has there been so many poets and so much poetry as there is today. That is, so much *printed* poetry. But, literature was originally transmitted *orally,* and there is nothing else in literature quite so effective in literal vocalization as poetry. How often, however, does the average person in English-speaking cultures encounter poetry first as *sound,* and as presented by a poet himself. Not too often, we must admit. Poetry has become, increasingly, literature in poetic form and, as such, is experienced primarily through the medium of the printed page.

In the case of much older poetry—normally accepted today as "venerable classics"—this constitutes a tragedy. Much older poetry is uniquely resonant and melodious. The older classics of poetry are like magnificent pieces of music, but music which is rarely played or heard. The printed page, of itself, has neither feeling nor music nor magic, and many persons lack the requisite background or developed instinct to grasp by themselves the poetic experience which is potential on the printed page. And this is where a skilled poet-performer can render a genuine service by vocalizing the poetry—from memory and with gestures and with intense feeling—for the benefit of whatever audience has gathered to *listen* and *watch* and (hopefully) *feel.*

At a time when too many of our older English poets are known only through the medium of the printed page, a genuine service is especially rendered by performing (again; from memory and in a dramatic format) whole cantoes from Spenser's epic *The Faerie Queene*, the greatest work by our first great poet in (early) modern English.

As odd as it might seem to most people today—who would ordinarily think of Elizabethan times as "the Age of Shakespeare"—for Shakespeare himself and his fellow Elizabethans the great contemporary English classic would have been Edmund Spenser's great epic-romance-allegory.

On the surface, the poem is an unique Renaissance type of discursive romance with many subsidiary narratives, or romances. And one of the most cogent and cohesive ways for a single poet-performer to dramatize "the Prince of Poets in his tyme" is as an old-fashioned storyteller who has a few "tall tales" to relate, but in metre and rime. This is completely in character with the poem itself as well as with the romance tradition from which the poem comes, and upon which the poem draws.

The Faerie Queene not only sums up medieval epic, medieval romance, and medieval allegory but classical epic, Renaissance epic, and Renaissance pastoral as well. The influence, whether direct or indirect, that this highly idiosyncratic work has had on all later literature written in English, is (quite simply) enormous. *The Faerie Queene* influenced not only such immediate contemporaries as Christopher Marlowe and William Shakespeare or such immediate successors to the specific Spenserian tradition as John Milton but also (closer to our own time) the whole generation of English Romantic poets: Keats, Coleridge, Shelley, etc. Therefore, it is important to the poem's mere survival that it be recreated and reconstituted in a dramatic way so that an academic audience can be exposed to Spenser *as prime experience* and not merely as so much printed material.

There is no other work so thoroughly saturated with the Renaissance as *The Faerie Queene.* The English Renaissance comes at the end of the Continental Renaissance, and as such, it sums up (whether directly or symbolically) the entire cultural life of the Middle Ages and the Renaissance. *The Faerie Queene*'s particular achievement was immediately subsumed into the work of Spenser's contemporaries and successors. Yet, paradoxically, Spenser saved us from too thorough a renascence, a fact most perceptively pointed out by C. S. Lewis in his monograph *The Allegory of Love*. Thus, "the Prince of Poets in his tyme" remains the great intermediary betwixt Chaucer and Shakespeare, betwixt medieval times and modern times.

It is beyond the scope of this paper to show all the curious and arcane lore—symbology, astrology, numerology, folklore, etc.—that Spenser draws upon and utilizes with brilliant intellectual effect throughout his epic–romance–allegory. The ultimate core of meaning is as "dense" and as carefully "hidden" as the same in James Joyce's *Ulysses* and *Finnegans Wake*, or Vladimir Nabokov's *Pale Fire,* or the succinct fantasies of the Argentinian poet Jorge Luis Borges. However, over two dozen book-length monographs on Spenser have appeared in the past ten or twelve years. These studies help to define and elucidate many aspects of the poem formerly thought to be confused or misguided. And most of these studies clearly indicate whole avenues of approach and appreciation that have remained otherwise "lost" since sometime in the 1600s. Spenser was to remain "England's Arch-poet" until the late 1600s and the early 1700s when the apotheosis of Shakespeare began, thanks to the propagandizing of Samuel Johnson and others of the new Augustan Age. See "Some Notes on Spenser" taken from the introduction of *Songs and Sonnets Atlantean* for a compact summary of some of the book-length Spenserian studies mentioned immediately above.

All this is by way of prelude to a consideration of the Spenser poetry-act itself, already described in compact form at the very beginning of this paper. But, since the act is difficult to conceptualize from a mere abstract statement, it will probably be easier to grasp from an example. The example chosen is the poet-performer's most recent show, to wit, "Saint George and the Dragon," Canto XI of Book I of *The Faerie Queene.*

This particular canto recounts the traditional story of the virtuous and virtue-aspiring young knight battling the monstrous dragon—but, however, from the perspective of Renaissance "epic propriety." Thus,

Spenser arranges the fight so as to last three days. The characters are: Saint George, alias the Red Cross Knight, representing Holiness; the Lady Una, representing Truth; and "that old Dragon," representing Death. During the three days of the battle, the Lady Una is safely situated on a hill from which she can most effectively give her knight the considerable benefit of her moral support. The fight itself is highly comedic, and Spenser presents it in a highly stylized way, almost in the manner of a ballet. At the end of the first day's fight, the knight is saved purely by chance: the dragon knocks him backside into a conveniently located well—to wit, the Well of Life—whose waters possess miraculous powers of healing and refreshing. The well completely heals the knight of all his wounds and fatigue, and the morning of the second day sees him as good as new, battling the dragon once again. At the end of the second day's fight the knight is again saved purely by chance: he slips and falls into a copious stream of "precious balm" flowing from a likewise conveniently-located magical tree—to wit, The Tree of Life—which similarly possesses miraculous powers of healing and refreshing. Again, like the well, this tree—or rather its balm— completely heals the knight of all his wounds and fatigue. Needless to say, both the well and the tree are strictly "off limits" to the dragon— "for he of death was made." At last, on the third day, Sir George triumphs over the dragon—again purely by chance—the Lady Una comes down from her hill and congratulates her knight on his great victory, and "the greatest fight of all time" is over.

This brief summary allows us to perceive how adroitly Spenser makes the old legend new. The legend, being received information from the past, is akin to historical fact, and since Spenser knows we know the outcome of the story in advance, he is more or less free to develop the actual fight as he sees fit. In this way Spenser injects considerable suspense and comedy by making neither the dragon nor the knight particularly intelligent, and by having the knight win out over the dragon, purely by chance as it were, or (in the terms of early Puritan England) by "the eternal providence of God."

Also, as can be readily seen, this particular canto lends itself especially well to graphic storytelling. The "action" takes about an hour in all, and falls into four or five major divisions: the introduction describing the knight, the lady, their quest, and their first sighting of the dragon; then the elaborate description of the dragon; then the first day's fight; the second day's fight; and finally the third day's fight and the brief triumphant conclusion.

The poet-performer sharply defines these divers divisions of the over-all canto, especially those circumscribing the three days of the great battle. He slips both into, and out of, the narrative. He takes all the parts, delineating the three characters of the "dramatis personae" with appropriate changes in voice, gesture, and prop. He carefully glosses the references from classical mythology, as well as any and all recondite or difficult phases. There are also numerous "broad" asides that comment on the action, and that thus serve to heighten any humorous effect. The glosses and asides are delivered for the most part in a synthetic Cockney accent; this give an amusing contrast to the "refined" or "noble" mode of vocal projection that the poet-performer uses for most of Spenser's actual text.

The poet-performer in this particular canto has carefully prepared the text with a twentieth-century audience in mind. Thus, whilst certainly respecting Spenser's actual lines, the poet-performer has not hesitated to modernize some words and phrases. The greater communicability resulting from these modest changes, more than justifies the changes themselves.

The "action" is on occasion taken into and around the audience as the need or inspiration arises. Together with the poet-performer's motley Neo-Elizabethan costume, what emerges is a kind of free-form courtly *commedia dell'arte,* The narrative itself amounts to just about 500 lines—to say nothing of all the asides and glosses—all of which has had to be painstakingly prepared, memorized, and rehearsed.

Although there is never any substitute for a live performance, the description above does give some kind of idea as to the Spenser poetry-act's over-all style. Thus, the resultant performance is indeed "a new kind of literary art."

This poetry-act possesses certain precise analogies to the art of metric narrative as once practiced by the jongleurs, or before them by the pagan bards, or as still practiced by folk bards to this day. One important component, common to the bard or jongleur, is lacking however in the present case. That is, a musical instrument for accompaniment. While many bards have used harps or harp-like instruments, the jongleurs most commonly used the peculiar three-string medieval fiddle, to wit, the *vièle*: whilst bowing divers long bass notes with the peculiar medieval arched bow, the jongleurs would half-sing, half-chant, the successive strophes of medieval epic or medieval romance. Their musical art, however simple or "primitive" to a twentieth-century sensibility, created a monotonous but hypnotic apparatus, perfect for leading the listener's attention deeper into the divers ways and byways of any given story.

An art of more elaborate accompaniment was practiced by the troubadours in the south of France, in the north of Italy, and in the northeast of Spain; by the trouvères in the north of France; and by the minnesingers at the German-speaking courts in the middle and north of Europe. During the 1000s on into the 1300s, many of these poets sang their lyrics to the accompaniment of the vièle, or of the little medieval harp with metal strings, or of the early medieval lute. This last came into Europe via Spain, Italy, and the Balkan states about the time of the First Crusade. The lute at first had only four single strings, plucked with a metal pick or with a large (quill) feather. Later, the four strings evolved into four pairs of strings, and still later, the medieval lute transformed into the Renaissance lute with yet further pairs of strings, and played no longer with a plectrum but with the fingertips in a delicately arpeggiated style. Whilst singing or narrating, the jongleurs had often accompanied themselves on an earlier simpler style of lute called the mandola, or mandora, and with one small variant of it surviving to this day as the mandolin (and still very much alive in such eminently popular genres of music as American country western, etc.), or mandolino.

Something of the troubadour and minnesinger yet lingered on in the lutenist–composer–singers of the Renaissance who created and sang the lyrics of their own songs, or who adapted the lyrics (i.e., the *written* lyrics) of others as the basis for conscious art songs, or sung poems. Mention must also be made of the poetic "rhapsodists" at divers Renaissance courts. Those of such courtiers and courtly poets who were also good amateur musicians, would recite long passages from such favorite narrative poems as *Orlando Furioso* and *Orlando Innamorato*, whilst they would improvise on the lute to certain well-established melodic patterns called *arias* (used to denote certain musical schemes, such as the "Aria di Romanesca" or "Aria di Ruggiero," and not to be confused with the later operatic arias).

However, with the development of the poet-Renaissance or baroque lute, the lute proper now became, for the most part, the exclusive property of super-virtuosos, and was perforce abandoned by cultivated amateurs for the increasingly popular and simpler Spanish guitar. The baroque guitar and the early classic guitar consciously imitated the late lute technique and repertory. With the death of the last great lutanists around the mid-1700s, the instrument then passed into the hands of lesser musicians clearly incapable of continuing the great achievements of the lute's immediate past. Christian Gottlieb Scheidler, the so-called Last of the German Lutanists, ended his life as a guitarist and guitar teacher.

By 1800 the lute had become virtually extinct; but, in the German-speaking countries the lute never completely died out, and survived into the early twentieth century when first-class trained antiquarian-scholar musicians became interested in the instrument, and the modern revival of the classical lute began. Today, thanks to the pioneering efforts of Oscar Chilesotti, Emilio Pujol, Walter Gerwig, Julian Bream, Eugen Müller-Dombois, and others, the classical lute is now thoroughly re-established as a practical performing instrument. The once-lowly Spanish guitar has coincidentally become the king of the fretted instruments, and has fallen heir to much of the old lute literature for its earlier performing repertoire.

Thus, what the poet-performer now seeks in order to make his Spenser poetry-act complete and authentic both in style and character, is the musical component now lacking but nonetheless indigenous to the art of bards and lyricists widely separated by time and space. That is, the musical component in the form of an instrument for accompaniment.

Rather than the guitar, the "magic harp" of the lute is the ideal stringed instrument for the poet-musician. Its pure tone and harp-like technique lend themselves very well to the singing or chanting or (highly musical) reciting of verses. And a poet addressing himself to a "romance" style of music, would need to know the music of both the Middle Ages and the Renaissance, from the 1000s or 1100s on into the first two decades of the 1600s, the apogee of the late Renaissance lute, which reached at that particular time its largest range: ten courses, or nineteen strings. Around 1620 the late Renaissance lute began evolving into the early-baroque lute with its distinctively different style of tuning and playing. The poet-musician would need to know the melodies and words of troubadours, trouvères, and minnesingers, and *precisely* how they accompanied themselves on the lute, their characteristic melodic progressions, etc. He would need to know the lute songs of the Renaissance, and their characteristic styles. He would need to know his way among the great mass of purely instrumental music for the lute produced during the Renaissance and preserved in published "tablatures"—from the earliest preserved (the late 1400s and the early 1500s) to the culmination of the Renaissance lute style in the two collections of lute compositions by Robert Ballard, chief lutanist at the court of France from 1610 into 1617 (i.e., during the Regency of Marie de Medicis, mother of Louis XIII).

From this great wealth of music the poet-musician would then need to abstract those styles, cadences, and progressions best suited to the interlacing lines and rimes of Spenser's melodiously modulated stanzas. This is all a very large order of achievement. and would require extensive musical training anywhere from one year to three or four years. The poet would need to study lute and lute music at those places and institutions whose *precise* musical traditions would prove most beneficial and fruitful for the *precise* needs of the poet-musician.

That institution which most immediately comes to mind is the Schola Cantorum Basiliensis in Basel, Switzerland, founded in 1933 for the study and practice of "old" music, that is, from the High Middle Ages through the Renaissance on into the Late Baroque period ending around 1750. However, whilst their method and methodology are absolutely authentic, the Schola requires some previous musical training and ability that could only be obtained by a year's study (of beginning lute) at some other, most appropriate, German-speaking musical institution of impeccable and unbroken "romance" traditions.

The place which then most immediately comes to mind is Vienna, Austria, to the general east of Basel. Vienna has been a capital of music for over one thousand years, and a great imperial seat from the time of Marcus Aurelius (the second century A.D.) to the abdication of Karl I, the last of the Austro-Hungarian emperors. Some of the most signal developments in the Medieval-Renaissance-Baroque-Classical-Romantic tradition occurred in Vienna, and her specific "romance" and poet-musician traditions go directly back to the brilliant ducal court of the Babenbergs in the High Middle Ages. Some of the greatest minnesingers found employment as court poet-singers at the court of the Babenbergs. Indeed, this court nurtured the early career of Walter Von der Vogelweide, later to develop into the greatest medieval poet of the German-speaking peoples. Especial note should be made of the fact that these minnesingers accompanied their singing both with harp and with lute. When the late-romantic movement in music reached its ultimate development in the late nineteenth century on into the early twentieth, most of it transpired in Vienna whose musico-romantic traditions thus revert back (in an unbroken line of culture, it must be emphasized) to the heart of the Middle Ages.

The Vienna Academy of Music (formerly the Vienna Conservatory) and its affiliated Hochschule für Musik reflect in their own tradition the thousand years and more of this uninterrupted Viennese musical culture. The Academy could thus give the poet-musician the necessary training prerequisite to the regimen established by the Schola Cantorum Basiliensis. For this training the poet-musician will require a late Renaissance lute of special design and make (ten courses, or nineteen strings), as well as his tuition and basic living expenses (room and board). The poet-performer has been preparing himself for this musical training since late 1971 when he began teaching himself the rudiments of music, the decipherment of simple musical notation, the art of tuning with wooden pegs, etc., all on a mandola-guitar with the six strings tuned (from top to bottom) E B G DAD. He has taught himself as much as he can, and now requires such regular musical training in lute as only such authentic institutions as the Schola Cantorum Basiliensis and the Wiener Academie could provide. With such training and preparation, the Last of the Courtly Poets could then endow his Spenser poetry-act with the most authentic musical atmosphere and accompaniment possible. He would also be able to compose and perform all manner of musical settings for a wide variety of single lyrics, medieval, Renaissance, or late romantic.

The style of accompaniment for the Spenser material would not be "close" (that is, one bar or measure of music for each line of poet-

ry, etc.) but would be "interpolative" (that is, featuring little composi-
tions and passages for lute, at the beginning and the end of any given
canto, as well as in the half-dozen or so natural breaks that 'occur
within any longer narrative passage).

The poet-performer's ultimate Spenser repertoire will include
three two-hour shows, each with intermission, as follows:

SAINT GEORGE AND THE DRAGON
(Cantoes XI *and* XII of Book I of *The Faerie Queene*)
THE HOUSE OF PRIDE
(Cantoes IV *and* V of Book I of *The Faerie Queene*)
THE MUTABILITIE CANTOES
(Cantoes VI *and* VII of Book VII of *The Faerie Queene*)

Each of these three shows will be eventually furnished with authentic
lute music carefully chosen and fitted to the particular needs of each
canto. For such a large order of work, the poet-performer manifestly
will require some considerable financial assistance, whether such as-
sistance takes the form of scholarship or grant or fellowship. And the
poet-performer will also require the opportunity to concentrate his
main energies in preparing both the dramatic and musical aspect of
the Spenser shows listed immediately above.

The poet-performer and/or his (lecture) agents, in any future bro-
chures and publicity relative to his romance poetry-act, would always
make a point of mentioning, in some featured way, and help (as in
the form of a sizable grant) that the Renaissance Centre would see fit
to give him.

[N. B. The poet-performer did not receive the grant requested and
never achieved his ambitious program. This essay was written during
the summer of 1973. The appendices mentioned on pp. 77 and 79—
"a gallery of written reactions," reviews, and "recommendations," and
"Some Notes on Spencer"—are not included herein.]

Gaspard de la Nuit and the Poem in Prose

The character who gives his name to the one and only hook achieved by its author, Louis or Aloysius Bertrand (1807–1841), is obviously and intentionally a projection of that author, a fictional *doppelganger,* and is often invoked throughout that collection, it would seem interchangeably, in a half-serious or half-whimsical way. For example, the long introduction in prose "Gaspard de la Nuit" is signed by Louis Bertrand, and the "Preface" following it at once, is signed by Gaspard de la Nuit. Despite the author's charming and quite attractive whimsy in this and other instances, he manages to make some valid and eminently significant statements about the purpose of his highly structured compilation, *Gaspard de la Nuit,* first published at long last in late 1842, a year and a half after the author's untimely death in April of 1841.

The purpose of Bertrand's collection is the description or depiction through the words of *fantasies* (or *fantaisies,* the poet's own literal term) in the manner of Rembrandt and Caillot (no less than a dozen or more of other celebrated artists whether ancient or comparatively modern). By fantasies the author intends imaginary paintings, that is, through the medium of prose, in clear but highly condensed prose. Nowhere does Bertrand use the term that became common from at least Baudelaire onward, the poem in prose. But in essence, or quintessence, what Bertrand had accomplished, while achieving his objective purpose, the creation of otherwise non-existent paintings, was this: that he had created a new form, the *poème en prose,* and had created extensively within that form.

Even though something like it had existed before his collection, whether in French or in English, it tended to do so in isolation, or as part of something else, a novel, a short story, a book of prose translations from verse originals whether genuine or feigned. It was Bertrand's example that influenced Baudelaire and others to take up the form and to expand its purpose and capabilities. In the case of Baudelaire, who had already translated, or actually rewritten, all of the then available prose (in English) of Edgar Allan Poe into French, the example of certain short and compact pieces of prose, such as *Eleanora, The Masque of the Red Death, Shadow—A Parable, Silence—*

A Fable, as well as others, had exercised a strong influence, supplemental to be sure but still determining, on the French poet's own posthumously published volume of prose-poems known under two different titles, *Le Spleen de Paris,* or (more tellingly) the *Petits poèmes en prose* (1867).

Thus it was the example of Baudelaire, and then retroactively that of Bertrand through the example and influence of Baudelaire, that became decisive in the promulgation of the new form, whether during the latter 1800s or early 1900s, and in a variety of languages and their associated literatures. It is beyond the scope of this capsule essay to trace in detail the later evolution of the poem in prose, except for a few salient examples in English as embodied in two distinct collections—and except for one other curious and ironic development, quite unintended by Bertrand, Poe, and Baudelaire.

This unintentional consequence came about not only through itself, the later evolution of the poem in prose in French or in whatever other language in which it happened, but also through the even more influential example of Walt Whitman and his one collection *Leaves of Grass* (which nonetheless passed through several salient versions by the original poet himself). As I have written elsewhere, the long essay "Bertrand, Dijon and Gaspard" (in my translation and presentation of *Gaspard de la Nuit,* published by Black Coat Press in the Summer of 2004):—

> It was Bertrand's innovation of the actual form of the poem in prose—with all its deliberate condensation and hence its evocatory power of imaginative suggestion as exemplified on a sustained basis in *Gaspard de la Nuit*—that inspired Baudelaire to recreate the form into a flexible medium in prose of diversified length and character for his strategic volume [known alternately as either] *Le Spleen de Paris,* or [more definingly] *Petits poèmes en prose.* His admiration for Bertrand, as well as the example that Baudelaire himself supplied with his own volume, helped to popularize the form, or the medium, of the poem in prose with other writers whether French, British, Russian or American (that is, the Anglophone world of the U.S.A.) before it became indistinguishable from modern contemporary poetry written directly in any kind of prose arranged in any manner whatsoever.

Thus it is quite ironic that something created by such lovers of style and form as Bertrand, Poe, and Baudelaire, such lovers of polished work, albeit sometimes innovative, achieved in the traditional prosodies of their native languages, should have led, even if indirectly, to the dissolution of poetry as perceived in terms of rigorously strict forms. That poets in general should have done so in search, and in experimentation, of a new type of poetry responding to the conditions and exigencies of modern life, is not an issue of primary concern here, however validly that issue may land in the balance. As I raise the rhetorical question in the introduction just preceding this one:

> In a day and age when poets in general have freed themselves from the presumed shackles of the traditional prosodies in English and most other languages, is it any wonder that so many skilled practitioners of the art can achieve 12 to 14 volumes during their lifetime, or even as elevated a number as 30, as witness the total published by the late Kenneth Koch of New York City?

No matter the rhetoric or form or shape that poetry may assume, presumably it somehow remains poetry in some indefinable way, and achieves the much desired continuity, as from one generation of living creatures unto the succeeding one. However, the poem in prose, as exemplified in the works of Bertrand, Poe, and Baudelaire, has meanwhile fulfilled its own precise and rigorously defined recipe, and has achieved, and this is more strategic, its own explicit continuity. I cite here now the two most salient examples in English as embodied in two distinct collections: *Pastels in Prose* and *Ebony and Crystal, Poems in Verse and Prose.* The first collection, *Pastels in Prose,* published by Harper and Brothers at New York in 1890, was chosen and translated from the French of 32 authors by Stuart Merrill (1863–1915), with an introduction by William Dean Howells (1837–1920), that notable promulgator of American Realism in literary terms.

Pastels in Prose constitutes in its entirety a choice and remarkable anthology of what some of the most eminent French poets had achieved in this new genre (starting with Bertrand), rendered all the more effective by the supple and natural English accomplished by the author-editor in question. It is the only book published in English by Stuart Merrill who, although born in the U.S.A., passed most of his life in France, and wrote all his other books, and had them published, in French, becoming in the process a well-known and quite respected French poet of the then *fin-de-siècle,* the late 1800s and early 1900s.

It was around the start of the 1910s, probably as a result of his new friendship with George Sterling (begun in early 1911 but first through correspondence), that a copy of this remarkable collection came into the hands of the brilliant young California poet Clark Ashton Smith, who read it, and not only subjected it to intense perusal during the 1910s, but apparently read and re-read it throughout his lifetime, including his final years. The result of this intense perusal and assimilation found its just efflorescence in Smith's third poetry collection, but only second major one, *Ebony and Crystal, Poems in Verse and Prose,* published by Smith himself at Auburn in late 1922. Although this magisterial collection has never become that well-known, at least to the literary mainstream, Smith exhibited himself in it, among other accomplishments, as the sovereign master of this new form in English by virtue of the nine-and-twenty variegated poems in prose that end the volume. However, the undeniable influence of *Ebony and Crystal,* including that of the poems in prose chosen by the author-poet to appear in it, has remained for the most part restricted to the authors and poets working in the genre or genres of fantasy and science fiction, that is to say, of modern imaginative literature.

Thus my translation and presentation of *Gaspard de la Nuit,* as published recently by Black Coat Press, is a return not only to a seminal and consequential classic of French literature, a veritable compendium of the French Romanticism of the 1820s and 1830s, but above all else to the fountainhead of the poem in prose in any modern language whatsoever anywhere. Its decisive influence on Baudelaire has even made its impress in English, even if only in assimilated or transformed substance (rather alchemistically), through the divers translations of the *Petits poèmes en prose* that first began to appear in the late 1800s. In essence this recent publication of *Gaspard de la Nuit* through the medium of the popular press, rather than the academic (university) one, is a return of the poem in prose to its source, notwithstanding the fact that in English there have long existed the salient poetic experiments in prose of such a modern master as Edgar Allan Poe on the one hand, and of such a much older master as Sir Thomas Browne on the other hand.

Los Angeles, 19 March 2005

Continuity via *Songs and Sonnets Atlantean*

As befits a private publication, this is a personal statement, eschewing the editorial first person plural for the idiosyncratic first person singular. For me the three quintessential ingredients in poetry are music, magic, and continuity, all of which exist in abundance in the output of the California Romantic poets, a group or movement that extends from c. 1890 to c. 1930, from Ambrose Bierce through George Sterling and Nora May French, and then up through the first major phase of the poetic career of Clark Ashton Smith ending c. 1930, when he concentrated his poetic talents on his prose fantasies, thus a second career begun c. 1928 and finished c. 1938, when he again returned to poetry. I discovered the poetry of the California Romantics through Ashton Smith and his prose fantasies (I had begun reading those in the Spring of 1954), starting in the Spring of 1958 through his four early poetry collections, 1912, 1918, 1922, and 1925. Sometime after that spring I began reading the works of both George Sterling and Nora May French.

I had already studied much poetry, beginning in Latin with the first 6 of the 12 books making up *The Aeneid,* by the great Roman poet Virgil, during my last two years, 1951-1952, and 1952-1953, of high school in the city of my birth, New Bedford, Massachusetts. In a similar manner I also learned much about poetry during 1956-1961, my four years at U.C.L.A., when I studied French language and literature from the eleventh century through the twentieth, finding a particular affinity with the poets of the Renaissance and those of the 1800s, the French Romantics, Parnassians, Symbolists, etc. English-language poetry, whether British or American, I read and studied simply on my own, or as part of the regular curriculum in grammar school and high school. However, it was my reading and study in depth of *The Faerie Queene* (1590, 1596, 1609), the idiosyncratic epic by Edmund Spenser—a deliberate and intensive study conducted from February or March of 1961 through the following June—that proved pivotal in my case, as it has in that of many other poets and writers whether during Spenser's own period or subsequently during all the succeeding centuries, 1600s, 1700s, 1800s, and 1900s.

What led me to this intense perusal of such a vast and quite uncommon masterpiece and literary landmark was the sage and serious advice of several friends, first William Farmer during the Summer of 1960, when I worked at a temporary summer job in Auburn, California (Ashton Smith's birthplace), and second, Fritz and Jonquil Leiber, whom I met in February of 1961, when all three of us resided in the Los Angeles basin, they alternating between Santa Monica and Pacific Palisades, and I in the same Pacific Palisades during the same period, in my case from c. 1957 or 1958 through the Summer of 1965. It was the sustained examination and experience of *The Faerie Queene* that not only made me into a poet, but that pulled together all that I had previously learned about poetry whether in Latin, French, Italian, Spanish, or German, whether in terms of subject matter or technique.

Apart from Spenser's unique style and stanza and subject matter, what especially fascinated me was the elder poet's use of myth and legend, as extensive in its manner as the similar but even more radical use of the same mythopoeic elements in the poetry of Clark Ashton Smith, who moreover had invented much new myth and legend not only in his poetry of 1910–1930, but especially his prose fantasies of 1928–1938. It was inevitable that I would continue not only Ashton Smith's uncompromising Romanticism but just as much his mythopoeic qualities. I had only gradually come to the realization of Smith's true grandeur as poet and thinker, but by the Summer of 1960, partially as a result of my discussions about Smith and other writers with my great and good friend William Farmer, this belief in Smith's greatness as a poet had become my firm and unyielding conviction.

For me it was fabulous that Ashton Smith still was very much alive, a survivor from another age—just as George Sterling, a product of the Romantic Century born in 1869, still was very much alive up through late 1926, thus during Smith's years as a young adult {1911–1926)— and that Smith was living in Pacific Grove with Carol Jones Dorman (married late in 1954). By means of his long-term friend Ethel Heiple in Auburn, I met and visited the elder poet himself at his home near Monterey, first in the late Summer of 1958, and then in the early Summer of 1959. I realize now that what I perceived then in Ashton Smith was the Lost Tradition of High Romance Poetry, lost or at least intellectually disdained from the early 1920s on into the latter 1950s. When I began writing my own mature poetry in March of 1961, it was very much under the double aegis of romance provided by Edmund Spenser and Clark Ashton Smith.

When I created the first dozen poems or so for what became the

First Series of *Songs and Sonnets Atlantean* (it took me some three years to get them more or less the way that I purposed) and then sent a copy of them as a token of my own interior life to August Derleth, but not as an overt submission per se for Arkham House—he had just sent me a copy of his own *Walden West* some little time before-hand—well, I was completely unprepared not only for his gracious acceptance, but especially for his warm encouragement to continue the MS. in the same fashion, which he promised implicitly to publish.

Seven years later I finally completed the volume, and moreover with the valuable addition of the introduction and notes by Dr. Ibid M. Andor (since deceased), the then foremost Atlantologist in the world. August lived up to his word, and published the entire volume as I had conceived it. The edition of 2000 copies gradually sold out over a period of twenty years, that is, during 1971 through 1991, more or less.

Over-all the book received excellent critical reaction: my long-term and patient labor, not to mention gamble, had paid off, at least artistically, or (if you will) aesthetically. Poetry scrivened more or less in strict form, employing meter and rime, requires a considerable amount of painstaking travail and relentless testing. Strict poems in prose like those of Edgar Allan Poe, Aloysius Bertrand, Baudelaire, and Clark Ashton Smith also demand the same things in equal measure.

In a day and age when poets in general have freed themselves from the presumed shackles of the traditional prosodies in English and most other languages, is it any wonder that so many skilled practitioners of the art can achieve 12 to 14 volumes during their lifetime, or even as elevated a number as 30, as witness the total published by the late Kenneth Koch of New York City? Aloysius Bertrand achieved *one* almost perfect volume of poems in prose *Gaspard de la Nuit,* and Baudelaire himself accomplished only *two* original collections, *Les Fleurs du Mal* and *the Petits Poèmes en Prose.* Walt Whitman crafted one *Leaves of Grass.*

Of all the favorable reviews that my little but substantial book received, none could have given me greater pleasure than the one accorded it by Earl J. Dias in the *Standard-Times* of New Bedford, Massachusetts (where I spent the first 18 years of my life) for Sunday, 5 March 1972, a review wherein he opined: "Sidney-Fryer has created in his fictional Atlantis an entire civilization and a body of absorbing literature. The book should appeal to lovers of poetry, devotees of science fiction, and to those who admire writers who can fashion a realistic world from the materials of mythology and speculation."

This review gave me great pleasure not just because it was favorable but simply because it had emanated from the pen of someone with whose multifarious critical writings I had grown up. Earl J. Dias was a practising and quite evenhanded critic for many years, and contributed innumerable reviews of books, plays, films, concerts, etc., to the *Standard-Times*, the leading newspaper of southeastern Massachusetts. However, he worked primarily as a professor of English at Southeastern Massachusetts University, where he taught drama and Shakespeare. As critic, teacher, and person, Dias was highly regarded.

In the latter 1980s, directly inspired by the warm encouragement of Stanley D. McNail, poet, poetry editor, and poetry publisher, I began a second collection, the Second Series of *Songs and Sonnets Atlantean.* Then to a circle of close and long-term friends I issued some of the individual sections in a series of photocopied booklets, thus privately published, and they made their appearance in 1991, 1992, 1996, and 1997, respectively. I completed the MS. of the entire collection in June of 1998, two months before I moved back to Los Angeles, and began submitting it to less than a handful of publishers, Donald M. Grant, Arkham House, and Fedogan and Bremer, among others. Although it did not find acceptance at any of these firms (all specializing in imaginative literature), I finally submitted it to John G. Betancourt of Wildside Press, thanks to the welcome established for it there by friend and colleague Don Herron. There it found acceptance, and made its appearance at last sometime Summer of 2003.

From August through December of 2001 I became involved with the late science-fiction poet, as well as publisher of science-fiction poetry in book form, Keith Allen Daniels, owner of Anamnesis Press, who tentatively planned to bring my second collection out. However, due to his ongoing battle with cancer from March onward, ending in his death c. mid-December, this possibility did not materialize. Nevertheless, I am indebted to Keith not only for his kind and generous friendship (from April of 2000 until his death), but more particularly for the warm encouragement that he gave me to continue the creation of new poetry. Our exchange of poetics had proven utterly cordial.

Thus I began thinking of a third collection as a real possibility, the Third Series of *Songs and Sonnets Atlantean.* Casting off my diffidence, and implicitly trusting to my faith in the Muse—that goddess inspiring poets and looking after them—I began to create the series in the Winter of 2001-2002, and managed to complete it in the Winter of 2004-2005. During the three years required to create and complete the collection, I issued—again to a circle of close and long-term friends—some of the individual sections in a series of photocopied booklets, thus privately published, and they made their appearance in 2002, 2003, 2004, and 2005, respectively. It is now ready for publication by Black Coat Press (formerly of Los Angeles, California, and now resettled at Chalabre, France, south-west of Carcassonne), and is presently scheduled to appear sometime Summer of 2005.

And this brings me back to the Winter of 1960-1961, where it all began for me as a Modern Romantic poet continuing the tradition of the California Romantics, as given renewed inspiration from Spenser as the fountainhead of romance in Early Modern English. At about the same time that I first began reading Spenser's great epic-romance-allegory *The Faerie Queene,* and putting down on paper the first of the poems that constitute the First Series of *Songs and Sonnets Atlantean*—this was in March of 1961—I was also seriously looking into the *oeuvre* of Algernon Charles Swinburne for the first time. I was doing so to discover a direct alleged link (per Lin Carter) between the output of Swinburne and that of Clark Ashton Smith. This link I did not find, although I discovered why someone like Ashton Smith would have admired quite a bit the work of a poet like Swinburne. I also discovered what was for me personally the work of an extraordinary, even Titanic author, noticeably distinct from Spenser.

Spenser is one of the very few great elder poets in English disdained by Swinburne, and likewise, I am confident, Spenser would have found Swinburne quite antagonistic to his own tastes whether in temperament or in poetics. Be that as it may, Swinburne's over-all output, with his many collections of lyrical poetry by themselves—never mind his poetic dramas, and his many volumes of essays and other studies—remains a colossal achievement not just in terms of size but just as much in terms of technical innovation, no less than technical virtuosity. Among the collections there stand out the three series of *Poems and Ballads,* the first two being particularly remarkable and copious. If I could achieve in the manner of Swinburne a total of only three series of my own *Songs and Sonnets Atlantean* as my life's poetic *oeuvre,* then I should rest content. Or so I thought, and as I still think.

The thought or desire that I scarcely permitted myself to think back in the Winter and Spring of 1961—"Would it be possible for me, just beginning as an adult poet, to achieve three series of my own poems, numerically speaking, in the manner of Swinburne and his *Poems and Ballads?*"—has found fulfillment, *mirabile dictum!* I have now created three series of *Songs and Sonnets Atlantean,* and may now rest content at least in regard to that wish-fulfillment. I remain grateful to the Muse forevermore. Whereas the first two series each required ten or more years, the third and final one has taken me only three years, a feat that for me must rank as incredibly fast.

But what is more, the creation of some innovative poetry in traditionalist form has allowed me through thick and thin, no matter the artistic or political climate through which I happened to find myself surviving, to cultivate my own garden, as per Voltaire's injunction at the end of *Candide,* his delicious and compact fable-romance, a cautionary tale if ever there was one. This capacity for the creation of new poetry has proven a marvelous personal resource, whether through periods of elation or depression, especially the latter. One has always a secret incantation with which to revive an interior enchantment!

It is thus with a renewed sense of music, magic, and continuity that I present here, courtesy of my friend Scott Connors, not only the reviews accorded the Second Series of *Songs and Sonnets Atlantean,* published in the Summer of 2003, but also those given to my translation and presentation of *Gaspard de la Nuit* by Aloysius Bertrand, published in the Summer of 2004, the fountainhead of the poem in prose not just in French but in any modern language whatsoever anywhere.

Why choose Atlantis for subject matter?

Why not? As a subject for poetry it is almost unexploited. Whatever else that Atlantis may have been, or wherever it may have found itself extant as a real place, it was not in Africa, or Europe, or South America, or North America, except perhaps tangentially, as colonies or peripheral areas. As trumpeted every now and then in the press, the ancient land or island of Atlantis is periodically found or discovered, say, in Ireland, or Spain, or the Sahara—or whatever geographical candidate that the investigator wishes to postulate—but in general such discoveries or speculations are a complete waste of time. The only source of Atlantis, *qua* Atlantis, at least in the terms postulated by Plato is that worthy's two dialogues, the *Timaeus* and the *Critias.* Neither the name nor the story as detailed by Plato exists before him and his accounts, notwithstanding whatever sources, real or imaginary, that he may have been using, or whatever genuine historical place or events that he may have been invoking.

Plato, the Greek philosopher, has it as a tale told to Solon, the Athenian lawgiver, by some Egyptian priests, as recorded in hieroglyphics on some temple walls, wherever the lane or fanes in question may have existed, most likely in some ancient city somewhere in or near the delta of the river Nile. The events relative to Atlantis, such as its foundering beneath the sea, as described by Plato, are recorded as happening some 9,000 years before Solon's time. It has been suggested that 900 or 1,000 years before Solon might be more accurate, and that 9,000 is an accidental conflation of the more likely 900. Plato's dates are usually now given as c. 428–c. 348 (or 347) B.C., and those for Solon as c. 640 (or 630)-c. 560 B.C. Presumably the story was passed down from Solon to Plato via family or other close connections.

If Plato's Atlantis does in fact refer to a real place and a real catastrophe, it is most likely as discovered and theorized by the archaeologist Spyridon Marinatos in the early 1930s, but not announced by him in the public press until the early 1970s, at which time he functioned as the Inspector General of Antiquities under the Government of Greece. As formulated by Marinatos, it all took place on the ancient island of Thera, or the modern Santorin, c. 1520 B.C., recently updated to c. 1630 B.C. Not unlike the much later explosion of Krakatoa, the volcanic island that is part of Indonesia, located between Sumatra and Java, and that erupted in August of 1883; a series of earthquakes preceded a volcanic cataclysm that exploded and gutted the Greek island, eradicating not only the brilliant Minoan civilization there but above all else on the northern littoral of Crete, as well as inland of it, this large island lying only 70 miles away south of Thera. The tsunamis generated by this explosion, never mind the volcanic fallout that preceded and/or accompanied them, immediately developed immense height and speed, all triggered by the collapse of Thera's volcanic cone, the height and speed being estimated at 300 feet, and 200 miles an hour, respectively.

These tsunamis would probably have reached Crete almost at *once, or at least in less* than half an hour, piling up on the island's northern shores. Of course, such a catastrophe and these tsunamis would have affected all the Aegean Sea, and much, if not most, of the Eastern Mediterranean. The Minoan civilization on Crete was functioning at the height of its power and efflorescence, and the effect of such an eruption would have destroyed that civilization then and there almost at once. If there ever was one, this catastrophe would have formed one perfect Atlantean doom. For obvious reasons the Minoan civilization never recovered. If we extrapolate about one thousand years back from Solon's life-time, the 900 or 1,000 conflated from the 9,000 years quoted by Plato seems to fit in remarkably well with the c. 1520 B.C., or c. 1630 B.C. for the explosion of the huge volcano that dominated Minoan Thera's island mass.

It is easy to see how such an event would have impressed itself on all the people in the Aegean as well as the Eastern Mediterranean and the lands contiguous thereunto. Marinatos cautiously suggests, to form an adequate concept of the convulsion that shook the Aegean as the result of Thera's gigantic explosion, that we multiply the Krakatoa convulsion by a factor of four! The recent earthquake and consequent tsunamis generated off the northwest coast of Sumatra in the Indian Ocean during the latter half of December of 2004, albeit extremely minor compared to what happened in either Krakatoa or Thera, can serve nonetheless as some kind of reminder of just how devastating such natural catastrophes may turn out in terms of human death and damage. It is also easy to see how such a catastrophe as that caused by the explosion of the volcano dominating Thera could have led to Plato's Atlantis Mythos.

Aye, but there's the rub! Atlantis as described by Plato is the glittering dream of an island empire centered in the North Atlantic Ocean, that is, a central island kingdom or island continent with nine other but much smaller island kingdoms environing it, and some of them obviously at some real distance from the archkingdom. No, Plato does not describe Crete or Thera or any other place in the Aegean or the Eastern Mediterranean as the locale of this empire, even if Thera and Crete may have served as the specific but otherwise forgotten inspiration for Plato's fable. And, yes, he unequivocally indicates that this great maritime empire is located in the North Atlantic Ocean for the most part, that it is very old in the manner of ancient Egypt, and that the dynasty ruling over the empire and its lesser island kingdoms is the same one that founded it, let's say, some three thousand years before the Great Catastrophe that destroyed and submerged it.

Into this rich welter of pseudo-history or scientifictional speculation, the Theosophists have injected some potent mythopoeic insights or pseudo-facts of their own. As far as I can figure it out in real time, according to this conjectural pre-history or proto-history, Atlantis as described by Plato, or the major part of it, submerged about 13,000 B.C., about the time that the last ice age was ending. The heightened ocean level that resulted from the melting ice opened up the Straits of Gibraltar, and inundated and connected the western and eastern basins of the Mediterranean, hitherto separated, and made them into one vast, almost landlocked body of water. However, the cataclysm that led to the submergence of Atlantis yet left a substantial island behind, the former central mountain heartland, that the Theosophists have identified as Poseidonis. This major fragment then lasted another 3,000 years. Then it also submerged, about 10,000 B.C., leaving the present Azores, Madeira, and other islands mostly located in the North Atlantic.

Thus it is implicitly suggested that this ancient empire and world of Atlantis, as formulated by Plato, is in some sense an antiquity beyond antiquity, that is, an even more distant antiquity long before the classical Graeco-Roman antiquity whose breakdown led inevitably to our modern Western world. In that sense Plato's Atlantis is a gigantic "What if?!" Thus it was in such terms as these that I created and extrapolated my own version of *his* Atlantis, with great care and a certain logic, treating it as a real place with real people and with a real history, and yet emphasizing at every opportunity the inherently poetic aspects of this ancient empire and world as inherited from Plato's fable. The poems and notes contained in the three series of *Songs and Sonnets Atlantean* are essentially a secondary development from this extrapolation.

Whether or not Atlantis was actually a real place, metaphorically and symbolically it is real in an emotional sense, and represents at least for myself all splendor and all beauty irretrievably lost and poignantly adumbrated in art, music, and literature, as indicated by the poem "A Symbol for All Splendor Lost," included in the First Series. To some extent, for myself in a purely personal sense, it likewise adumbrates the once great seaport in which I was born, i.e., New Bedford, Massachusetts, the greatest whaling port anywhere in the world in the 1800s, a port that reached the zenith of its efflorescence and economic power in the early 1860s, when it briefly became the most affluent city on the entire Eastern Seaboard of the U.S.A. Thus as a rich and enigmatic symbol or metaphor Atlantis possesses many foci, many shifting layers of definition and meaning.

Los Angeles, 17 March 2005

Afterword

Some afterthoughts on Atlantis, High Romance, innovation in traditional poetry (that is, in the English language), the once great whaling port of New Bedford, Massachusetts, perceived as a symbolic Atlantis, and other matters.

I

Sometimes at a reading-signing or even at a performance, one or more of the public will ask the author or performer about his modus operandi, his method of creation or composition. Contrary to the practise of many poets, who redact a number of miscellaneous works, and then put a collection together, usually carefully chosen from this output, I have always created my poems to belong to a given collection, that is, given a common theme or subject, and as in my case, Plato's Atlantis Mythos. This insures a certain continuity or integrity, even if the collections might superficially seem to be no more than miscellaneous collections without any readily apparent structure. All three of my collections are thus carefully structured.

Some poets do not need to do this, but their different volumes are all of a piece within themselves, or so it would appear in many cases. For example, in the case of Clark Ashton Smith, *The Star-Treader* (1912) has a distinct personality from that of *Ebony and Crystal* (1922), or that of *Sandalwood* (1925), even if they are manifestly the work of the same poet. The first volume collects the output primarily from the years 1910, 1911, and 1912. The second volume gathers that of 1912 or 1913–1922, and the third volume that of 1922 or 1923–1925. However, in such things, as a matter of course, different poets employ different methods of composition, compilation, organization, and structuring, but whatever method the poet uses cannot but influence the nature of the given collection as a finished product. I have chosen my own method of creating a collection for my own good reasons, which should nonetheless come to the surface, obviously enough, in the book when published.

"It was inevitable that I would continue not only Ashton Smith's uncompromising Romanticism, but just as much his mythopoeic qualities." But I would achieve this in my very own way, thanks to Edmund Spenser, his own mythopoeic imagination, and the wonderful stanza that he created for *The Faerie Queene,* not to mention his own sonnet form, and then thanks to my particular extrapolation of Plato's Atlantis Mythos, which I had been cultivating since late adolescence, when I entered military service, and read among other monographs, L. Sprague de Camp's admirable and copious popularization *Lost Continents,* one of the first books, if not *the* first one, to examine the theme in modern times and in modern terms.

Partially as a result of World War I, the whole tradition of High Romance essentially went underground sometimes during the 1920s. Beginning with the attention focused on T. S. Eliot as a result of his long poem, of over 400 lines, his epic of spiritual desolation, *The Waste Land,* published in 1922, which won the $2000 Dial Award; the concept of High Romance with all its rich inheritance of imaginative fantasy underwent a great and thorough devaluation, at least in serious intellectual terms, and encountered in general nothing but disdain and ridicule.

This began in the early 1920s, and continued up until the Beatles, whose advent in the U.S.A. during 1964 (thus the year after the assassination of John F. Kennedy, the 35th President of America) sparked an entire new Renaissance and not just in the arts but also in the lives and lifestyles of people throughout the world, especially the Anglophone one. The huge success of Tolkien's paramount opus *The Lord of the Rings* throughout that same Anglophone world—above all as a prose epic of High Fantasy—more or less coincided with the Renaissance inspired by the Beatles and others, and led to many beneficial developments in a literary sense, as well as in others.

Not least of these was the launching by Ballantine Books of its wide-reaching Adult Fantasy Series, as edited by the sophisticated and quite knowledgeable connoisseur of literary fantasy Lin Carter, who deliberately built on what Arkham House under August Derleth in Sauk City, Wisconsin, had achieved in hardcover book form during the 1940s, 1950s, and 1960s, up to Derleth's demise in mid-1971.

Derleth's achievement gave new life and some kind of permanence to those better authors especially fostered by *Weird Tales,* the premier fiction magazine of imaginative fiction (founded in 1923) that expired in late 1954. We speak here of H. P. Lovecraft, Henry S. Whitehead, Robert E. Howard, Clark Ashton Smith, and Ray Bradbury, but there were other notable writers, even if not as prolific as the quality scriveners just mentioned.

The weird or highly fantastical story such as the magazine *Weird Tales* made a point of featuring is essentially a creation of the Middle Ages, as developed in verse by the genres of mediaeval epic, mediaeval romance, mediaeval satire, not to mention the late mediaeval prose romances, the direct ancestors of today's fantasy adventures. The Renaissance then gave new life and a new formulation to the fantastic narrative as exemplified in the unique epics of Ariosto (1474–1533), Tasso (1544–1595), and last but not least Edmund Spenser (1552–1599), in whose work the mediaeval is almost co-equal to the Renaissance elements.

Some two hundred years after Spenser, the 1800s, the Romantic Century par excellence (as defined by Jacques Barzun), gave the weird or fantastic tale a new definitive form in prose not only through the English Romantics and Victorians but just as much through such American writers as Washington Irving and Edgar Allan Poe. How many aficionados of the modern weird or fantastic tale are aware of this type of narrative's high pedigree going back probably to the time of Charlemagne (c. 800 A.D.) or William the Conqueror (the Battle of Hastings, 1066 A.D.)–?! The fantastic, the weird, the daemonic, all these together constituted very much a solid part of the mediaeval imagination whether in written or oral form—this held true all across Europe—even on through the Renaissance and later, until its vibrant rebirth yet again in the late 1700s, all of the 1800s, and then on into the early 1900s. Then it suffered some kind of eclipse in strict intellectual terms in the Anglophone world following World War I until the great rebirth fomented by the huge success of Tolkien and his magisterial epic in prose.

In spite of the disdain or disregard that the weird and fantastic, to say nothing of the case of High Romance, has undergone it has often enjoyed enormous favor in the popular arts. Witness the meticulous paintings of Maxfield Parrish: both his early fantasy scenic tableaux work and his later primarily scenic tableaux celebrating impossible but gorgeous fairy-tale subjects and milieux. Parrish's copious *oeuvre* still enjoys universal popularity in the U.S.A. Witness the specialist magazine, the generically named *Weird Tales,* which somehow survived for over three decades. But most of all witness the huge and continuing success of the once new art and industry of the motion picture, which during the 1920s, 1930s, and 1940s specialized among other genres in story-book romance and make-believe—an industry which lavished extraordinary sums of money on movies of purely imaginative nature, or of elaborate historical reconstruction, closely akin in one sense to story-book romance, and near impossible to separate in some instances, given the common necessity for imaginative projection.

For someone growing up on the movies of the late 1930s and then of the 1940s, why should romanticism not have seemed a perfectly legitimate and honored perspective—with all its ancient connotations of fantasy, Carolingian, Arthurian, the Pagan or Christian Marvellous, etc., etc.—?! And why should it not have seemed thus, despite the disdain or disregard that it suffered in austere intellectual circles from c. 1922 to c. 1964? Although I formerly regarded authors like George Sterling, Ashton Smith, and myself as Late Romantics, and as an extension, in serious emotional and intellectual terms, of the authors of the 1800s and early 1900s, that is, before World War I—which in one sense they are—I have now changed my mind, my over-all perspective, and perceive all of them, myself no less, as indeed what they really are, to wit, Modern Romantics.

To repeat, "I realize now that what I perceived then in Ashton Smith [and then concomitantly in George Sterling, Ambrose Bierce, Nora May French, together with others] was the Lost Tradition of High Romance Poetry, lost or at least intellectually disdained from the early 1920s on into the latter 1950s. When I began writing my own mature poetry in March of 1961, it was very much under the double aegis of romance provided by Edmund Spenser and Clark Ashton Smith." Thus I began, have flourished, and shall end "as a Modern Romantic poet continuing the tradition of the California Romantics, as given renewed inspiration from Spenser as the fountainhead of romance in Early Modern English."

II

"Whether or not Atlantis was actually a real place, metaphorically and symbolically it is real in an emotional sense, and represents at least for myself all splendor and all beauty irretrievably lost and poignantly adumbrated in art, music, and literature. . . . To some extent, for myself in a purely personal sense, it likewise adumbrates the once great seaport in which I was born, i.e., New Bedford, Massachusetts. . . ."

In enumerating the various *literary* influences upon his own development, a poet or other type of author often tends to over-look the equally important but *non-literary* ones that have shaped him and his writing. In my own case I have alluded to the fact of my birth and early life in my home town, the venerable and once great whaling capital of the world in the 1800s, with all the vestiges of previous affluence and other grandeur. As a once-renowned urban locale, this old city simply by and of itself exercised a considerable, if not overwhelming, influence upon me. How could it not have? The remains of its once great maritime splendor loom up on all sides in the older parts of the city, primarily the central section extending from the deep-water harbor formed by the Acushnet River all the gradual ascent up to the all-pervasive ridge more or less marked by County Street, the most spectacular of the older residential thoroughfares—river, ridge, and street all aligned on a north-south axis.

Since it was my recent but unexpected pleasure to revisit this old New England city—to pay my respects at my Mother's grave (she died in January of 1979), and then to spend a few hours with my half-brother Scott Fryer in nearby North Dartmouth, whom I had not seen for about 40 years—and since the experience still is fresh in my mind—a brief description or impression of Old New Bedford might have some value. Taken in the company of my nephew James Fryer, who drove us from his home in mid-Connecticut to Providence, R.I., and New Bedford, Mass., and then back to mid-Connecticut all on the same day this visit took place on Friday, 29 April (2005), a clear and exceptionally beautiful day. Before visiting my mother's grave and then my half-brother at his ancient cottage in North Dartmouth, we drove around the historic center of Old New Bedford. It proved a genuine architectural revelation to look at all the old mansions and institutional buildings of the whaling period all over again. The structures exercise their centuried magick and historic charm still.

The New Bedford variation of the American stately mansion is distinctive and individual, and although you find the same or similar big houses in other whaling communities—Fall River, Fairhaven, Martha's Vineyard, Nantucket, Sag Harbor, and a few other towns—New Bedford has the greatest concentration of such structures, and the type may generically be designated as the classic New Bedford whaling mansion as built largely by wealthy whaling captains and merchants. Most of the extant structures of this type came into existence in the course of the 1800s. Placed over a full cellar or basement, the main part of block of such a house assumes the shape of a great big two-story square, often with somewhat flat or slightly sloping roof, often highlighted with gables centrally placed athwart three of the four sides, usually oriented to the four chief points of the compass, with everything more or less disposed symmetrically.

The front or main door, often protected by a small but aptly scaled porch with simple column-posts, appears in the middle of the front side. Similarly styled, a large wing, usually two stories, projects out of the back side, thus adding considerably to the interior volume. This wing contains the kitchen and other service areas on the first floor. There is often or usually a full basement underneath the wing as well. Both main house and wing often possess finished attic spaces over their chambered interiors.

The main house or square has a central hall, spacious enough and endowed with impressive but not overly fancy staircases, with two or three rooms on either side, both downstairs and upstairs. Downstairs there are usually a double parlor with the rooms opening up into each other, a library, a drawing room, and a dining room. Upstairs there are four or five ample bedrooms, the largest one the master bedroom. The wing upstairs has more bedrooms, sometimes used by the servants, unless they slept in the rooms or spaces in the attic or attics. The single most recognizable feature of the main house on the outside finds its characteristic form always placed centrally on the roof: this is the multi-windowed cupola, often flat-roofed, that was round, octagonal, or square, usually but not always encircled by a balustered widow's walk, so called.

Although designed in a variety of styles, and even sometimes using elements from Graeco-Roman architecture—and constructed of wood, stone, or brick, or a variety of such solid substances, the wooden elements even sometimes fabricated by the expert carpenters who were shipbuilders—the houses generally do not look like the Greek Revival mansions characteristic of much of the 1800s in the USA Some of the houses possess graceful curves that suggest some kind of Chinese or Japanese or other Far Eastern style of architecture; and many of the most striking examples of this generic whaling mansion are conveniently displayed along County Street, the old main residential thoroughfare, and obviously dominate their respective lots, often beautifully landscaped. Some of the fancier mansions have notably ample space around them, especially landscaped with gardens, and sporting sometimes a small conservatory, either separate or attached to the main block of the house. Before the destruction wrought by the Dutch Elm disease in the 1930s and 1940s, County Street at one time possessed innumerable elm trees renowned for their shade and the high graceful Gothic arches that their upper branches created like a canopy over the roadbed.

There are several mansions of greater size and elaboration, both of architecture and of setting, that stand out at once, and merit special mention. These are the Greek Revival mansions that exist in a class by themselves, apparently built in the 1830s and/or 1840s, as were similar mansions up and down the Atlantic coast, as well as inland. The Greek Revival mansions of the Deep South are celebrated, but those in the North-east, some no less spectacular, are still relatively unknown. One major point of distinction between them is that the walls of the Greek Revival houses of the Northeast are often constructed out of granite blocks, often imparting to these mansions a certain attractively stern or austere quality.

Union Street, running east and west, comes up from the harbor area, and more or less bisects County Street, which crowns the crest of the long ridge that runs north and south, all the way from the south end of New Bedford to the city's north end. The town is thus long and narrow. Several imposing structures from the whaling days, the red-brick Wamsutta Club (a family mansion considerably altered or expanded from its original state), the Unitarian Church with its dark Gothic stone, and others, distinguish this intersection. About half a mile south of it along County Street, as the ridge itself gradually descends, there still stand two extraordinary Greek Revival mansions, noticeably larger than similar ones in the old center of Nantucket, otherwise exquisite examples.

On the west, set way back amid an unusually large space, and approached by a single cobblestoned driveway that goes directly back to some stable, passing close to the grandiose full-fledged portico, with four deeply fluted, two-story Doric columns, the Grinnell mansion lifts up its imposing mass. Its four columns are unusually massive, some of the largest that I have ever observed on any Greek Revival mansion. The main block itself of the house is predominantly squarish, possessing two full stories and a lesser attic story. Although the massive columns are made of wood, the structure itself is made of specially quarried granite blocks. The chambers on both first and second floors boast noticeably high ceilings. For years the building served as a private school, and the structure has recently and patently undergone considerable refurbishing both in and out. The large windows have the usual wooden shutters on the outside—this part of New England often endures the great storms called hurricanes that come up out of the Caribbean or the adjacent Atlantic Ocean—and have as well carefully and solidly made folding shutters on the inside. These could ensure privacy and further storm protection even without the heavy drapes and valances preferred in the 1800s, and demanded by the architectural style. The over-all impression of such a structure is of wealth, substance, and severity; and the Grinnell mansion serves as an ineluctable reminder that in the 1800s most of the wealthy whaling captains and merchants were born, and remained, fairly strict Quakers throughout their individual existences.

A little north of the Grinnell mansion, but on the opposite or eastern side of the thoroughfare, on a very large corner lot, if not indeed on its very own block, another imposing Greek Revival mansion lifts up, larger and even more elaborate, flat-roofed, and enclosed within a masonry wall of medium height, and approached by a semi-circular drive indicated by two gateways for carriages or automobiles to enter and exit. Whereas the Grinnell mansion has four two-story Doric pillars of massive proportions, this grandiose house, which has functioned for years as New Bedford's own Jewish Community Center, has a portico made up of six elegant and large two-story Corinthian columns, deeply fluted like those on the Grinnell mansion. Similar to the latter this mansion on both first and second floors boasts noticeably high ceilings. On the bottom floor a wide front hall goes back to a much larger back hall, on the left of the front hall a library and a drawing room, and on the right a double parlor with the rooms opening up into each other. Although the library may be proportionately smaller, it could still hold a considerable quantity of books of all descriptions and sizes.

A peculiarity of these public rooms needs particular mention. Not only do they have wide entrances but also flat pedimented porticos flanked by columns, which impart an unusual but undeniable grandeur. The drawing room at least has one enormous mural, possibly two on the opposite east and west walls. (I recall this detail from memory, c. 1950. Caveat lector!) This mansion is obviously larger, and goes much further back, than the Grinnell house.

However, it is the back hall that provides the further and completely unexpected surprise. The front hall gives way to a much wider space that occupies the full two stories, the ceiling of which features a vast skylight with transpicuous but not transparent glass, decorated all around the edges with a handsome Grecian key design. This back hall (behind which the kitchen and service rooms are located) houses quite a large and elaborate staircase, with one flight of stairs (directly approached from the front hall) dividing into two lateral flights that lead to the almost equally large upper story. It may seem incredible, but it certainly serves as a reminder of just how much more our money used to be worth, that the original owner had a house of this magnitude and elaboration designed and constructed back in the 1830s or 1840s for $25,000 or $35,000!

Nevertheless, there still remains one other and final Greek Revival mansion for us to consider, the greatest example of all, also on the eastern side of County Street, but perhaps a mile north of the intersection at Union Street. In many long-established New England communities, going back to the earliest period of European settlement, there exists a special park, now rich with trees, bushes, and flowerbeds, usually designated as the common. This is where the local citizens once pastured their cows and other farm animals "in common." New Bedford has its own such common, longer than it is wide, that extends easterly downhill from County Street to the flat area marked by Purchase or Pleasant Street, and not far from the Acushnet River with its north-south axis.

Immediately south of the common is a large city block now mostly noteworthy for its large and handsome family houses mostly of two stories with attics, located on wide, successively descending terraces. On the southern side of this block, and thus away from the side facing the common, rises a solid medium-sized house with its own one-storied but modestly proportioned portico distinguished by Ionic columns. This mini-mansion (for such it seems) stands out from the other houses by the smooth and carefully dressed granite blocks that constitute its outer walls, no less than by its Greek Revival style of architecture.

This fragment, for such in fact is all that it is, is the southern wing of the largest mansion ever built in New Bedford, a mansion whose entire ground or estate once occupied this entire city block, and for which the ground was leveled not just on the highest and largest piece of earth next to County Street, but especially on the hillside's descending terrain as molded into a series of wide terraces, each one with its own retaining wall. These terraces once featured a series of gardens with the usual embowering trees, bushes, and flowerbeds, not to mention the then ubiquitous kitchen garden or gardens, once a standard necessity for almost all homesteads. Of course, the entire estate originally had its own stone wall surrounding it, but at the highest level a typical and substantial iron fence, made up of what would appear to be (from photos of the period or later) solid iron spears, or emblematical harpoons, as Herman Melville notes very early on in his unique and epic novel *Moby-Dick,* where he mentions such a fence surrounding some typical mansion of the period.

On the largest and highest piece of ground—approached by a semicircular drive marked at either end by two widely-separated gates fronting County Street—there once stood the chief pile of the house, not only built out of the usual granite blocks, and moreover with two wings one on the north and one on the south; but distinguished both on its western and eastern facades by full-fledged porticos running the entire length of these façades, with each portico composed of six two-story Ionic columns, deeply fluted like the Corinthian columns on the Jewish Community Center, or like the massive Doric columns on the Grinnell mansion.

To the best of my knowledge this double portico is unique, or at least quite uncommon, not only to New Bedford but to the entire Northeast of the USA While the mansion must have looked quite impressive from County Street, the view of it from the east, looking up at and out over its ascendant terraces with all the verdure of its gardens, must have proven spectacular. The view from the eastern portico, looking out over the handsome and bustling seaport must have been equally spectacular. As far as I can infer, the property was purchased by some developer, the house and its north wing were demolished, the gardens were obliterated, and new large family homes were then constructed both on the highest and chief level, and on the descending terraces—all of this before World War I. Only exceptional circumstances would have permitted the survival of such an estate as this must have been on into the late 1900s or early 2000s.

In the main section of town, especially near the waterfront, the Acushnet River and the later main business thoroughfare, many of New Bedford's original cobbled streets exist to this day, the stone cobbles constituting an especially tough and resistant surface. Not far from the harbor still stand several warehouses made of brick apparently from the Georgian period, which originally served as homes for some of the earliest wealthy families of the town in the late 1700s or early 1800s. One can still trace much of the original structures of Colonial or Federal architecture encased inside the later warehouses.

However, it was the many multi-masted whaling and other ships that tied up to the docks on the river—a veritable forest of ships' masts—that must have furnished not only a typical sight, but a fantastical one as well, speaking as they did of the innumerable spaces of water once visited by the whalers in their endless quest for those cetaceans that bore the desired oil and other products, and that fostered the whaling industry, until the inevitable near-extinction of the whales in general brought American whaling to its foreordained end.

The former New Bedford of the 1800s with its world-renowned whaling industry, with its grandiose mansions, Greek Revival and otherwise, I now can see more clearly for what it was, and still is, to me: my first symbolic adumbration of Plato's Atlantis, harkening as it does back to an antiquity beyond antiquity, to a kind of flourishing paradise otherwise forgotten or obliterated. One further point: as the whaling industry declined in the later 1800s, the people of wealth in my home town established textile factories, which dominated the local economy through much of the 1900s, until the great depression of 1929 and the early 1930s caused them to move to the South because of the cheaper labor. However, New Bedford still retains the title of the foremost salt-water fishing center on the east coast.

Postscriptum

"Thus as a rich and enigmatic symbol or metaphor Atlantis possesses many foci, many shifting layers of definition and meaning."

One of the seeming and more curious contradictions that has existed in the life and culture of the USA, a democratic republic as well as a self-proclaimed protector of democratic values worldwide, resides in the popular and continuing fascination with royalty, particularly with British royalty, from whose empire we, the Americans of the USA, deliberately broke away during 1775-1783. I mention this in connection with the conspicuous references to royalty, Atlantean and otherwise, throughout the three series of *Songs and Sonnets Atlantean.* In bringing up this especial subject, let me state at once that I do so not for reasons of political correctness, or of any pious humbuggery. Royalty, or glorified chieftainship, has existed since the need for leaders on a continuing basis has existed, and needs no political justification or apology from me. As a method of governing a group of people, it has given rise, just as democracy itself has, to both good and bad rulers, a mixed record at best, just like that demonstrated by democracy, or by most other political systems.

Nevertheless, the sometimes immense popularity generated at times by royal figures, whether British and otherwise, in the USA, the presumed home or haven of modern democracy, remains one of the more curious paradoxes in the mainstream culture of American life. One might well ask why such immense popularity *per se* comes about, as indeed it does on occasion, e.g., the coronation of Queen Elizabeth II (1952), or the wedding of Princess Elizabeth and Prince Philip (1947). The response to such a question would probably turn out to be fairly complex, but I warrant that such things as glamour and nostalgia would have much to do with it. We tend to forget that the whole concept of nationhood or nationality, in our modern sense, grew up around the person of the sovereign thus regarded as the personification of the given state or country. Thus the glorification of the sovereign, including outright flattery, became transmuted into patriotism, or the glorification of one's own country, just one more step in the long evolution of political institutions as created by human beings on planet Earth.

I must confess that I, no less than others, have often had a certain friendly feeling or curiosity concerning the now largely historical institution of royalty, which seems to have existed and often flourished since time immemorial (at least in human terms), that is, up until just after World War I, or the Great War. Then, as one result of such a destructive and sanguinary conflict, the whole institution of "kings, courts, and monarchy" (the title of a non-fiction best-seller in the latter 1900s) virtually disappeared, with the exception of British royalty, no less than the bicycle monarchies as thus once dubbed by a disdainful Queen Elizabeth II (born 1926). These bicycle monarchies would include Belgium, the Netherlands, Denmark, Norway, and Sweden. Incidentally, although without any real power, British royalty is just about the only institution of this type that has otherwise retained the full paraphernalia of its traditional pomp, appanage, and panoply. Concomitantly, following the end of World War I, much of the map of Europe became drastically reconfigured. The effect of all these changes for much of Europe, especially Mitteleuropa, proved nothing less than devastating, above all for the smaller states or principalities.

Essentially built around the paramount kingdom of Prussia, the German Empire reformed itself into modern Germany, losing not just Alsace-Lorraine (Elsass-Lothringen) but much of its eastern territories. As it was painfully changing itself into the Soviet Union, the Russian Empire lost its very westernmost possessions. The Austro-Hungarian Empire, that vast crazy-quilt or patchwork made up, it would seem, of every imaginable kind of Graustarkian kingdom, princedom, and often semi-autonomous territory, fell apart—and the primarily Germanophone portion shrank down to the heartland of so-called Germany-Austria (the present-day country). To avoid the further horror of a civil struggle, yet another internal conflict, especially after the slaughter involved in the Great War—an internal conflict as fomented by royalist partisans wanting to restore the monarchy there in Austria itself—the imperial family of the Hapsburgs had unselfishly and voluntarily gone into exile in Switzerland, shorn of all their estates and both personal and official income.

A few very positive developments emerged from this débâcle. Finland regained its independence, losing its former status of Grand Duchy belonging to Tsarist Russia. Poland at long last reappeared as a brand-new republic, and thus had regained its independence like Finland. Poland had vanished for almost a century and a half as a separate political entity with genuine autonomy because of the partitioning of this nation among Russia, Prussia, and Austria during 1772,

1793, and 1795. Other new nations appeared, or old ones reappeared: Lithuania, Latvia, and Estonia, all regained their independence as autonomous nations after belonging to Tsarist Russia. Meanwhile, however, the smaller states or principalities, which had functioned quite well, or even prospered, as dependent or semi-autonomous regions of the Austro-Hungarian Empire, and had needed that close union for economic and other reasons, now fell by the wayside, and some of them would have an especially grueling time of it, from the early 1920s until the latter 1980s, whether economically, politically, or ideologically, first independently, and then under the Nazis, the Soviets, and the (native) Communists.

I was born in latter 1934, and first studied geography as a separate subject when I was in the fourth grade of grammar school (during 1943-1944). Therefore I grew up with maps of Europe that revealed the configuration of countries there both before and after World War I. Between that before and after, there was quite some difference! I became especially intrigued by the peculiarly shaped Austro-Hungarian Empire that had vanished completely, or so it seemed. As I learned later, it had vanished after it had existed as the great and extensive dominion of Mitteleuropa, but in divers forms under divers names—the Holy Roman Empire, the Austrian Empire, the Austro-Hungarian Empire—first, for over one thousand years, as reckoned from the crowning of Charlemagne as Emperor of the West at Rome in 800 A.D., or second, for over nine hundred years, as reckoned from the reign of Otto II, 962-973 A.D. (As is obvious, the Holy Roman Empire included at divers times what later became the separate countries or empires of France, Germany, and Austria.)

For not quite seven full centuries it had been primarily the Hapsburgs who had reigned over this vast, and often shifting, political entity, and moreover had ruled well, steadfastly, and conscientiously. This German Swiss family or dynasty had originated in the town and castle of Habsburg in the canton of Aargau located in north central Switzerland. Moreover, a fine testimony to the high-mindedness and general competence of the Hapsburgs, the Electors of the Holy Roman Empire—the temporal and ecclesiastical princes who were entitled to take part in selecting that emperor—had consistently chosen to vote the successive rulers of that family into that paramount office. Often without real political power, the Holy Roman Emperor achieved his aims without war and through the prestige of his person or of his office.

This then was the empire in one form or another that had van-
ished—this then was the ruling family that had lost all their power and
almost all their possessions, and had retreated into exile back into the
mountain fastnesses where they had originated. I never quite realized
the full impact of that massive change, that massive disappearance,
until the spring of 1989, when I came upon the obituaries in divers
periodicals for Zita von Hapsburg, (born von Bourbon-Parma in
1892), who died on 14 March 1989, and received on Saturday, 1
April 1989, a magnificent funeral as well as a traditional burial in Vi-
enna, the last Hapsburg capital. As I read these obituaries, I suddenly
realized the full scope of the huge void left by that empire's dissolu-
tion, not to mention (above all) how many innocent people suffered
and/or died as the result of that same dissolution! How much pathos
and poignancy did that funeral and burial encapsulate in Vienna!

(As a parenthetical aside, mention should be made here that we,
the Western World, have still not made a full accounting of the cul-
tural efflorescence, whether artistic, literary, musical, or scientific, that
took place in Vienna during the latter 1700s, the over-all 1800s, and
the first half and more of the 1900s—that entire period alone!—and
that came about as the direct result, or under the general patronage,
of the Hapsburgs. The product himself of that empire, and now con-
sidered the last representative of the First Vienna School of music,
which began with Haydn, Mozart, and Beethoven, and ended with
Brahms, Bruckner, and Mahler; Franz Schmidt—born in 1874, and
deceased in 1939, and thus after the Anschluss in 1938, the annexa-
tion of Austria to Germany engineered by the Nazis—regarded his
own music, especially his profound, unique, and large-scale organ
works, 1914–1939, as a sustained evocation, no less than tribute, to
the Austro-Hungarian Empire and its monarchy, under which he had
passed his youth and early adulthood. Indeed, one seems constantly
to hear in those organ works the final echoes, the final imperial fan-
fares as it were, of the splendor, grandeur, and sheer accomplishment
of that empire as it had existed since 800 A.D., and perhaps even
since Roman times under such emperors as Marcus Aurelius, who
made Roman Vienna, or Vindabona, his headquarters—with his own
imperial palace whose construction he had ordered thereat—during
the second century A.D.)

As I continued growing up, and read more and more, and contin-
ued learning more and more about all the political and other changes

that had happened just in the fifty years or so before my birth in 1934; I could not help but feel haunted by the many kingdoms and empires that had suddenly disappeared as the chief result of World War I (1914-1918), together with all their royal or imperial families (exiled when not murdered), with all the traditions and customs—particularly of a positive nature—that had accumulated over centuries and centuries, and even over millennia. Thus it was this free-floating romance or mystique of a whole vanished world with all its pomp and circumstance, and somehow going back to ancient Rome and the Hellenistic period—otherwise undefined and unheralded, or unpublicized as such—that captured and intrigued my juvenile and adolescent imagination, something secreted away in my subconscious only to surface many years later.

Moreover, the fact that this whole mysterious and somehow glamorous world (that existed in various forms for over 2,000 years) had vanished—and just some twenty-five or thirty years before I became aware of it—only added to the over-all glamour and romance, and somehow became assimilated for me in the collective popular imagination on into Plato's Atlantis Mythos. This over-all gestalt of romance fructified for me the Greek philosopher's own conception of a great maritime Empire of Atlantis with a central island kingdom or continent and nine lesser island kingdoms among other far-flung territories. As thus formulated or adumbrated by Plato himself, the various dynasties ruling over this empire and its component kingdoms have inter-married among themselves, and have become interrelated over thousands of years. All of this then, whether historically real or pseudo-historical, formed part of what has gone into my perception or conception, extrapolated with immense care, of Plato's Atlantis Mythos.

One Final Afterthought: Atlantis as a metaphor for for the concept of romance itself.

There is one final afterthought that is completely germane to the utilization of Atlantis as a subject matter for modern poetry, as an antiquity somewhere beyond antiquity, that I have failed to discuss up to this time. Chronologically it involves the two millennia that have elapsed since the reign of Augustus, and the beginning of the Roman Empire, qua Empire. However one might define romance, romanticism, and the romantic, it has existed as a cultural and/or emotional reality in the Western World, the European and Neo-European universe of culture (thus including the three Americas), for some 15 or 16 centuries, and presumably still exists, even if not in any official or authoritative sense. If it still exists, and moreover at the margin of things and in remote crannies and corners, it has obviously become dethroned from its once dominant position, but only after it has enjoyed an exceptionally long run in one form or fashion after another. It is something more than just the product of the Middle Ages, of the troubadour or trouvère society. I have tried to define this romance and romanticism in the broadest possible sense in my monograph-review *The Last of the Great Romantic Poets,* published under the aegis of Harry Morris, Jr., by the Silver Scarab Press, Albuquerque, New Mexico, during 1973. This monograph deals with the *Selected Poems* of Clark Ashton Smith, published by Arkham House, Sauk City, Wisconsin, in November of 1971, no less than that volume's existential implications.

The earliest romanticism (emphasis on the Roman) goes all the way back in the most universal sense to the profound nostalgia (always a prime ingredient in any and all romanticism) intensely experienced by many survivors of the Western Roman Empire after the central authority animating it had finally collapsed in the tumultuous course of the fifth century A.D. This nostalgia embodied the near universal regret on the part of its manifold citizens for the loss of the relatively secure and stable world that (at least) had once extended all around the Mediterranean sea, that the Romans had established under Augustus as the first authentic Roman emperor during 30 B.C-14 A.D., and that they had maintained in an unbroken continuity, more or less, on into the fifth century. Classical antiquity is often construed as more or less ending in 410 A.D. with the sacking of the city itself of Rome, the heart of its far-flung empire, by Alaric and his Visigothic hordes. Similarly the Middle Ages are often considered as beginning with this frightening and unprecedented event, and could be said to have concluded with the long-delayed fall of Constantinople (the Eastern Roman Empire) to the Turks under Mohammed II in 1453 A.D. soon after he became sultan.

Much energy and thought became deployed in the course of the thousand or so years making up the Middle Ages towards restoring something of that once universal hegemony of ancient Rome. Much of the deeply dismembered and shattered world that had constituted the Western Roman Empire had regained a real something of its former integrity by the time that Leo III, the then Pope, crowned Charlemagne as the Emperor of the Holy Roman Empire at Rome on Christmas, 800 A.D., an empire that incorporated much of what later became modern Austria, Germany, France, and Italy. Alternating with periods of decline and shifting political boundaries, major periods of political stability and artistic efflorescence occurring under divers rulers managed to take place; during the High Middle Ages, chiefly the 1200s and 1300s, before the waning of the Middle Ages over-all in the 1300s and 1400s; during the Renaissance, the 1300s through the 1500s, and even on into the early 1600s, the long transitional period between the mediaeval and the modern; and finally during the Romantic Period or Century, the late 1700s, all of the 1800s, and thus the Romantic Century par excellence, and on into the first half of the 1900s. The modern political world could be said to have begun with the American Revolution (1775-1783) and the French Revolution (1789-1799) with their distinctive and epochal challenge to the divine right of kings, the duly constituted authority of monarchs and prelates who had become entrenched in an ironlike collaboration often exercised to suppress the population at large, as well as any dissent therefrom.

So where precisely does the over-all series, one, two, three of *Song and Sonnets Atlantean* fit into this over-all scheme or time-frame, above all in regard to the world of romance and romanticism? (Seemingly we descend from the significant to the trivial in asking such a question, but it all depends on the value that the individual assigns to the arts and sciences.) Essentially dated from March of 1961 through March of 2005 in a creative sense (although only about 23 of those 44 years were devoted more or less directly to the creation of the poems themselves)—the three volumes containing the three cycles or series of the ostensible songs and sonnets, etc., have thus appeared in published form during 1971, 2003, and 2005, respectively—these three series represent (to quote the blurb on the back cover of *The Third Series}* "an unique poetic experiment . . . a deliberate and sustained extension . . . from the poetic output by the California Romantics, that group of poets headed by Ambrose Bierce but embodied primarily in George Sterling, Nora May French, and Clark Ashton Smith." The California Romantics and their efflorescence took place during

c. 1890 through c. 1961 (ending apparently with the death of Ashton Smith in mid-August of 1961). The extension of this group's output as embodied in the poetic output of myself as Donald Sidney-Fryer and as a Modern Romantic has occurred all under the mythopoeic aegis of Edmund Spenser and his unique epic *The Faerie Queene*.

For myself as the self-conscious inheritor of the certainly genuine romanticism of the California Romantics, Atlantis per se is a metaphor for the concept of romance itself, perceived in the highest possible terms, as an infinitely precious cultural commodity otherwise lost or almost lost, surviving from the Age of Rome through the Dark Ages and then through the Age of Chivalry on into the Age of Space.

Brave World Old and New:
The Atlantis Theme in the Poetry and
Fiction of Clark Ashton Smith

One of the themes pivotal to the oeuvre of the late Clark Ashton Smith is that which may be identified, specifically and generically, as the Atlantis theme, whether it assumes the name of Atlantis or that of some other Atlantis-like locale, such as Mu or Lemuria, or Hyperborea or Zothique for that matter. It is a theme or background that runs through the tapestry of a lifetime in word-weaving from virtually his first published work to literally his last. Of all the writers who have used, or extrapolated from, Plato's "quaint conceit," the Atlantis myth (as detailed in the two dialogues, the *Timaeus* and the *Critias*), few have done so with the taste, invention, and seriousness that Smith has demonstrated in his handling of this theme and/or background.

This is probably because Smith—of all such writers—is the closest to Plato in the quality of sheer poetic imagination. Just as much as Plato who created the Atlantis myth for didactic purposes, Smith has utilized it for his own serious ends, whether in verse or in prose. And Smith is undeniably the only major poet in English who has to date featured it in his own poetry and prose on a comparatively important scale, all discussion of novels by romancers of hackneyed imagination swept aside. This is odd when one considers the rare possibilities for splendor and "glamour" that this Platonic near-utopia proffers to the original poet.

Whatever the reasons for its neglect as a source of poetry, Smith in his literary output overall is the first and foremost poet in English to achieve, radiating from this theme, a sizeable body of poetry that possesses genuine substance and beauty. However, Smith's great patron and poetic mentor George Sterling had included in his magisterial narrative in verse "A Wine of Wizardry" (first published in the *Cosmopolitan* for September 1907, in which issue the young Smith first read the poem) an implicitly Atlantean passage, as follows (ll. 151–54):

> Shapes of men that were
> Point, weeping, at tremendous dooms to be,

> When pillared pomps and thrones supreme shall stir,
> Unstable as the foam-dreams of the sea.

This especial passage, among others from the same source, would fructify the younger poet's imagination and haunt it, long after he had first read and conned Sterling's poem, not only in Smith's own early but first mature poetry but just as much in his later tales of Atlantis, or (in his own employment of the fabled background) its embodiment as a good-sized final fragment, "Poseidonis," a concept that Smith apparently derived from the Theosophist writings of Helena Blavatsky.

The most salient examples in which Smith gives expression to the Atlantis theme are found for the most part not so much in his miscellaneously published poetry as in his collections of poetry, whether appearing early or late in his career. The first examples characteristically occur in Smith's first volume of verse, *The Star-Treader and Other Poems* (1912). And the very first example, proto-Atlantean, is contained in the first stanza of the poem "The Cloud-Islands."

> What islands marvellous are these,
>   That gem the sunset's tides of light—
> Opals aglow in saffron seas?
>   How beautiful they lie, and bright,
> Like some new-found Hesperides! (*ST* 50)

In Greek mythology, the Hesperides were those islands in the extreme west (i.e., as such appeared to the ancient Greeks living in Greece itself), and which contained the gardens wherein grew the golden apples guarded by nymphs (also called Hesperides) with the aid of a dragon. Presumably these islands lay somewhere in the Atlantic Ocean. Atlantis, according to Plato, lay somewhere in the North Atlantic and west of the Pillars of Heracles or Hercules (the Straits of Gibraltar), and hence was undoubtedly a hesperian island continent. The Hesperides prefigure Atlantis and possibly may have served, together with other islands, as a model for the Atlantis of Plato, an island empery remarkable for its wealth, extent, and antiquity, as well as for its almost utopian justice and order.

The next example, the sonnet "Atlantis" (*ST* 56), gives us an impressive submarine tableau of the sunken capital of the empire of Atlantis:

Above its domes the gulfs accumulate
    To where the sea-winds trumpet forth their screed;
    But here the buried waters take no heed—
Deaf, and with closéd lips from press of weight
Imposed by ocean. Dim, inanimate,
    On temples of an unremembered creed
    Involved in long, slow tentacles of weed,
The dead tide lies immovable as Fate.

From out the ponderous-vaulted ocean-dome,
    A clouded light is questionably shed
On altars of a goddess garlanded
    With blossoms of some weird and hueless vine;
And wingèd, fleet, through skies beneath the foam,
    Like silent birds the sea-things dart and shine.

In particular, amongst many other things, we might note what a subtle visual effect is achieved by line 10: "A clouded light is questionably shed"—but the sonnet is a highly creditable achievement throughout.

Smith's third volume of verse—and his second major collection of poetry—*Ebony and Crystal: Poems in Verse and Prose* (published by Smith himself in 1922), contains some half-dozen references to Atlantis or Atlantis-like places. While these references may for the most part be but peripheral, they hint at a proto-historic world of unimaginable glamour and beauty.

Rosa Mystica

The secret rose we vainly dream to find,
Was blown in grey Atlantis long ago,
Or in old summers of the realms of snow,
Its attar lulled the pole-arisen wind;
Or once its broad and breathless petals pined
In gardens of Persepolis, aglow
With desert sunlight, and the fiery, slow
Red waves of sand, invincible and blind.

On orient isles, or isles hesperian,
Through mythic days ere mortal time began,

It flowered above the ever-flowering foam;
Or, legendless, in lands of yesteryear,
It flamed among the violets—near, how near,
To unenchanted fields and hills of home! (*EC* 7)

Note that the Atlantis mentioned above is "grey"—thus obliquely indicating that this is the post-cataclysmic Atlantis lying beneath the ocean, and evidently mantled with the grey of the deep-sea silt.

The second reference is to that Atlantis of the Pacific, the Mu postulated by James Churchward, or sometimes rendered as Lemuria (as in the present case), also postulated as extant in the Indian Ocean, stretching between Madagascar and the Indian subcontinent once upon a time. This reference appears in the sonnet "Mirrors," which Smith has cast in that metre somewhat rare in English (but not in French, where it serves as the basic line in classical prosody), the alexandrine, a metre he handles characteristically with incomparable dexterity.

Mirrors of steel or silver, gold or glass antique!
Whether in melancholy marble palaces
In some long trance you drew the dreamy loveliness
Of Roman queens, or queens barbarical, or Greek;
Or, further than the bright and sun-pursuing beak
Of argosy might fare, beheld the empresses
Of lost Lemuria; or behind the lattices
Alhambran, have returned forbidden smiles oblique

Of wan, mysterious women!—Mirrors, mirrors old,
Mirrors immutable, impassible as Fate,
Your bosoms held the perished beauty of the past
Nearer than straining love might ever hope to hold;
And fleeing faces, lips too phantom-frail to last,
Found in your magic depth a life re-duplicate. (*EC* 17)

Note the hyper-subtle effect the poet achieves by the enjambment in lines 6 through 9, an effect tantalizing in its half-palpable quality, as of images that disappear before they are fully formed in our minds but that hint at an extraordinary beauty just beyond our powers to imagine.

The third reference is to Lemuria and Atlantis both, and is found in lines 40–53 of Smith's elegy "To Nora May French."[1]

> If thy voice
> In any wise return, and word of thee,
> It is a lost, incognizable sigh,
> Upon the wind's oblivious woe, or blown,
> Antiphonal, from wave to plangent wave
> In the vast, unhuman sorrow of the main,
> On tides that lave the city-laden shores
> Of lands wherein the eternal vanities
> Are served at many altars; tides that wash
> Lemuria's unfathomable walls,
> And idly sway the weed-involvèd oars
> At wharves of lost Atlantis; tides that rise
> From coral-coffered bones of all the drowned,
> And sunless tombs of pearl that krakens guard. (*EC* 22)

The reader will have noted how naturally the references to Lemuria and Atlantis occur within the context of the given passage (with its imagery of sea-wind and sea-tide).

The fourth reference—or (rather) in this case, example—is the entire sonnet "In Lemuria," a masterpiece of compression and subtle suggestiveness. This otherworldly sonnet narrates its tale through a succession of exotic scenes or images, a succession that culminates in the hyper-exotic reference, the "jaspers from the moon."

> Rememberest thou? Enormous gongs of stone
> Were stricken, and the storming trumpeteers
> Acclaimed my deed to answering tides of spears,

---

1. Nora May French, a remarkably gifted poet, was born at Aurora, New York, in 1881 and died by her own hand at Carmel-by-the-Sea, California, in late 1907 while residing there as a guest of George and Carrie Sterling. (Sterling was the unofficial poet laureate of the west coast from about 1903 until his death in 1926.) Nora May's body was cremated, and a group of friends in a special ceremony scattered her ashes into the Pacific Ocean from Point Lobos just south of Carmel. Posthumously gathered and edited by Henry Anderson Lafler (with the help of Sterling and critic Porter Garnett), her one and only collection *Poems* appeared in 1910, as published by the Strange Company, San Francisco. (Porter Garnett himself did the actual printing of the volume.)

And spoke the names of monsters overthrown—
Griffins whose angry gold, and fervid store
Of sapphires wrenched from marble-plungèd mines—
Carnelians, opals, agates, almandines,
I brought to thee some scarlet eve of yore.

In the wide fane that shrined thee, Venus-wise,
The fallen clamours died. . . . I heard the tune
Of tiny bells of pearl and melanite,
Hung at thy knees, and arms of dreamt delight;
And placed my wealth before thy fabled eyes,
Pallid and pure as jaspers from the moon. (*EC* 24)

    Is it to a goddess or empress, statue or living woman, that the warrior-prince-narrator proffers the booty of conquest? It is a tribute to the author's adroitness that we do not definitely know. The only clue that we have is the tinkling of the "tiny bells of pearl and melanite," which might indicate a living person making the natural slight movements that a sitting person makes. Yet the tinkling could be caused by the wind or by some artificial means, as of a priest stirring those bells by hand or by some hidden mechanism in the statue, if the object in question is indeed a statue.

    The fifth Atlantean reference occurs in the sonnet "Symbols." In this lyric the poet abjures his already quite exotic style of imagery for one even more exotic, if possible. (The poem immediately precedes, in the original *Ebony and Crystal,* Smith's greatest and most imaginative effort, *The Hashish-Eater; or, The Apocalypse of Evil.*)

No more of gold and marble, nor of snow,
And sunlight, and vermilion, would I make
My vision and my symbols, nor would take
The auroral flame of some prismatic floe,
Nor iris of the frail and lunar bow,
Flung on the shafted waterfalls that wake
The night's blue slumber in a shadowy lake. . . .
To body forth my fantasies, and show
Communicable mystery, I would find,
In adamantine darkness of the earth,
Metals untouched of any sun; and bring

> Black azures of the nether sea to birth—
> Or fetch the secret, splendid leaves, and blind,
> Blue lilies of an Atlantean spring. (*EC* 48)

It seems clear from the context (lines 13–14) that the springtime to which Smith refers is not so much specifically that of Plato's lost continent as it is, more generally, a springtime indescribably primal. Observe the original way in which the poet indicates the fact that these "Blue lilies of an Atlantean spring" are buds—through the subtle epithet "blind."

The sixth reference, or example, is only implicitly Atlantean, and occurs in lines 105–13 of *The Hashish-Eater*. This is the vision or episode that closes the second of the overall ten sections (as originally published in 1922) that make up this compressed epic, sections two, three, and four consist of a relentless piling-up of one vision on top of another.

> I behold
> The slowly-thronging corals that usurp
> Some harbour of a million-masted sea
> And sun them on the league-long wharves of gold
> Bulks of enormous crimson, kraken-limbed
> And kraken-headed, lifting up as crowns
> The octiremes of perished emperors,
> And galleys fraught with royal gems, that sailed
> From a sea-deserted haven. (*EC* 51–52)

This vision suggests an ultramundane Atlantis which is in process of being overwhelmed, not by one great catastrophe of earthquake and tsunami but by a stranger doom requiring aeons of time.

The seventh and last Atlantean reference in *Ebony and Crystal* is to Atlantis and Lemuria both, and is found in the first and shorter of the two sections of the poem in prose "From a Letter":

> Will you not join me in Atlantis, where we will go down through streets of blue and yellow marble to the wharves of orichalch, and choose us a galley with a golden Eros for figurehead, and sails of Tyrian sendal? With mariners that knew Odysseus, and beautiful amber-breasted slaves from the mountain-vales of Lemuria, we will lift anchor for the unknown fortunate isles of the outer sea; and, sailing in the wake of an opal sunset, will lose that ancient land in the glaucous twilight, and

see from our couch of ivory and satin the rising of unknown stars and perished planets. (*EC* 145)

The above is one of the rare instances wherein the poet gives us a palpable envisioning of Plato's fabled city, complete with a mention of that fabulous alloy of copper and gold (mixed-in with some silver) called orichalch, or orichalcum, evidently a bright or pale flame-gold. Note in particular the magisterial handling of the rhythm in the second period, a rhythm which seems to lift anchor for us, and to rise and fall with the waves of the ocean herself—a rise and fall first stated in the two subordinate phrases opening the sentence, and then echoed or repeated in the last part of the last phrase, "the rising of unknown stars and perished planets."

Smith's fourth volume of verse—and his third major collection of poetry—*Sandalwood* (published by Smith himself in 1925), contains only two specifically Atlantean references. These occur in two sonnets, the first cast in alexandrines, the second in the usual decasyllabics.

The first sonnet, "Forgotten Sorrow," is one of the most delicate and subtle tasks that Smith ever assigned to himself, to give embodiment to a theme which threatens to disappear during the handling of it, due to its utter filmy character, or to be destroyed if the given embodiment prove too heavy. The razor-thin terrain wherein such manifestation can take place, the poet just achieves, no more and no less. The Atlantean allusion occurs in the final image, which contains both visual and aural clues. The final image occupies the entire fourteenth line, thus logically capping the rest of the sonnet. Smith is ever the master of style and form, discovering the perfect expression for his poetic substance.

> A stranger grief than any grief by music told
> Is mine: regret for unremembered loves, and faces
> Veiled by the night of some unknown farewell, or places
> Lost in the dusty ebb and lapse of kingdoms old
> On the slow desert, rises vague and manifold
> Within my heart at summer twilight. Through the spaces
> Of all oblivion, voidly then my soul retraces
> Her dead lives given to the marbles and the mould
> In dim Palmyra, or some pink, enormous city
> Whose falling columns now the boles of mightier trees

Support in far Siam. . . . All grievous love and pity,
All loveliness unheld for long, and long estranged,
Appeals with voices indistinguishably changed,
Like bells in deep Atlantis, tolled by summer seas. (*S* 9–10)

The second sonnet wherein we find an Atlantean reference is "Enchanted Mirrors." The entire piece possesses an abundance of those peculiarly Smithian elements of poetic magic, but the reference to Atlantis especially seems to possess, if possible, an even greater amount of this magical quality. We must call particular attention to the final lines of both the octet and the sestet which, although differing as to where the pauses or semi-pauses fall (in the vocal delivery of the lines), manage to achieve an almost similar rhythm or rhythmical effect, but with this one major distinction: the pauses in the last line of the sestet reverse those in the last line of the octet.

These are enchanted mirrors that I bring—
By daemons wrought from metals of the moon
To burnished forms of lune or plenilune;
Therein are faery faces vanishing,
And warm Pompeiian phantoms lovelier
Than mortal flesh or marble; and the gleam
Of Atlantean suns that rose in dream
And sank on golden worlds that never were.

Therein you shall behold unshapen dooms,
And ghoul-astounding shadows of the tombs;
Oblivion, with eyes like poppy-buds,
Or love, with blossoms plucked in Devachan,
In stillness of the lily-pillared woods—
But nevermore the moiling world of man.[2] (*S* 18)

Created at about the same time as the poems included in the original *Sandalwood* and, like those poems, first published in the *Auburn Journal,* are two quatrains that contain Atlantean or peripherally Atlantean references, and which are both similar in form, rhetoric, and ef-

---

2. Smith eliminated the reference to Atlantis when he revised this poem for *SP.* In the first published version of this poem, "the boughs of Eden" reads "the palms of Eden."

fect. (Smith included both "Dissidence" and "Lemurienne" in his collection of collections, *Selected Poems,* in the section "Sandalwood.") The first quatrain, "Dissidence" (first entitled "Diversity"), contains the peripherally Atlantean reference:

> Within your voice the boughs of Eden sigh
> In scented winds blown from the summer foam;
> But in your gaze the lulling hills of home
> Accept the silence of an autumn sky.[3] (*SP* 169)

The equation of Eden to the almost utopian, semi-paradisiacal world of Plato's Atlantis is borne out by one possible interpretation of lines 1–2. Restricting our examination to these two lines only, we may evolve two different interpretations of what exactly is the physical image that Smith intends within the context. The first reading is that the boughs of Eden sigh because of the scented winds blown from the summer foam (i.e., at the edge of the ocean littoral). The second reading is that, within the scented winds blown from the summer foam, we can hear the boughs of Eden sigh, and that the summer foam causes this sound as a memory, as an auditory resurrection, of an Eden lost or sunk, Atlantis-wise, beneath the sea. Which reading is the correct one, is impossible to tell due to the word-arrangement dictated by the exigencies of verse-rhetoric.

The second quatrain, "Lemurienne" (first entitled "The Lemurienne"), has a directly generical Atlantean reference, apart from the title (which apparently indicates a female inhabitant of that Atlantis of the Indian Ocean, or of the Pacific, Lemuria).

> From dawn to dawn your eyes of graven spar
> For ever change, with chill forgotten runes;
> But all the while your spirit lies afar,
> A sphinx that peers on prediluvian moons.[4] (*SP* 169)

Also created at approximately the same time (1923–25) as the poems in *Sandalwood* (including the pieces quoted above among oth-

---

3. In the first published version of the poem above, l. 4 reads: "A sphinx that peers on lost Lemuric moons."

4. The original version of this poem was republished in the *Arkham Collector* for Summer 1968.

ers) is an extensive series of epigrams and pensées first published in the *Auburn Journal*. This is one of the few places in his overall creativity where Smith makes a number of overt references to a narrow contemporaneity. Most of these epigrams might be characterized as up-to-date, smart, topical; and these have predictably dated the most. Some of them are still amusing, and some still possess genuine interest. In the *Auburn Journal* for Thursday, 15 November 1923, four items appear under the title "Points for the Pious." The second of these four items, one of the most perceptive of the real pensées, contains an unexpected reference to Atlantis:

> The terror of Lilith, the fear of beauty and its destructive potentialities, lies at the heart of all puritanism. Humanity has always been divided into those who loved beauty and those who were afraid of it. Doubtless there were witch-burners in ancient Atlantis. (*DN* 53)

These same years also saw Smith writing his first play, *The Fugitives,* which he failed to complete. This was a romantic drama composed in blank verse interspersed with songs. All the songs that Smith wrote for the play, he included in *Sandalwood:* "Song" or "The Fugitive"; "The Song of Aviol"; "The Love-Potion"; and "The Song of Cartha." In his letter to R. H. Barlow dated 23 November 1936, Smith described the plot, one surprisingly dealing with Atlantis, as follows:

> The plot was a simple and quite romantic one: it began with the mutual dawning of love in an Atlantean boy and girl, soon to be separated. Later, they were to meet again: the boy a wandering poet of recognized genius, the girl a king's concubine. Their old love reawakens, they flee from the Atlantean court and capital, to perish in the wilderness after several days and nights of mad happiness. (*SL* 275)

Such a play, developed in several acts and various tableaux, would have made a notable addition to the one play that he did complete, but evidently much later, *The Dead Will Cuckold You.*

In the summer of 1928, following the death of George Sterling in November 1926 (an event of great consequence for Smith as one of Sterling's closest friends), Smith began writing his mature fiction, a development marked by the brief prose fantasy "The Ninth Skeleton." Between 1928 and 1938 he was to write over one hundred and forty short stories and novelettes. In December 1929 he created some ten poems in prose

later designated as "prose pastels"—and in one of them, "To the Dae-
mon," composed on the 16th, the poet addresses his tutelary daemon,
or genius, asking this entity, suitably enough, to tell him "many tales"
but not necessarily of Atlantis, among other esoteric locations.

> Tell me many tales, O benign maleficent daemon, but tell me none
> that I have ever heard or have even dreamt of otherwise than obscurely or
> infrequently. Nay, tell me not of anything that lies between the bourns of
> time or the limits of space; for I am a little weary of all recorded years and
> chartered lands; and the isles that are westward of Cathay, and the sunset
> realms of Ind, are not remote enough to be made the abiding-place of my
> conceptions; and Atlantis is over-new for my thoughts to sojourn there,
> and Mu itself has gazed upon the sun in aeons that are too recent.
> Tell me many tales, but let them be of things that are past the lore of
> legend and of which there are no myths in our world or any world ad-
> joining. [. . .] Tell me tales of inconceivable fear and unimaginable love,
> in orbs whereto our sun is a nameless star, or unto which its rays have
> never reached. (*NU* 17-18)

However, be his request as it may have been, the daemon did tell
him something of Plato's lost world, for included in Smith's prose fic-
tions of 1928–38 are five tales of Atlantis, or (more correctly) "the last
isle of foundering Atlantis"—to wit, Poseidonis. These tales comprise
"The Last Incantation," "The Death of Malygris," "The Double
Shadow," "A Voyage to Sfanomoë" (the last word Smith pronounced
with the accent on the second syllable), and "A Vintage from Atlan-
tis." These must be ranked among Smith's finest efforts in prose. It is
very difficult to classify these tales, as it is most of Smith's fiction. In
form they are poems in prose; but conceptually and symbolically they
may be generally considered as fables, parables, allegories.

An important point to remember is that, while only five of his tales
concern Atlantis, or Poseidonis, precisely, Smith's other lost worlds, es-
pecially his other continents of Earth—which he has used or created as a
background for some of his other stories—are implicitly Atlantean in
concept-principle: Hyperborea, the first inhabited continent of Earth, a
sort of proto-Atlantis; and Zothique, the last continent of Earth, a sort of
infinitely latter-day Atlantis arisen out of the sea, while all the other for-
mer continents have subsided beneath the globe-wide oceans.

In one of the specifically Atlantean tales the poet vouchsafes us a
full-scale vision of Plato's ancient capital of Atlantis. This occurs in "A

Vintage from Atlantis," a tale that Smith created in November 1931. This vision is one of the great set-pieces of typically Smithian description, comparable to any of the same engineered by Edmund Spenser for his epic-romance-allegory *The Faerie Queene.*

The air about me seemed to brighten, with a redness of ghostly blood that was everywhere; a light that came not from the fire nor from the nocturnal heavens. I beheld the faces and forms of the drinkers [the fellow crew-members of the narrator], standing without shadow, as if mantled with a rosy phosphorescence. And beyond them, where they stared in troubled and restless wonder, the darkness was illumed with a strange light.

Mad and unholy was the vision that I saw: for the harbour waves no longer lapped on the sand, and the sea had wholly vanished. The *Black Falcon* was gone, and where the reefs had been, great marble walls ascended, flushed as if with the ruby of lost sunsets. Above them were haughty domes of heathen temples, and spires of pagan palaces; and beneath were mighty streets and causeys where people passed in a never-ending throng. I thought that I gazed upon some immemorial city, such as had flourished in Earth's prime; and I saw the trees of its terraced gardens, fairer than the palms of Eden. Listening, I heard the sound of dulcimers that were sweet as the moaning of women; and the cry of horns that told forgotten glorious things; and the wild sweet singing of people who passed to some hidden, sacred festival within the walls.

I saw that the light poured upward from the city, and was born of its streets and buildings. It blinded the heavens above; and the horizon beyond was lost in a shining mist. One building there was, a high fane above the rest, from which the light streamed in a ruddier flood; and from its open portals music came, sorcerous and beguiling as the far voices of bygone years. And the revellers passed gayly into its portals, but none came forth. The weird music seemed to call me and entice me; and I longed to tread the streets of the alien city, and a deep desire was upon me to mingle with its people and pass into the glowing Lane.

Verily I knew why the drinkers had stared at the darkness and had muttered among themselves in wonder. I knew that they also longed to descend into the city. And I saw that a great causey, built of marble and gleaming with the red luster, ran downward from their very feet over meadows of unknown blossoms to the foremost buildings.

Then, as I watched and listened, the singing grew sweeter, the music stranger, and the rosy luster brightened. Then, with no backward glance, no word or gesture of injunction to his men, Captain Dwale went slowly forward, treading the marble causey like a dreamer who walks in his dream. And after him, one by one, Roger Aglone and the crew followed in the same manner, going toward the city.

Haply I too should have followed, drawn by the witching music. For truly it seemed that I had trod the ways of that city in former time, and had known the things whereof the music told and the voices sang. Well did I remember why the people passed eternally into the fane, and why they came not forth; and there, it seemed, I should meet familiar and beloved faces, and take part in mysteries recalled from the foundered years.

All this, which the wine had remembered through its sleep in the ocean depths, was mine to behold and conceive for a moment. And well it was that I had drunk less of that evil and pagan vintage than the others, and was less besotted than they with its luring vision. For even as Captain Dwale and his crew went toward the city, it appeared to me that the rosy glow began to fade a little. The walls took on a wavering thinness, and the domes grew insubstantial. The rose departed, the light was pale as a phosphor of the tomb; and the people went to and fro like phantoms, with a thin crying of ghostly horns and a ghostly singing. Dimly above the sunken causey the harbor waves returned; and Red Barnaby and his men walked down beneath them. Slowly the waters darkened above the fading spires and walls; and the midnight blackened upon the sea; and the city was lost like the vanished bubbles of wine. (*AY* 52–54)

It is of interest to note—among the abundance of many other details in this overall vision—that, toward the end of the second paragraph quoted, we have a repeat or echo of "the palms of Eden" from the original version of "Dissidence"—"and I saw the trees of its terraced gardens, fairer than the palms of Eden."

After 1938, Smith virtually gave up the writing of prose fiction, at least in any real amount, and had returned to his first love, the creation of poetry in verse. In some of this later lyric poetry we find some scattered Atlantean references, and even a few full-scale Atlantean poems. Smith's new, rejuvenated poetic drive or impulsion would last almost up until the time of his death, fueled as it was by two remarkable and lasting love affairs.

In 1951, Arkham House, after bringing out three collections of Smith's highly imaginative fiction (in 1942, 1944, and 1948), published its first collection of poetry by the same author, *The Dark Chateau,* three of whose pieces contain Atlantean references. In the sixth and seventh stanzas of "Dominium in Excelsis" we note "the fabled Atlantean doom," but now coupled with a resurrection out of the condition of such a catastrophic death.

Thou shalt respire the flame and fume
Of Beltis' altars drowned in gloom
Under her sharded fanes; or share
The fabled Atlantean doom,

And rise unharmed to light and air
Out of old death, once more to dare
With antinomian deed and thought
The planet of thy slain despair—(*DC* 17-18)

In the second and third stanzas of "Malediction" there occurs a reference to Atlantis but the Atlantis in question is imaged as being "accurst." (We also quote the sixth stanza as well as the final single line that follows it for an easier syntactical comprehension by the reader.)

While the worms, apart from light,
Eat the page where magians pored;
While the kraken, blind and white,

Guards the greening books abhorred
Where the evil oghams rust—
In accurst Atlantis stored;

[. . .]

Never shall the spell be done
And the curse be lifted never
That shall find and leave you one

With forgotten things for ever. (*DC* 26)

And in the final lines (47-54) of "Revenant" we note an allusion to "atlantean fanes" but clearly intended by the poet in a generic rather than a specific usage, as clearly demonstrated by his abandonment of the upper-case *a* at the start of the adjective "atlantean."

Mummied and ceremented,
I sit in councils of the kingly dead,
And oftentimes for vestiture I wear
The granite of great idols looming darkly
In atlantean fanes;

Or closely now and starkly,
I cling as clings the attenuating air
Above the ruins bare. (*DC 54*)

In 1958, Arkham House published its second collection of poetry
by Smith, *Spells and Philtres,* which has two Atlantean references. Our
first example Atlantean is the entire poem of "Tolometh," featuring as
it does a major god of Poseidonis, the large island that Smith presents
as the last major fragment of foundering Atlantis, evidently taking a clue
from the Theosophist writings of Helena Blavatsky:

In billow-lost Poseidonis
I was the black god of the abyss;
My three horns were of similor
Above my double diadem;
My one eye was a moon-bright gem
Found in a monstrous meteor.

Incredible far peoples came,
Called by the thunders of my fame,
And passed below my terraced throne
Where titan pards and lions stood,
As pours a never-lapsing flood
Before the wind of winter blown.

Below my glooming architraves
One brown eternal file of slaves
Came in from mines of chalcedon,
And camels from the long plateaus
Laid down their sard and peridoz,
Their incense and their cinnamon.

The star-born evil that I brought
Through all that ancient land was wrought;
All women took my yoke of shame;
I reared, through sunless centuries,
The thrones of hell-black wizardries,
The hecatombs of blood and flame.

But now, within my sunken walls,
The slow blind ocean-serpent crawls,
And sea-worms are my ministers,
And wandering fishes pass me now
Or press before mine eyeless brow
As once the thronging worshippers. . . .

And yet, in ways outpassing thought,
Men worship me that know me not.
They work my will. I shall arise
In that last dawn of atom-fire,
To stand upon the planet's pyre
And cast my shadow on the skies. (*SP* 274–75)

Our second example Atlantean occurs in "The Prophet Speaks," which devotes its full second stanza to an Atlantean allusion but, as in the case of "Malediction" included in *The Dark Chateau,* the Atlantis in question the poet views through a glass darkly. (We quote the first full stanza as well on behalf of the reader's easier comprehension.)

City forbanned by seer and god and devil!
In glory less than Tyre or fabled Ys,
But more than they in mere, surpassing evil!

Yea, black Atlantis, fallen beneath dim seas
For sinful lore and rites to demons done,
Bore not the weight of such iniquities. (*SP* 276)

For our final examples of Atlanteana from Smith's overall corpus of published poetry, we turn to the final section of his final and finally published collection of collections, *Selected Poems,* brought out by Arkham House in late 1971. This final section embodies the cycle of love poems *The Hill of Dionysus,* which evolved out of the great friendship or deep love that Smith shared with the younger poet Eric Barker and his wife, the dancer Madelynne Greene.[5] Their friendship began in early 1938 and did not end until Smith's death in August

---

5. The young Madelynne Greene was a strikingly beautiful woman of Irish descent with dark auburn hair, green eyes, and well-shaped body, which she kept supple, strong, and well-toned by means of her daily dance exercises.

1961, but waxed at its strongest in the period 1938–55, the poems themselves apparently coming into being in the years 1939–47.

Smith's mother Fanny, or Frances, Gaylord Smith, had passed on in early September 1935, and his father in late December 1937. The family had lived together since the poet's birth, and just as his parents had nurtured him both as person and as poet, so their son had nurtured and nursed the parents, both of them in turn, through their final phase of old age or terminal ill health. Thus the family had always been very close, that is, had lived as almost constant companions for over four full decades, from the early 1890s on into the mid-1930s. By early 1938 Smith found himself not only very much alone but also very lonely. Into this real void the Barkers arrived, and their friendship filled and fulfilled a true need in Smith's life. The three of them would visit back and forth between Auburn and the California coast (mostly San Rafael, San Francisco, and the Monterey, Carmel, and Big Sur area) during the next twenty years. They would share many pleasant hours of companionship, not to mention a number of whimsical adventures. How much this love meant to Smith, and in particular the love that he consummated with Madelynne, the poet reveals in "Wizard's Love," one of the earliest poems in the cycle *The Hill of Dionysus,* a favorite hill in San Rafael covered with giant oak trees where they loved to have picnics and similar outings.

> O perfect love, unhoped-for, past despair!
> I had not thought to find
> Your face betwixt the terrene earth and air:
> But deemed you lost in fabulous old lands
> And rose-lit years to darkness long resigned.
> O child, you cannot know
> What magic and what miracles you bring
> Within your tender hands;
> What griefs are lulled to blissful slumbering,
> Cushioned upon your deep and fragrant hair;
> What gall-black bitterness of long ago,
> Within my bosom sealed,
> Ebbs gradually as might some desert well

Under your beauty's heaven warm and fair,
And the green suns of your vertumnal eyes.

O beauty wrought of rapture and surprise,
Too dear for heart to know, or tongue to tell! (*SP* 366–67)

The lucid statement of profound emotion in "Wizard's Love" informs us without equivocation just how much value Smith placed on the supreme adventure of love, a value also borne out emphatically by the two final paragraphs from "The Enchantress of Sylaire," one of Smith's Averoigne chronicles. The two main characters are the poet Anselme and the enchantress herself:

> Again the clinging deliciousness of Sephora was in his arms, and her fruit-soft mouth was crushed beneath his hungry lips.
> The strongest of all enchantments held them in its golden circle. (*AY* 140)

As we know from her letter to Donald Sidney-Fryer, written in the spring of 1967 (*Emperor of Dreams* 154), the love that bound Ashton, Eric, and Madelynne together, and that Madelynne fully shared, inspired the three of them in so many different ways. However, as Madelynne made it clear to Sidney-Fryer in the course of their friendship (from late 1966 until her death at the age of fifty-eight in the early or middle 1970s), Smith had often wanted Eric and herself to move to Auburn so that they could all reside together or close by each other. Nevertheless, Madelynne as dancer and as teacher of dance needed the conveniences and advantages of a big city like San Francisco. She confided that, as much as she loved Ashton, and loved spending long sojourns with him near Auburn or on the coast, she could never have lived with him on a regular basis. As Madelynne expressed this, and with real regret, she found Smith such a melancholy man that she found it much too depressing to stay with him indefinitely. She and Eric later introduced Smith to Carol Jones Dorman sometime during latter 1954. Eric was living at that time as a caretaker on some property in Little Sur (not far from Big Sur), and Smith had come to visit on an occasion when Carol also happened to be there as a friend to both Eric and Madelynne. Smith and Carol fell in love almost immediately, and were married in mid-November 1954.

Too many readers or critics, at least those of male gender, have underestimated or have simply ignored the specific love poems by Smith, beginning with those included in *Ebony and Crystal* and *Sandalwood,* continuing through *The Jasmine Girdle,* and concluding with *The Hill of Dionysus* (which remains Smith's last major cycle of poems of any description). Such poems unequivocally make us intimate with the hope and even optimism that Smith reveals in this one area of experience, even in the face of unavoidable doom. *Maître de conférence* and specialist in highly imaginative literature in the English department at the University of Nantes (the major city in northwest France at the mouth of the river Loire, just southeast of Brittany), Lauric Guillaud has asked in a recent and excellent critical evaluation of Smith's oeuvre the following question: "Yet is it correct to assume that Smith's universe is really barren of any hope?" (207). In answering his own question, Guillaud typically neglects or overlooks the evidence to be found in Smith's overt love poetry.

The final stanza of "Resurrection" embodies our first specific Atlantean reference from *The Hill of Dionysus:*

> Witch belovèd from of old
> When upon Atlantis rolled
> All the dire and wrathful deep,
> You had kissed mine eyes asleep.
> On my lids shall fall your lips
> In the final sun's eclipse;
> And your hand shall take my hand
> In the last and utmost land. (*SP* 368)

Our next Atlantean reference we find in the opening and closing of "Bond," with its poignant statement of love's eternal return with the same lovers reincarnating from century to century:

> By the red seal redoubled of that kiss
> When thy lips parted softly to my own
> Ere the sun sank from doomed Poseidonis;
> [. . .]

By the sealed ways no prophet has foreshown,
Whereon our lips shall meet, our footsteps go:—
By these, by these I claim thee for mine own. . . .

Even as I have claimed thee long ago. (*SP* 378)

Some especially poignant Atlantean references feature in the opening and closing of *"Amor Hesternalis."* The opening stanza is particularly haunting:

Our blood is swayed by sunken moons
And lulled by midnights long foredone;
We waken to a foundered sun
In Atlantean afternoons:
Our blood is swayed by sunken moons.
[. . .]
We are the specters of past years:
But soon Atlantis from the main
Shall lift; and Sappho bring again,
Risen from ancient brine and tears,
The living Lesbos of past years. (*SP* 387)

The entire lyric that is "Sea Cycle" adumbrates, but only implicitly, an Atlantean content as the opening and closing of the poem in question clearly demonstrate:

Below the cliff, before the granite stair,
The foam-crests curl and feather in blue air,
Numberless as the helmet-plumes of hosts
Resurgent from millennium-foundered coasts.
[. . .]
Though prayer be vain, this thing shall come to pass,
For still the solemn cycles wane and flow,
Bringing again the lost and long ago.
All that the sea has taken, the sea restores:
Somehow, somewhere, on ocean-winnowed shores,
Again we two shall wander, and shall not stay,
Finding the golden wrack of yesterday. (*SP* 399–400)

Another example of a lyric doing so implicitly, the very final poem in the entire cycle, the sonnet "Avowal," adumbrates many an Atlantis arising out of the far future—deep in "the cosmic sea sublime"—but all of which shall arise in vain, if it does not restore to us the pristine beauty, wonder, love, and mystery from our collective past, immeasurable and immemorial:

> Whatever alien fruits and changeling faces
> And pleasances of mutable perfume
> The flambeaux of the senses shall illume
> Amid the night-filled labyrinthine spaces,
> In lives to be, in unestablished places,
> All, all were vain as the rock-raveled spume
> If no strange close restore the Paphian bloom,
> No path return the moon-shod maenad's paces.
>
> Yea, for the lover of lost pagan things,
> No vintage grown in islands unascended
> Shall quite supplant the old Bacchantic urn,
> No mouth that new Canopic suns make splendid
> Content the mouth of sealed rememberings
> Where still the nymph's uncleaving kisses burn. (*SP* 403)

The last completed poem that Smith created (insofar as our present information allows us to state) is the sonnet in alexandrines, "Cycles," written on 4 June 1961, a little more than two months before his death on 14 August 1961. Donald Sidney-Fryer commissioned this lyric expressly for his *Emperor of Dreams: A Clark Ashton Smith Bibliography,* omitted therefrom by happenstance. This thus contains Smith's very last reference to Atlantis in print:

> The sorcerer departs . . . and his high tower is drowned
> Slowly by low flat communal seas that level all . . .
> While crowding centuries retreat, return and fall
> Into the cyclic gulf that girds the cosmos round,
> Widening, deepening ever outward without bound . . .
> Till the oft-rerisen bells from young Atlantis call;
> And again the wizard-mortised tower upbuilds its wall
> Above a re-beginning cycle, turret-crowned.

New-born, the mage re-summons stronger spells, and spirits
With dazzling darkness clad about, and fierier flame
Renewed by aeon-curtained slumber. All the powers
Of genii and Solomon the sage inherits;
And there, to blaze with blinding glory the bored hours,
He calls upon Shem-hamphorash, the nameless Name. (*LO* 174)

The love specifically taking place between Smith and Madelynne, which waxed at its strongest, it would seem, during 1939–47 (approximately), had enabled Smith to discover a late-blossoming period of intensely poetic activity and creativity. During the middle to latter 1940s the poet was concurrently preparing the enormous typescript of his *Selected Poems,* a task that represented a huge challenge for him in terms of collating manuscripts, and of rethinking and retyping a vast amount of material. The whole task became hampered and complicated by the fact that during much of the process Smith was experiencing serious eye trouble.

Nevertheless, despite such problems, out of this enormously fruitful period, like some unexpected Atlantis arising out from the ocean of time and memory, there came into palpable being his last major cycle of new poetry, and of new love poems at that. This new corpus of pure but accessible lyricism presents a remarkable efflorescence of creativity, indeed, for a poet at the half-century mark of his lifetime, when some commentators might have considered him already to be past his most fruitful prime. As formulated elsewhere, "Phoenix-like, the poet had been reborn out of the ashes of the fiction-writer" (Sidney-Fryer, 19).

Acknowledgments

Together with other materials by other authors, this essay was originally prepared for a special issue (No. 5) of the then promising semiprozine *Anubis.* The issue was projected to appear sometime during the late 1960s (or the early 1970s). Most of the contents were written or compiled c. 1966 or 1967. For a variety of reasons not quite explained or made clear, the number in question has never made its appearance, nor has any other issue of *Anubis,* for that matter.

When a photocopy of this essay (as laid out on sheets readied for photopublishing), together with a copy of a map of Poseidonis by Tim Kirk, found their way back into the hands of the present author (courtesy of Don Herron and Ronald S. Hilger) in May 2002, the original conclusion was completely missing (i.e., following the first mention of the 1958 Arkham House collection of poems *Spells and Philtres*). The present author perforce had to re-create it from a re-reading of the cycle of love poems *The Hill of Dionysus* and other materials, with a discussion of which he had originally finished the essay. To this he has added some biographical details never before vouchsafed concerning the relationship among the poet Eric Barker, the dancer Madelynne Greene, and Clark Ashton Smith himself.

Otherwise, during the latter half of September 2002, the present author has also revised this essay in ways both major and minor. In particular he would like to thank his personal friends Don Herron, Ronald Hilger, and Rah Hoffman for verifying information or for the use of books and other materials.

Works Cited

Greene, Madelynne. Letter. In Donald Sidney-Fryer. *Emperor of Dreams: A Clark Ashton Smith Bibliography.* West Kingston, RI: Donald M. Grant, 1978, p. 154.

Guillard, Lauric. "Fantasy and Decadence in the Work of Clark Ashton Smith." *Paradoxa 5* (1999–2000): 189–212.

Sidney-Fryer, Donald. *The Sorcerer Departs.* 1963. West Hills, CA: Tsathoggua Press, 1997.

Smith, Clark Ashton. *The Abominations of Yondo.* Sauk City, WI: Arkham House, 1960. [*AY*]

————. *The Dark Chateau.* Sauk City, WI: Arkham House, 1951. [*DC*]

————. *Ebony and Crystal: Poems in Verse and Prose.* Auburn, CA: Auburn Press, 1922. [*EC*]

————. *The Last Oblivion: Best Fantastic Poems of Clark Ashton Smith.* Ed. S. T. Joshi and David E. Schultz. New York: Hippocampus Press, 2002. [*LO*]

————. *Sandalwood.* Auburn, CA: Auburn Press, 1925. [*S*]

————. *Selected Poems.* Sauk City, WI: Arkham House, 1971. [*SP*]

————. *The Star-Treader and Other Poems.* San Francisco: A. M. Robertson, 1912. [*ST*]

Sterling, George. *Complete Poetry.* Ed. S. T. Joshi and David E. Schultz. New York: Hippocampus Press, 2013.

Klarkash-Ton and "Greek"

Preface

This commemorative essay is being written on the eve of the one hundred and tenth anniversary of Clark Ashton Smith's birth, 13 January 2003. On that occasion a group of friends and admirers will dedicate a monument to Smith's memory in Bicentennial Park in Old Auburn, California. This essay seeks to honor not only Smith as a great poet but also that other great poet without whom there might not have existed any Smith as poet at all: George Sterling.

It is important that, in conjunction with the life and career of Smith, we review those proper to Sterling himself. What Sterling accomplished, initially under the tutelage of Ambrose Bierce, led inexorably to what Smith in turn achieved. The group that we have labelled the California Romantics, and that flourished from c. 1890 to c. 1930, or slightly refigured, to c. 1960, included other significant figures, but with the one exception perhaps of Nora May French, Sterling and Smith remain two eagles flying high over flocks of sparrows.

As the leading California Romantic, Clark Ashton Smith—poet, storyteller, painter, and sculptor—inherited from George Sterling the figurative Cloak of Elijah bequeathed him by Ambrose Bierce. It is their shared and uncompromising vision, their vision of what they perceived as the truth—and the burning need to communicate it in the manner of the Biblical prophet Elijah, that is, with utter passion—that we commemorate in this essay.

George and Clark, Respectively

George Sterling emigrated to Oakland, California, from his birthplace Sag Harbor, New York, in 1890. While working, during the period 1890–1915, as personal secretary for his uncle, Frank C. Havens, his mother's brother, a wealthy real-estate operator in Oakland, Sterling met a variety of significant literary figures there during the mid-1890s, including Joaquin Miller, Ina Donna Coolbrith, Ambrose Bierce, and Jack London. London belonged to the same generation as Sterling,

144

and the others represented an important survival from California's first "Golden Age" of literature that had also included Bret Harte, Mark Twain, and Robert Louis Stevenson, among many others. Sterling became good friends with each of his new acquaintances, but a special bond soon united Sterling and London. Kindred spirits in many respects, they became the closest of friends: truly, drinking buddies and boon companions. Whereas Sterling called London "Wolf," London called Sterling "Greek." Although London would go on to become one of the most popular authors of his time, Sterling's fame would remain restricted more or less to the United States, Britain, and especially California. Because Joaquin Miller and Bierce had established a sort of literary beach-head in Britain during the 1870s, this foothold had served as a special mode of communication between the London and San Francisco literary scenes, a conduit that benefited many California poets and writers from the 1870s on into the 1920s at least. It helped many littérateurs who would not otherwise have become known abroad. These figures would include both Sterling and Clark Ashton Smith in their turn.

Jack London admired Sterling enormously as person and poet. Later, in the novel *Martin Eden,* he painted a glamorous portrait of him as the elegant and cultured Russ Brissenden. Sterling for his part thought so highly of London's ability as storyteller that he volunteered to edit and proofread all London's books published from the late 1890s up to his death, apparently by suicide, in 1916. Later still, during the 1920s, after H. P. Lovecraft and Clark Ashton Smith (as Sterling's own chief protégé) became close friends, but only through correspondence, Lovecraft often addressed Smith as Klarkash-Ton. However, in their own correspondence and friendship that lasted from January 1911 until the elder poet died in November 1926, Sterling and Smith simply called each other George and Clark, respectively.

Today many admirers of Smith's highly imaginative stories know Sterling only through Smith, and it would seem that, just as Sterling "carried" Smith in a sense under his protective aegis (during 1911–26), so now it seems likely that, as time goes on, Smith will return the favor and increasingly will "carry" his long-term friend and mentor under the aegis of his own ever-expanding international reputation as a unique and inimitable author. Nevertheless, Sterling in his time created an extraordinary legend of his own as a poet, and as the popular ideal of a poet in his public persona.

George Sterling: Poet Laureate of the Far West

At some point during the 1890s George Sterling (born in 1869, and thus in his twenties at that time) began writing his first mature poetry under the direction more or less of the satirist and storyteller Ambrose Bierce, who had agreed to act as Sterling's poetic mentor. Poetically the two had much in common: a disdain for the then fashionable sentimentality and a preference for traditional meter, form, and rhyme. Very much the product of the *fin-de-siècle,* Sterling's first major poem (in two extended sections) emerged as *The Testimony of the Suns,* a striking and grandiose appraisal of the cosmos at large. The first section is dated December 1901, and the second February 1902. The poem became the dominant feature, as well as title poem, of Sterling's first collection, published by W. E. Wood of San Francisco in 1903. It remains an austere and very sober disquisition on the uncharted and star-strewn immensities of the cosmic-astronomic spaces, as well as the utter indifference of the cosmos at large to human beings and their concerns while residing and evolving on a small and inconspicuous planet circling around an insignificant sun located almost at the edge of the Milky Way, one galaxy among billions. This long, rather digressive, but certainly impressive poem still represents the strongest statement of cosmic pessimism or nihilism ever penned.

The poem and the collection, by the scope of the subject matter and the quality of the execution, established Sterling as the foremost poet of San Francisco and California, if not indeed on the entire west coast of the U.S.—although he did not become recognized as such until the publication (under Bierce's aegis) of his next major poem, "A Wine of Wizardry," in the *Cosmopolitan* during the summer of 1907. Meanwhile, changes were happening in Sterling's life, of a radical but positive nature. In 1905 his aunt, Mrs. Frank C. Havens, gave her nephew his "freedom money," and with this gift he left the San Francisco Bay Area to settle on the Monterey Peninsula. He purchased some land in the village of Carmel-by-the-Sea, built a house there (as well as a cabin farther back on his property), and proceeded to devote his time to writing, fishing for abalone, hunting small game, growing a vegetable garden, and fostering other forms of do-it-yourself husbandry. Soon other writers and artists, inspired by Sterling's example, came down from the Bay Area to set up a Bohemian existence in Carmel. The town owes its early development and character almost completely to Sterling as San Francisco's "King of Bohemia" (as the journalist Idwal Jones nicknamed him). Apart from occasional sojourns back in the City and elsewhere, Sterling's principal residence from 1905 until 1913 remained the developing town of Carmel.

Whatever reputation he may have won from *The Testimony of the Suns,* the young poet soon saw it eclipsed when, through Bierce's influence, the *Cosmopolitan* for September 1907 published "A Wine of Wizardry," a glittering and highly colored fantasy in sumptuous rhymed verse. Sterling's poetic mentor outrageously trumpeted the poem's praises in his accompanying essay. The poem and the poet, no less than the claims made for them by Bierce, aroused an astonishing and often inimical chorus of controversy from all over the U.S. But the controversy produced Bierce's desired effect: it established Sterling as the poet laureate of the Far West, even if uncrowned as such. It placed poem and poet solidly on the literary map of America. Among other connoisseurs of the weird and fantastic, the science fiction writer Fritz Leiber has judged "A Wine of Wizardry" equal in value to Coleridge's ineffable effusion "Kubla Khan," that Holy Writ of the high romantic imagination.

Meanwhile, the performance that same summer of Sterling's first verse drama, *The Triumph of Bohemia,* had proven eminently successful for what it was, a hastily composed although competent poetic drama of no great merit, but amusing and appropriate. It depicted with naive idealism the triumphant battle waged by the good forces of Nature against the evil strategems of Mammon, seeking to cut the Bohemian Grove itself down for mere filthy lucre. Sterling had written the play for the Bohemian Club of San Francisco (to which he belonged) for its annual revels, or High Jinks, that took place every summer at the Bohemian Grove on the Russian River up in Marin County north of the City. This was a small forest of giant redwoods and of great beauty. The Bohemian Club subsequently published the play in 1907

as the second of Sterling's books of poetry. The national notoriety de-
riving from the magazine publication of "A Wine of Wizardry," no
less than the local fame generated anew by his Grove Play, produced
another and very positive result. It brought Sterling to the attention of
the eminent bookseller and publisher A. M. Robertson, who owned
and operated a successful bookstore in San Francisco, a significant cul-
tural institution of its type known throughout the Bay Area.

Living chiefly in Carmel and making occasional sojourns up to the
City, Sterling himself was very little affected by the great earthquake
and fire that devastated much of San Francisco during April 1906,
although he did go up there at the time to lend what aid that he could
to those dear and close to him. Like everyone and everything in the
areas surrounding the City, whether near or far, he felt the shocks,
which had proven of unprecedented severity within living memory.

Both the major new poem and his first verse play now made up
the principal contents of Sterling's next collection, *A Wine of Wiz-
ardry,* brought out in 1909, the first of ten volumes of poetry pub-
lished by A. M. Robertson. Their titles evoke not only the poet's lush
and exotic romanticism but also (some of them) their *raison d'être* in
contemporary places and events of San Francisco and California,
no less than in the world at large: *The House of Orchids* (1911),
one of his best single collections; *Beyond the Breakers* (1914);
*Ode on the Opening of the Panama-Pacific International Exposi-
tion* (1915), actually celebrated in honor of the completion of the
Panama Canal in 1914, and at the resplendent fair grounds in both
San Francisco and San Diego; *The Evanescent City* (1915), a series
of three connected poems detailing the building, then the animated
existence, and finally the demolition of the San Francisco fair's gran-
diose but ephemeral structures; *Yosemite: An Ode* (1915), celebrat-
ing one of California's greatest natural wonders.

But now the Great War that raged in Europe during 1914–18
obtruded into the lives of Americans everywhere when, in part be-
cause of the sinking of the British liner *Lusitania* (with American
citizens aboard) by German submarine action in May 1915, the
U.S. entered the war in April 1917, staying the course until the Ar-
mistice in November 1918. As part of his new role as San Francis-
co's unofficial poet laureate, several books by Sterling at this time

reflect the war and connected events, as was perhaps expected, even if it did not result in some of his best work: *The Caged Eagle* (1916) and *The Binding of the Beast* (1917), a collection of war sonnets. (Although both the last two volumes reflect the Great War in Europe, the latter title does so much more than the former.) A special mention must be made here of a rare volume not brought out by A. M. Robertson, and one of the few books of poetry ever published by the Book Club of California based in San Francisco: *Thirty-five Sonnets* (1917), honoring Sterling's acknowledged supremacy in this form, almost invariably of the Petrarchan type. *Rosamund* (1920), another verse drama, and the collection *Sails and Mirage* (1921), one of his best, are the last volumes by Sterling published by A. M. Robertson. Most, if not all, of these ten books constitute elegant examples not only of Art Nouveau binding but above all excellent printing by various fine-art printers of San Francisco during the period of 1909–23.

A variety of publishers, located outside California with two exceptions, issued Sterling's remaining seven volumes during his lifetime or afterwards: *Selected Poems* (New York: Henry Holt, 1923), his single most important collection by its very nature; *Truth* (Chicago: The Bookfellows, 1923), another verse drama; *Truth* (San Francisco: The Bohemian Club, 1926), a revised version; *Robinson Jeffers: The Man and the Artist* (New York: Boni & Liveright, 1926). Finally there are three posthumous collections: *Sonnets to Craig* (New York: Albert and Charles Boni, 1928); *Poems to Vera* (New York: Oxford University Press, 1938); and *After Sunset* (San Francisco: Howell, 1939). Of Sterling's four verse dramas, only two have been produced and performed, and moreover successfully, *The Triumph of Bohemia* in 1907 and *Truth* in 1926, both by the Bohemian Club. Both *Rosamund* and *Lilith* (1919) appear eminently stageworthy in a practical sense, and it might make a fascinating experiment for the Bohemian Club or some other appropriate organization in San Francisco to produce and perform these plays.

Along with an occasional negative criticism (as usually caused by his perceived lack of modernism), many honors came to Sterling in the course of the years between 1907 and 1926, and most of them he richly deserved. Following his unsuccessful sojourn back east (mostly in New York City) from the spring of 1914 until the spring of 1915, he returned to San Francisco, welcomed back as its unofficial poet laureate, a role that he played to perfection until his death late in 1926. The architraves of the grandiose edifices erected on the fair grounds of the Panama-Pacific International Exposition presented (in carved or engraved form) apposite quotations not only from the poetry of Shakespeare, Milton, Dante, Firdausi, etc., but also from that of Sterling as San Francisco's own adopted son. Somewhat later the San Diego version of the same exposition (constructed in Balboa Park) honored him with a "George Sterling Day." Following the fair in Bagdad-by-the-Bay, the vast piece of real estate that had provided the fairgrounds became the Marina District, the northernmost section of San Francisco southeast of the Golden Gate at its most narrow location. The land was mostly fill.

All these honors represented the greatest public accolades that Sterling was ever to receive. It happened coincidentally during early 1915 that the governor and legislature of the state proffered to Sterling the position of poet laureate of California, seemingly created expressly for him as the state's most visible poet as well as its most flamboyant public figure of a poet. This was a very great and unprecedented honor, indeed! However, with characteristic self-effacement and generosity he did that which most people in his position would never have done: he declined the honor, insisting instead that such should go by all poetic justice to Ina Donna Coolbrith, that now rare survivor from California's first "Golden Age" of literature. With deserved acclaim Coolbrith fulfilled this position from 1915 until her death in 1928, thus outliving Sterling himself by several years. But, let us remember and emphasize, she could not have done so without Sterling's fine gesture of self-sacrifice. Only he would have known of all the help and encouragement that she had given as librarian at the Oakland Free Library to so many emerging minds, such as Jack London and the dancer Isadora Duncan, guiding their adventurous reading among the great books inherited from the past. After all, Sterling had honors to spare, universally if unofficially acknowledged as he was as the poet laureate not just of San Francisco but of the Far West.

Having changed almost overnight from artistic revolutionary or outlaw (at least as perceived in 1907 because of "A Wine of Wizardry") to virtual civic institution, Sterling entered the final phase of his life and career from 1915 to 1926, thus recognized as the very spirit of the City's now long-lasting Bohemia. In this role he functioned as the on-site but unofficial ambassador or master of ceremonies for San Francisco, entertaining a great variety of celebrities literary and otherwise. Whether in person or through correspondence, whether before or after 1915—in fact, almost from the very start of his life in California and lasting until his death—Sterling maintained an enormous range and number of friendships and acquaintances, and as indulged by San Francisco's city fathers, he performed various picturesque pranks on occasion, such as the celebrated swimming in the nude in one or more ponds or lakes of Golden Gate Park in the company of some attractive lady friend, also nude.

The poet, it must be remarked, was tall, slender, well knit, and spectacularly handsome. Many people referred to him as an Apollo, and he had great charm. He was also athletic, an excellent boxer, swimmer, etc. At Carmel he seemed to be a veritable ocean deity, frequently diving for abalone and other shellfish, and performing the task with skill and panache. Given his looks and charming personality, it is not a surprise that many females found Sterling irresistibly attractive, and that, with no strings attached, he consummated relationships with an innumerable succession of willing and beautiful women. Almost throughout the entire period of his marriage to Carrie, from 1896 through 1913 (they had separated in 1911 and were divorced in early 1914), Sterling had made love with a great many other women besides his wife. Carrie committed suicide by poison in 1918.

During all this very busy life and career Sterling not only had had his poetry and prose very widely published in all manner of periodicals and collections nationally circulated, but as always he found the time and energy to help, encourage, and instruct innumerable poets, both men and women. Apparently he regarded this as a sacred obligation, the passing of the "sacred fire" of art from one generation to another, and it is the one thing that remains as a genuine credit, in a very personal sense, to his memory, and that possesses a real nobility and selflessness. Although he had others, his one outstanding protégé was Clark Ashton Smith, "The Bard of Auburn." In addition, as we have already indicated, Sterling was one of the first to "discover" Robinson Jeffers, and with his monograph on Jeffers (the very first ever dedicated to him) to play a pivotal role in establishing him as a major new poet.

Paradoxically, as he approached the end of his life and career, Sterling increasingly felt himself to be a failure, so much had poetic tastes changed since the *fin-de-siècle* when he had come of age. During the 1920s the whole trend of literary art, at least in English, was radically changing from the long-established romance tradition, that is, from the highly imaginative, to the disillusioned and ironic nitty-gritty of modern realism. In a bold and innovative fashion Sterling had specialized in creating highly imaginative poetry, but quite apart from his *manner,* his *matter* had presumably much less relevance and appeal to the young intellectuals taking over the emerging literary establishment.

Despite this radical and catastrophic shift in literary taste—catastrophic at least from the elder poet's perspective—Sterling nonetheless managed to leave behind him quite a substantial output, especially from the very last decade of his life: eight collections of lyrical poems, three volumes of occasional pieces, four or five verse dramas, one study of a fellow poet; and then between 1928 and 1939 three posthumous collections appeared. Sterling scholars rate his last three verse plays as ranking among his very best work, comparable to such early extended pieces as *The Testimony of the Suns* and "A Wine of Wizardry."

Just as important, perhaps, Sterling also left behind him one protégé and poet similar to himself in style and substance, but with far greater depth. This person would not only redeem Sterling's own type of make-believe, as the direct inheritance of the full-blown romantic tradition, but would also redeem—incidentally and in an indirect manner—Sterling's own substantial poetic output, and justify its existence despite the condition of half-oblivion into which it would lapse, leaving behind it a curious legend as of fabulous treasures but remotely known and unintentionally buried amid the shifting sands of time. This person was the still young "Bard of Auburn."

evolution. Twenty years later he described this discovery in "George Sterling—An Appreciation," published in the *Overland Monthly* for March 1927:

> Likewise memorable, and touched with more than the glamour of childhood dreams, was my first reading, two years later, of "A Wine of Wizardry," in the pages of the old *Cosmopolitan.* The poem with its necromantic music and splendours as of sunset on jewels and cathedral windows, was veritably all that its title implied; and—to pile marvel upon enchantment—there was the knowledge that it had been written in my own time, by someone who lived little more than a hundred miles away. In the ruck of magazine verse it was a fire-opal of the Titans in a potato-bin; and, after finding it, I ransacked all available contemporary periodicals for verse by George Sterling, to be rewarded, not too frequently, with some marmoreal sonnet or "molten golden" lyric. I am sure that I more than agreed, at the time, with the dictum of Ambrose Bierce, who placed "A Wine of Wizardry" with the best work of Keats, Poe and Coleridge; and I still hold, in the teeth of our new Didactic School, the protagonists of the "human" and the "vital," that Bierce's judgement will be the ultimate one regarding this poem, as well as Sterling's work in general. Bierce, whose own fine qualities as a poet are mentioned with singular infrequency, was an almost infallible critic. (*SU* 294)

This poem represented Smith's introduction to Sterling, and it would haunt and fructify the younger poet's mature work in verse and in prose from start to finish, and not just in the most obvious way. True, generically Sterling's poem anticipates, it is patent, Smith's later (and greater) compressed epic *The Hashish-Eater,* and many episodes in the latter poem anticipate some of Smith's later short stories; but by the same token Sterling's earlier poem not only prefigures Smith's own mature fiction of 1928–38, but at least one episode or passage, the one involving Satan and Lilith (not far from the poem's conclusion), directly anticipates one of Smith's very last stories, "Schizoid Creator."

At some point after his initial discovery of Sterling, Smith would have obtained the elder poet's first two collections *The Testimony of the Suns* and *A Wine of Wizardry,* and from *The House of Orchids* onward Sterling himself would have supplied Smith with copies of his own books as they came off the press. In January 1911 the two poets began their correspondence, the elder poet taking on the role of poetic mentor to the younger one and advising him during

1911 and 1912 not just concerning the first mature poems that Smith was creating at the age of eighteen and nineteen but just as much concerning which poems would constitute his first collection, *The Star-Treader,* brought out by Sterling's own publisher in November 1912. The subjects range from the cosmic-astronomic spaces and Graeco-Roman mythology to charming nature vignettes and little-known archaeological or mythic topics. Despite Sterling's obvious influence in terms of cosmic-astronomic subjects, this first book of poetry still remains very much Smith's own.

Meanwhile, during June and July 1912 poetic mentor and younger poet met in person when Sterling had Smith come down from Auburn to Carmel to spend an idyllic month of great happiness, during which the latter shared almost all aspects of the older poet's ideal Bohemian existence. It proved a major eye-opener for Smith, and in quite a positive way. It was the younger poet's first prolonged exposure to residing by the sea, and it left a lasting impression on him (as found among other instances in the gorgeous lyric in alexandrines "Sea-Memory," created at the same time as analogous lyrics included in *Ebony and Crystal*). Things now happened rapidly in Smith's ongoing literary career after he returned home to Auburn.

By means of San Francisco's half a dozen daily and weekly newspapers, a wealthy property owner in Placer County, Boutwell Dunlap, who had just discovered Smith and his poetry for himself, triggered in August 1912 the official public discovery of Smith as a youthful poetic genius. The resultant uproar of publicity thus prepared poetry lovers, as well as the general public in California and elsewhere, to receive both poet and first volume with heightened interest, and (just as important) actually moved them to purchase copies of that first volume, which at one hundred pages made up a substantial volume of solid poetry. All this alerted the east-coast critics to the presence of a significant new voice. Despite the inevitable negative reactions incited by all the publicity—relatively low-key and not amounting to much numerically—Clark Ashton Smith had made his entrance, and then some, on the American literary scene.

Interviewing the poet Witter Bynner in *Town Talk: The Pacific Weekly,* in the issue for Saturday, 7 September 1912, Edward F. O'Day (he and editor-in-chief Theodore Bonnet served as the weekly's principal literary critics) provides us with an amusing side-light on Smith's new-found fame, and how he and Sterling became yoked as poetic partners in the public's collective mentality. This interview or profile appears in the department "Varied Types," invariably written by O'Day himself.

> Bynner and George Sterling are friends, such good friends that Bynner is not afraid to speak freely of Sterling's poetry.
> "It is too stellar for me," he says. "There's too much Aldebaran in it. It gives me cosmic indigestion. Somebody at the Bohemian jinks called Sterling and this young poet Clark Ashton Smith the Star Dust Twins. It is shocking to me to see such a young man write poetry which might be written by Sterling. In saying so I'm not deprecating Sterling. The young poet has some prodigious lines. But as Harry Lafler says, two are less than one. I like Sterling best when he comes closest to earth. For that reason I was delighted with that little poem of his about the coyote. I regard that poem as a most hopeful sign in Sterling's development."

The poem about the coyote is "Father Coyote," later gathered by Sterling into his fourth major collection, *Beyond the Breakers.* Already recognized nationally, Witter Bynner would go on to have a very long life and career, outliving both Sterling and Smith. His patronizing remarks about Smith imitating Sterling, however, are typical of other such comments at the time as well as later. Also, how two are less than one is at best a moot point. To have written cosmic-astronomic poetry such as Smith wrote—with the same depth and power of emotion, insight, and imagination as the younger poet commanded—would have been impossible for Sterling, all evidence to the contrary. He wrote only one such poem, and it remains his greatest, *The Testimony of the Suns,* even if the general sensibility permeates his overall output. To judge from Bynner's remarks, the significance of Sterling's as well as Smith's greatest achievements in verse completely passed over Mr. Bynner's head.

Yet for all their poetic and even personal similarities the two figures and their respective bodies of work are noticeably distinct, even without the difference in age between them. On the one hand, whereas privately Sterling was a true artist who took his art quite seriously, he went out of his way publicly to disguise the fact: that he had had often to work hard at his poetry. In addition to the demands made on him by his own creativity, he increasingly had to play the role of a public figure as the most conspicuous poet in California, and hence as the poet laureate of the Far West. Here his Apollonian good looks, his great charm, his practiced ease in society helped him enormously in such a role. On the other hand, although very poor in a monetary sense most of his life, Smith managed to have the luxury of leading a more or less quiet private existence during which he could concentrate on his own creativity almost completely. Relative to the extraverted Sterling, Smith was almost painfully shy and ill at ease around groups.

If Sterling reigned as the poet laureate of the Far West for the period of 1903–26, then his protégé would soon reveal himself as the uncontested poet laureate of the otherworldly, as "the emperor of dreams," and moreover one who would reign as such for a termless while. Whereas Sterling's life seems at times rife with bustle and animation, Smith's uneventful existence appeared to come to life only when his ongoing creativity manifested itself externally from time to time in a book of poetry and later in a book of short stories, not to mention the rare exhibit of drawings and paintings, together with his small but fascinating sculptures (which he would begin during the spring of 1935 and continue the rest of his life). The external uneventfulness of Smith's existence compels us to concentrate on the products and events of his creativity almost exclusively as the source of the greatest excitement.

Meanwhile, as formerly, Sterling did not let up in his advocacy for Smith. During his brief period back on the east coast (mostly based in New York City), from spring 1914 to spring 1915, when invited to read aloud from his own output before a group of influential or wealthy littérateurs and other solid members of the arts community there, Sterling instead insisted on reading largely from Smith's works. Then, late in 1915, before the Panama-Pacific International Exposition closed up for the last time, Smith came down from Auburn to see the fair during a visit to San Francisco with Sterling as his cicerone. The exposition's exuberant and grandiose architecture impressed and pleased the young poet, but not the amusement zone. All this occurred while, from January 1911 onward, the two poets were exchanging letters as well as manuscripts of their new and old poems, no less than the occasional clipping from newspaper or periodical.

In the year following the publication of Sterling's own *Thirty-five Sonnets* (1917), the Book Club of California brought out a small selection of only fifteen pieces of Smith's poetry, under the title *Odes and Sonnets*. Like Sterling's own volume, this is one of the few books of poetry ever published by this book club, probably the oldest in the U.S. Just as Sterling had secured publication for Smith's very first book of poetry, by his very own publisher, the elder poet's advocacy without a doubt played a decisive part in the publication of *Odes and Sonnets* in a small but elegant Art Nouveau *édition de luxe* of only 300 copies. The volume has only thirty pages. Each page is surrounded by the same decorative design by Florence Lundborg of New York, a design featuring peacocks, grapes, and pomegranates.

Distributed only to the club's members, like all their editions, this choice volume did not appear for sale in bookstores. Much more than general advocacy, Sterling had provided the succinct and pithy foreword (dated "Bohemian Club, / April 17, 1918"). Among other cogent statements, the foreword maintained that, vis-à-vis the "devotees of [poetic] austerity" (that is, the adherents of non-traditional modern poetry), "an even partial use of the intelligence that is their one asset will cause them to shrink from the stern conclusions involved in some of the passages of this book—to turn from its terrible vistas. Clark Ashton Smith is unlikely to be afflicted with present-day popularity" (*SU* 289–90). If this statement emerged as a true prediction—and it did at that time—then such was the price to be paid by the poet who donned the figurative Cloak of Elijah in the manner of Ambrose Bierce.

Although a great honor to the young but evolving author, *Odes and Sonnets* at best served as a mere stopgap or update on his progress as a poet. Whatever he may have achieved with *The Star-Treader* in late 1912—a volume that had gained in sustaining power during the ten following years—it now paled before *Ebony and Crystal: Poems in Verse and Prose,* issued by Smith himself in December 1922 (printed by the *Auburn Journal* press)—one of the most remarkable volumes of pure poetry ever published in any language. Once again Sterling had continued his advocacy with another preface (dated "San Francisco, October 28, 1922"), making even more audacious claims than he had made on behalf of *Odes and Sonnets.* As it turned out, his claims were and are completely justified. We quote his first paragraph in full.

> Who of us care to be present at the *accouchement* of the immortal? I think that we so attend who are first to take this book in our hands. A bold assertion, truly, and one demonstrable only in years remote from these; and—dust wages no war with dust. But it is one of those things that I should most "like to come back and see." (*SU* 290)

Because Smith published his second major collection himself, the edition totalled only 500 copies, rather than the 2,000 that Robertson had brought out of *The Star-Treader* in 1912, this figure being the usual number of copies mandated for the collections by Sterling that Robertson issued. Because Smith had self-published, Sterling took it upon himself, in person or by mail, to distribute the review copies that Smith sent him, with most of them going to the San Francisco daily newspapers and other periodicals. With such copies distributed under Sterling's aegis, Smith's latest major production was virtually guaranteed critical attention.

At over 150 pages, with over 90 short to medium-length poems in verse, almost 30 poems in prose, and one very long poem (totalling almost 600 lines) positioned after the first third of the volume, *Ebony and Crystal* ran almost two-thirds longer than any collection by Sterling in actual material, with the exception of Sterling's *Selected Poems.* The one very long poem, *The Hashish-Eater,* could have better and more profitably appeared as a separate book. Printed as it was at almost forty lines per page, and filling sixteen very full pages, the format just avoids being too crowded for its typeset layout. Whereas *The Star-Treader* sold for $1.25 per copy, *Ebony and Crystal* went on sale at $2.00 per copy, an incredible bargain even for 1922, given the extremely high quality of the contents, no less than its overflowing abundance.

In general the book received excellent reviews wherever it managed to get them, and it managed to get them principally because of Sterling's assiduous and effectual ministrations. In addition to his general and long-term advocacy on behalf of Smith's poetry, Sterling in a direct manner had contributed to the physical welfare and maintenance of both Smith and his parents. Sometime during the

1910s the elder poet managed to get a pittance mailed to the Smiths on a regular basis from one of California's authentic multimillionaires. He had convinced "Old Man" Templeton Crocker to send the family the monthly sum of $10.00, which must have proven useful, and which still represented something of real value back in the second decade of the 1900s, however small it may seem to us today. Then, beginning sometime in the later 1910s or early 1920s, two well-known patrons of the arts mailed Smith a small quarterly allowance, one of them being the well-known bibliophile and *fin-de-siècle* Bohemian Albert M. Bender (actually a successful lawyer) and the other being James Duval Phelan, one of the U.S. senators from California. Bender sent Smith the allowance from the later 1910s until sometime in the early to middle 1930s. Phelan sent Smith the allowance from the later 1910s or early 1920s until sometime in the later 1920s.

Despite all these positive developments in Smith's life and career, the still young poet (he was almost thirty when *Ebony and Crystal* made its appearance) had just committed two major tactical errors in his career, as it has now become apparent in hindsight. Although he had submitted the manuscript of his second major collection to at least one New York publisher (Knopf, which turned it down with no more ado than with the customary form letter of rejection), for some reason or other he did not want to submit it to A. M. Robertson, although Sterling encouraged him to do so. Smith stated that he did not like the manner in which Robertson had conducted business with Smith in regard to *The Star-Treader.* Possibly Smith felt cheated, but in his letters to Sterling he did not state that overtly. However, Robertson's books regularly received reviews, and generally good ones, on both the west and east coasts, he had perfectly adequate book distribution, and whatever the business part of the deals he struck with his authors may have involved, he promoted them and their books efficiently and effectively.

Had he accepted the manuscript of *Ebony and Crystal* for publication, Robertson probably would have suggested that *The Hashish-Eater* be detached from the main mass of the contents and brought out in a separate edition, printed in the same style as any of Sterling's collections, thus allowing about twenty lines of blank verse per page, and furnished with a short preface by Sterling or some other notable, not to mention a brief introduction about the poem and its purpose by the poet himself. Such an edition would have totalled somewhere around 35 to 40 pages on good rag paper, and Robertson could have issued it as a companion volume to *Ebony and Crystal.* The chief volume, presented in a similar format but with far more pages, probably would have totalled around 240 pages, quite a large book of poetry for that time. Whether he liked or disliked Robertson's mode of business, Smith could have achieved much, much more career-wise if the San Francisco bookseller-publisher had issued his latest major collection, in however many volumes it might have required. The poems in prose could easily have constituted their own separate volume, say, as in the manner of *The Hashish-Eater* suggested above. The young poet certainly missed out on what could have developed into a major chance not necessarily for fame and fortune but simply overall recognition for him as a major poet by the literary mainstream.

The second tactical error in his career that Smith had just made involved the *Smart Set,* and sending a copy of *Ebony and Crystal* to the magazine for review. Mencken himself would probably have reviewed it, and quite favorably. He had already published in the magazine a number of the poems in verse and in prose that Smith had included in *Ebony and Crystal,* he certainly knew the high regard in which Sterling held Smith and his poetry, and he probably shared something of the same high value that Sterling put on the poems of his protégé. Mencken, like Bierce, had quite a fondness for romantic poetry, especially when profound and intelligent thought might lie behind the romantic effusions.

George Jean Nathan and H. L. Mencken edited the *Smart Set,* the distinguished precursor to the *New Yorker,* from 1914 to 1923, and Sterling in his letters to Smith had mentioned the possibility of sending a copy to Mencken to review. Smith decided not to do so, thinking that the book would not prove to Mencken's taste. Whatever else such a review might have been worth, Smith would not have lost anything even if the only thing he might have received at the hands of Mencken was a mere capsule review. Such a review published in a magazine of national circulation and acknowledged prestige might have accomplished much for Smith in terms of national recognition at this time in his career. But it was not to be. The decision would haunt the young poet into the early 1940s.

In 1923 the New York publisher Henry Holt brought out the definitive collection of Sterling's own *Selected Poems,* which gathered all his best work into one volume. Because they had appeared in published form within half a year or less of each other, Benjamin De Casseres reviewed both *Ebony and Crystal* and Sterling's own volume, a large one, together for the magazine *Arts and Decorations* in the issue for August 1923, in De Casseres' regular department "And a Little Book Shall Lead Them." Once again the two poets were yoked together as a team in the public's collective mentality. Although this critic gave the books a favorable reaction, he himself had apparently burned out on poetry in general around that time.

The printing and binding costs for the 500 copies of his own new collection had forced Smith to become indebted to B. A. Cassidy, the editor and owner of the *Auburn Journal* and its press. Although the edition was apparently selling well enough, the sales did not suffice in themselves to take care of Smith's indebtedness to Cassidy, who nevertheless offered the poet another way to handle it. He suggested that, if Smith contributed a column more or less for each weekly issue, as prorated over a period of a few years, this would repay the newspaper's owner-editor for having printed *Ebony and Crystal.*

The poet was free to make of his column what he wished, to feature poems or epigrams or whatever in it. Clearly this represented an exceptional deal, and Smith agreed. Thus it was that Smith became a journalist, and "Clark Ashton Smith's Column" came into being. The new department would now see some of the newest, as well as most remarkable, pure poetry, no less than some of the most adroit and profound epigrams and pensées, ever produced in America during the next three years.

During the first half of the 1920s the *Auburn Journal* published 101 installments of "Clark Ashton Smith's Column"—the first dated 5 April 1923, the last 7 January 1926. The columns highlighted both poems and epigrams, but mostly poems: overall, 81 poems (59 original ones and 22 translations from Baudelaire), plus 329 original, and 17 selected, epigrams, etc. To the *Journal* overall, Smith contributed 84 poems. Most of the poems in *Sandalwood*—that is, 49 of the total 61 poems in that collection (37 of the 42 original ones and 12 of the 19 translations from Baudelaire)—made their first appearance in this column or department. Although most of the poems first published in the *Journal* have since reappeared elsewhere, almost all of the 329, or 346, epigrams and penseés have not, that is, until recently, languishing uncollected in the files of Auburn's leading local newspaper for over half a century.

Some east-coast publisher tentatively considered publishing a selection of them (as made by Smith himself) during the early 1940s. The epigrams and penseés appeared in the *Journal* under the following titles: "Epigrams" (once), "Cocktails and Creme de Menthe," "Points for the Pious," "Unpopular Sayings" (once), "New Teeth for Old Saws" (once), "The Devil's Note-Book," and "Paradox and Persiflage." "The Devil's Note-Book," as a title, has obvious analogies with Ambrose Bierce's *The Devil's Dictionary,* originally named *The Cynic's Word-Book.* At long last, after sixty-five years of languishing uncollected and unpublished in book form, a complete collection of Smith's epigrams and apothegms, as published by Starmont House, came forth in December 1990, compiled by Donald Sidney-Fryer, and edited with an introduction and notes by Don Herron, and under the overall title *The Devil's Notebook.* This chapbook-sized and softbound booklet totalled almost 100 pages. Smith's epigrams and penseés have obvious affinities with Bierce's definitions in *The Devil's Dictionary.*

Because once more Smith published another major collection of poems himself—his third, under the title *Sandalwood,* in October 1925—the edition totalled only 250 copies (plus the usual extra ones), and thus only half of that for *Ebony and Crystal.* The book, dedicated to Sterling, is about the same size in terms of width and height, but is paperbound, rather than hardcover, and at about only fifty pages overall, totalling about only sixty poems, *Sandalwood* contains about only one-third the amount of material that had gone into the second major collection. The book went on sale at only $1.00 per copy, another incredible bargain, given the extremely high quality of the contents, even if much less abundant than those of the previous volume. Whereas much of *Ebony and Crystal* seems epic in subject matter and monumental in tone, the character and subject matter of the original poems in *Sandalwood* appear much more gossamer and evanescent.

Once again Sterling took it upon himself, both in person and through the post office, to distribute the review copies that Smith sent him, with most of them going to the San Francisco daily newspapers. However, this time a book of poems by Smith received less than half a dozen reviews, even though the critical reaction proved favorable in general wherever the collection managed to get it. Because of its less than widespread distribution in a limited edition, *Sandalwood* at first underwent the same fate as *Ebony and Crystal* of being little better than unknown, and in fact of being even more unknown than the former volume. Nevertheless, whether in terms of technique, inspiration, or new directions in an imaginative sense, the new volume is no less remarkable and innovative than the last one. In particular the twenty or so translations from *Les Fleurs du mal* of Baudelaire represent a real triumph on behalf of Smith's technical mastery, inasmuch as he had learned sufficient French to make his translations in something less than a year, no mean accomplishment. Fancifully speaking, perhaps we can perceive in his mastering a new language some possible evidence of "ancestral memory," descended as he was from Norman-French counts and barons on his mother's side, the Gaylords or Gaillards, who had fled to Britain from France when the Edict of Nantes was revoked.

Let us ponder some of the implications of Smith's creativity during 1911–25, and the various personal and poetic statistics, that we have cited. When he is eighteen and nineteen, during 1911–12, he composes his first mature poetry, resulting in *The Star-Treader,* published in late 1912. However, a long period of self-education and apprenticeship has preceded this, from 1906 to 1910, during which he writes his earliest or juvenile poetry, imitations of Poe's extant poetry, as well as of Edward FitzGerald's version of the *Rubaiyat* of Omar Khayyam, among other models. The greatest influence has derived from Poe and (even more) Sterling's own opus "A Wine of Wizardry." The five years of this apprentice work suddenly results in a period of rapid and fervent creativity, 1911–12, and his first book. A period of mature apprenticeship ensues during 1912–22, when everything slows down again as during 1906 to 1910. Then in early 1920 things pick up speed again when from mid-January to mid-February he creates his greatest and longest poem, *The Hashish-Eater,* finishing it on 20 February, and totalling almost 600 lines of highly imaginative blank verse, most of it the result of white-hot inspiration.

The whole decade of 1912-22 culminates in *Ebony and Crystal,* published in late 1922. However, following the decade in question, things do not slow down, but throughout 1923-26 Smith maintains the speed, facility, and high quality of his poetic productiveness, over eighty original poems at least and two dozen or more translations. Although his productiveness and speed lessen somewhat, possibly by as much as half, he remains quite prolific all during 1926-30. By the latter date fictioneering takes over almost exclusively until 1934, when he resumes creating poems in verse in some noticeable quantity. Obviously we are dealing here with a great or major poet, but rather strangely, following his greatest period of productiveness in poetry, say, 1911-25, there is no major mainstream recognition of Smith as the great poet that he has patently become, a great poet who has just produced a major body of work as represented in three major collections, published in 1912, 1922, and 1925, respectively. (The highly productive years of 1923-25 have culminated in *Sandalwood,* issued in late 1925.) Has his long and patient apprenticeship under the poetic tutelage or mentorship of George Sterling amounted to nothing more than three or four volumes acclaimed only by a small chorus of discerning voices in California and Britain? Thus it would appear. Something is gravely wrong in this configuration.

Let us look around at the national and international situation regarding poetry (at least in English), and see if we can find a clue as to what else may have conspired against Smith receiving his just recognition as a major poet. The year 1922 saw the beginning of the apotheosis for that modernist poet par excellence, T. S. Eliot. During that year he won the Dial Award of $2,000 for his 434-line poem *The Waste Land,* which (including the fascinating notes) he had carefully prepared for publication with the help and advice of Ezra Pound. The latter figure would reveal his own poetic vision in all its abundance a little later in his own major work *The Cantos.* These two great poems, along with works by other significant modern poets, anticipated or signalized in advance the major shift in taste and sensibility that was occurring early in the 1920s, and that gained critical momentum as the decade progressed. In the case of his own major poem Eliot, only in his mid-thirties at the time, had summed up, in a thoroughly novel and then modern manner, the disillusionment and the disenchantment that had become prevalent among the younger generation following the catastrophe of World War I.

The implications of the triumph attendant on Eliot's own success, and later that of Ezra Pound, along with other modernist figures, can only be imagined for those poetic masters whose work had been painstakingly cast in the traditional prosody, regardless of the grandeur of the vision and thought behind their verses. Right in the forefront of these traditionalist masters Sterling and Smith occupied a prominent place, for those cognoscenti who knew their work in depth. The two poets in their final exchange of letters during 1926 show themselves quite conscious of the major shift in poetic taste and sensibility that was occurring, and also sensitive to the implications for their own respective outputs. Whether by deliberate or accidental suicide Sterling as the poet laureate of the Far West, the foremost public defender of the classico-romantic tradition, died in late 1926. True, his death represented a great loss to that tradition, not to mention personally to Clark Ashton Smith, but Sterling had accomplished almost everything that he could have on behalf of traditionalist poetry in English, that is, as it had evolved up through the first quarter of the twentieth century.

Just what could Smith do now, stranded as he was, almost "in the teeth of our new Didactic School, the protagonists of the *human* and the *vital,"* the newly triumphant masters of the modern mode in poetry? Left behind in the countryside of rolling hills near Auburn, a thousand feet above sea level, Smith as the poet laureate of the otherworldly continued to live with his parents from the mid-1920s to the mid-1930s; but now, thanks to the earnest encouragement of Smith's friend Genevieve K. Sully, who, during the summer of 1927 when they were visiting Crater (now Hyperboreal) Ridge, urged him to write fiction for the emerging pulp magazines, the young poet would ignore his former mentor's advice to give up "this macabre prose" and would produce between the late 1920s and late 1930s some 140 completed stories. There is a certain irony here because, just as "A Wine of Wizardry" anticipates *The Hashish-Eater,* and the latter poem anticipates much of Smith's fantastic fiction of that decade (1928–38), so does "A Wine of Wizardry" clearly prefigure in a generic way the extremely picturesque or pictorial character of many of Smith's typical, far-ranging, and most polished fantasies, his extended poems in prose.

At least one episode in "A Wine of Wizardry," the one involving Satan and Lilith (lines 155–64) directly anticipates one of the details or episodes near the end of one of Smith's very last stories of any type whatsoever as published in the fantasy and science fiction magazines of the early 1950s.

> But Fancy still is fugitive, and turns
> To caverns where a demon altar burns,
> And Satan, yawning on his brazen seat,
> Fondles a screaming thing his fiends have flayed,
> Ere Lilith come his indolence to greet,
> Who leads from Hell his whitest queens, arrayed
> In chains so heated at their master's fire
> That one new-damned had thought their bright attire
> Indeed were coral, till the dazzling dance
> So terribly that brilliance shall enhance. (*CF* 1.80–81)

In its issue for November 1953 the magazine *Fantasy Fiction* published a late and rather mordant story "Schizoid Creator." Near the end of the narrative one of his lieutenants, Bifrons, comes to report to Satan.

> He found that Master of that picturesque region occupied in caressing a half-flayed girl. The flaying had been done to render the caresses more intimate and more exquisitely agonizing.
> Satan listened gravely [. . .] His tapering artistic fingers, with long-pointed nails of polished jet, ceased their occupation; and a furrow appeared like a black triangle between his luminous brows.
> [. . .]
> When Bifrons departed, Satan summoned his chief lieutenants before him in the halls of Pandemonium.
> "I am going away for awhile," he told them. "There are certain obligations of a pressing nature that call me—and I must not neglect them too long. In my absence, I consign the management of Hell to your competent hands."
> [. . .]
> When they had gone, he descended from his globed throne and passed through many corridors and by upward-winding stairs to the small postern gate of Hell.

The door swung open without touch of any visible hand. A long white robe seemed to weave itself from the air about Satan's form. His infernal attributes withered and dropped away. And the long white beard of the Elohim sprouted and flowed down over his bosom as he stepped across the sill into Heaven. (*TSS* 219-20)

But it is less in the specific passages and details of "A Wine of Wizardry," and more in the *manner* of envisioning any fantastic scene or tableau, and of shaping it into words, that we can trace the genuine continuity from the variegated contents of Sterling's second greatest poem to many scenes and settings in Smith's mature fiction of 1928-38. (The greatest influence on Smith's early or juvenile fiction seems to have been *The Arabian Nights,* coupled with the standard fairy tales.) However, it is beyond the scope of this essay to pursue this continuity from Sterling (and not just from "A Wine of Wizardry," but from his four earliest collections of poetry) to Smith in detail, apart from our one token example. The compressed or compact mode of presentation so typical of poetry, including "A Wine of Wizardry," obviously carries over to the clear but compact prose typical of Smith's best short stories, those which justify the designation of extended poems in prose.

It is precisely by the veritable flood or avalanche of Smith's often dark and mordant fantasies in prose, with their cosmic indifference (rather than pessimism or nihilism), that Sterling's protégé redeems not only Sterling's own type of make-believe (marked by his own profound cosmic pessimism), as the direct but very late inheritance of the full-blown romantic tradition, but redeems no less, even if indirectly, Sterling's own substantial poetic output. Without the latter there might not have existed any Smith at all whether as poet or as prosateur of fantasy, or of the uninhibited human imagination. This creative influence from the older poet to the younger one, like father to son, or older brother to younger one, will always remain as the greatest possible monument or homage to Sterling as a fructifying force of literature.

What of Sterling's bold assertion or prophecy that he made on behalf of Smith in late October 1922 while writing the foreword for *Ebony and Crystal?* "Who of us care to be present at the *accouchement*

of the immortal? I think that we so attend who are first to take this
book in our hands. A bold assertion, truly, and one demonstrable only
in years remote from these; and—dust wages no war with dust." The
first step to immortality for any author or poet is to have his output in
whole or in part printed and then reprinted. Produced by Smith during
1944–49 as a manuscript, and published in November 1971 by Ark-
ham House, the *Selected Poems,* totalling almost 425 pages, resurrects
not only his first three major collections but makes available for the first
time his later collections or cycles of poems, created in the later 1920s,
the 1930s, and the 1940s, such as *The Jasmine Girdle, Incantations,
The Hill of Dionysus,* and *Experiments in Haiku. Selected Poems*
contains about 500 selections, and hence a major part of Smith's ma-
ture poetic output. Published in 1923, Sterling's own *Selected Poems* at
over 230 pages contains his best work, but only one major portion of
his overall output of poems. Sometime after 1970, a specialist publish-
er for libraries reprinted Sterling's own volume on acid-free paper in a
facsimile edition by photolithography, the copies being sturdily bound
in library-style hardcovers, made to withstand a great deal of handling.
Thus the poems of both Smith and Sterling, at least in part, have man-
aged to take the first important step on the way to immortality: their
poetic output, or the best of it, has undergone reprinting. *Vivat liber!*
Long live the book!

Postscript

Although probably interpreted by most readers as a mythic presen-
timent of a major new poetic voice, Sterling's sonnet "The Coming
Singer" (first collected in *Beyond the Breakers* in 1914) was privately
dedicated to Smith, but never in print. It remains the most ideal trib-
ute ever paid to Klarkash-Ton.

> The Veil before the mystery of things
> Shall stir for him with iris and with light;
> Chaos shall have no terror in his sight
> Nor Earth a bond to chafe his urgent wings;
> With sandals beaten from the crowns of kings
> Shall he tread down the altars of their night,

And stand with Silence on her breathless height,
To hear what song the star of morning sings.

With perished beauty in his hands as clay,
Shall he restore futurity its dream.
Behold! his feet shall take a heavenly way
Of choric silver and of chanting fire,
Till in his hands unshapen planets gleam,
'Mid murmurs from the Lion and the Lyre. (*CP* 1.240)

Works Cited

Benediktsson, Thomas E. *George Sterling.* Boston: Twayne, 1980.
Smith, Clark Ashton. *The Complete Poetry and Translations.* Edited by S. T. Joshi and David E. Schultz. New York: Hippocampus Press, 2012. [*CPT*]
————. *Tales of Science and Sorcery.* Sauk City, WI: Arkham House, 1964. [*TSS*]
————, and George Sterling. *The Shadow of the Unattained: The Letters of George Sterling and Clark Ashton Smith.* Ed. David E. Schultz and S. T. Joshi. a. New York: Hippocampus Press, 2005.
Sterling, George. *Complete Poetry.* Ed. S. T. Joshi and David E. Schultz. New York: Hippocampus Press, 2013. [*CP*]

A Report from Clark Ashton Smith Country

The recent death of Carolyn Jones Dorman Smith (Mrs. Clark Ashton Smith) on January 10, 1973, has left the estate of her late husband to her three children; she had made some English professor the literary executor sometime before her death. Mrs. Smith had terminal cancer and had been staying in a convalescent home in Carmichael (north Sacramento area) not far from the home of William Dorman, that one of her two sons who teaches in the journalism department at California State University at Sacramento, formerly Sacramento State College. Mrs. Smith shortly before her death had contracted the flu, and her body could not cope with both maladies. She was however spared the long, lingering, painful, expensive illness which terminal cancer often visits upon its victims, and which she had feared would prove her lot. According to a close personal friend of hers, Carolyn died with dignity, beauty, and serenity. The present writer will never forget the kindness both Clark and Carolyn showed him when he visited them in Pacific Grove in 1958 and 1959. Carolyn was in her latter sixties when she died. She had lived long enough to see both foreign and paperback publication of her late husband's works, to say nothing of the long-deferred publishing of Smith's *Selected Poems* by Arkham House. Thus, both wider readership and wider recognition of Smith's works became a reality in the last decade of Carolyn's life, surely some kind of consummation. She remained devoted to the cause and promulgation of Smith's *oeuvre* to the end of her life. REQUIESCAT IN PEACE!

A series of recent visits to the old Smith acres just outside Auburn to the southeast reveals a number of interesting developments. When Timeus Smith died in late 1937, his son Clark sold most of the forty or so acres of the old Smith property to a local Auburn contractor, in order to finance the funeral and burial of the father. The sale left about two and a half acres, including the land on which the cabin stood. During early 1938 Clark himself built the small wall of large and medium-sized stones just west and north of the cabin. In late August 1957 the cabin burned down, and Smith long suspected arson.

172

After his death in August 1961, his widow Carolyn Smith attempted in vain to give the remaining two and a half acres as a memorial park to the State of California.

The land sold back in 1938 has been subsequently developed as a series of housing tracts by the local Auburn contractor, who continues to make new additions. For quite a few years the way to the Smith property lay via the Auburn–Folsom highway (running north and south), then Carolyn Street (running east and west), then Katherine Way (running north and south), and then a vaguely-marked trail and finally a well-marked dirt road going southeast up to that part of Indian Ridge (also called Boulder Ridge) where the Smiths lived. (These compass directions are all approximate.) Barbed-wire fences (not hard of passage) surrounded both the Smith acres as well as the undeveloped portion of the land owned by the local Auburn contractor. Katherine Way deadended at its then southern end into a gate (also easy of passage).

Now both gate and barbed-wire fences are gone. Branching off Carolyn Street to the north is "Smith Court"—a few blocks in from the highway; branching off the same street but to the south, are two new streets (east of and parallel to Katherine Way), to wit, Ginger Drive and then "Poet Smith Drive." Attractive, unpretentious houses line both sides of both the new streets. Poet Smith Drive deadends into the remaining Smith acres, running virtually on the summit of Indian Ridge. Katherine Way now continues south and then the roadway swings northeast and links into Ginger Drive. The new streets are not yet paved but the sidewalks are in. Now the easiest way to pass into the Smith property is by Ginger Drive, and then the Klarkash-Tonophile pilgrim can readily find his way up the upper portion of the well-marked dirt road leading to the site of the Smith cabin.

The neighborhood children have evidently commandeered the remaining Smith land as a natural playground, and have placed part of a wooden pallet (the same as those used in warehouses, outdoor storage depots, etc.) up in the branches of one of the trees growing on the gradual slope that descends west of the cabin site, thus making a kind of tree-house. The actual site of the cabin itself appears to contain more refuse than formerly (but this is not obvious until one is virtually on the spot), some of it from the nearby construction. The

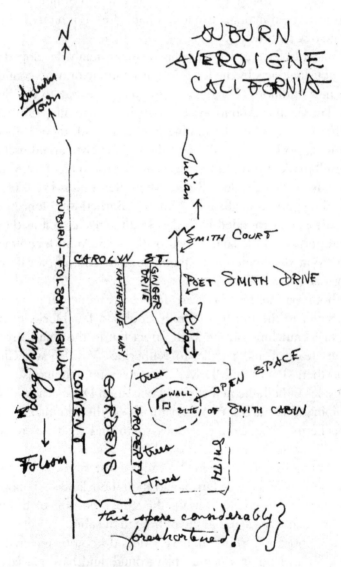

neighborhood children, just as much as any casual picnickers, may be responsible for this. Over-all, however, the property has not been really damaged, and many spots are flourishing that were favorites with Clark Ashton Smith. The natural vegetation (trees and grasses, etc.) appears healthy, and largely undiminished.

The spot where Smith used to sleep outdoors (northwest of the cabin and beyond the stone wall) and do most of his writing (that is, when he wrote outdoors, which was as much as the weather would allow), is covered by particularly lush grasses right now, due to the heavy Californian winter rains there.

One especial item: Much of the wall built by Smith has fallen down. If not casual picnickers, then the local children must be responsible for this through their general horsing around.

The Roman Catholic Novitiate (lying to the west between the Smith land and the Auburn–Folsom highway) has had considerable additions made to the older buildings. The gardens lying east of the Novitiate are as extensive and lovely as ever; in the spring divers groups tour through them free of charge. Smith used to refer to the convent as "the Nunnery of Averoigne"—indeed, the whole countryside roundabout does resemble Smith's mythical province of Medieval France.

The old Gaylord house in Long Valley (where Smith was born), the building that started out as the little red schoolhouse of the district (which Smith attended up through the first six grammar grades), and other places in Long Valley associated with Smith in his youth, are still extant, and have changed very little. Over-all, Long Valley, long a farming and fruit growing area, appears as lovely and as lush as ever.

Auburn has a new city and county library west of the Auburn District Cemetery and Old Auburn. The new library rather resembles a small campus and is quite attractive. Meanwhile the old Auburn Public Library building has turned into a Senior Citizens Center; the library was originally built and endowed from one of the library grants established by Scottish-American millionaire Andrew Carnegie. Smith not only used the old library as a place for his own reading but as one of the settings in the short story "The Devotee of Evil." Picturesquely situated in its extensive bower of trees and shrubbery, the house of "The Devotee of Evil" still sits up on the hill behind Old Auburn.

The young Smith (around 1909 or 1910) toyed with the idea of using "Ashton Smith" (with or without a hyphen) as his surname (to distinguish himself from any other writer by the name of Smith). Indeed, some of his poems and tales published during 1910 through 1912 bear the byline of "C. Ashton Smith." The recent British reprints (by Neville Spearman Ltd.) of the first four Smith, Arkham House, prose collections bear on their spines (both books and dust-jackets) Smith's name with the "Clark" just above the "Ashton Smith."

As ever-growing suburbia continues to spread around the remaining Smith acres, its eventual metamorphosis into a memorial park (operated by the State of California) seems more and more a reasonable possibility.

A final pensée: Is Smith the only American poet *and* writer of fantasy and science fiction to have one or two streets named after him?

A Roundup of Recent Reviews

Providentially Speaking Again

T.E.D. KLEIN. *Providence After Dark and Other Writings.* New York: Hippocampus Press, 2019. 591 pp. $30.00 tpb. ISBN 978-1-61498-268-5.

During the year 2019 it has happened as my great good fortune to have reviewed three or four major publications from Derrick Hussey and his Hippocampus Press, both of which now seem as magical and numinous as August Derleth and his Arkham House. All this, plus the ongoing and abundant volumes of the Lovecraft correspondence. First at my request there came from designer David Schultz a proof copy of Leah Bodine Drake's *The Song of the Sun,* her collected writings, at 767 pages, as largely and quite capably assembled and edited by Master Schultz. (Not yet released, some prose but mostly poetry.) Second, Arthur Machen's *Collected Fiction,* impeccably assembled and edited by S. T. Joshi, in three volumes; and a fourth volume of critical writings edited by Messieurs Mark Valentine and Timothy J. Jarvis; all four volumes totalling 2056 pages. Third, D. L. Myers's exceptional first volume of poetry, *Oracles from the Black Pool,* published like Klein's own much larger book in October 2019, but in Myers's case at 136 pages, which I review elsewhere, and quite positively—richly deserved.

The point that I am highlighting here? At 37 lines per page, whether prose or poetry, all these identified books constitute a considerable amount of discourse liberated for creative purposes. These publications, including the latest (by Ted Klein), represent strategic or important landmarks in the annals of modern imaginative literature, much of it speculative prose or poetry; as if all fiction is not in one sense speculative, even if nominally dealing with common reality.

Ted Klein is indeed a special case with his two classics of modern fiction, the novel *The Ceremonies* and the collection *Dark Gods.* Although never attested in print (in anything I have seen), Klein is a professional writer, a journalist writing for newspapers and magazines, like many of my favorite poets and prosateurs, including L. B. Drake, Louis Bertrand, Arthur Machen, or Margaret Munnerlyn Mitchell for that matter. In other words, Klein is a practiced and more than merely competent author; and it clearly shows in this exceptional tome of his, the *Collected Writings* now set before me.

On this opus I have spent a week carefully perusing it before committing pen to paper. A small note after the contents pages but before the official "Author's Note" informs me that, although Klein is in fact the author, S. T. Joshi is the instigator-assembler-editor of the collection. Therefore I have neatly written on the title page (where it should stand in print), an inch or so below the author's name, "Edited by S. T. Joshi." And as the back cover states in all truth, the compilation is indeed notable for "covering a remarkably wide range of topics with elegance and wit," a collection in which Klein in fact "reveals his skill as an essayist and reviewer," and impressively so.

In the current flux of publications emanating from Hippocampus Press, the author finds himself in distinguished company, some of them the literary objects of his fervid youthful admirations (or connected to them), Lovecraft, Machen, and Ramsey Campbell, among others. The titles of the six sections into which Joshi has ordered this gallimaufry of materials indicate these early but continuing enthusiasms: I. On Lovecraft; II. On Other Authors; III. *The Twilight Zone;* IV. On Film; V. On Other Topics; VI. Reviews. A nice and reassuring touch: each section ends with some earnest writer or reporter interviewing Klein, whereby we learn much about him and his literary output.

Among other activities he has edited several magazines including *The Twilight Zone* and *CrimeBeat.* He has had op-ed pieces published in the *New York Times,* the *Washington Post,* and so forth, a pretty impressive record.

The collection contains an incredible spectrum of intelligent and informed commentary on all manner of subjects, authors, books, magazines, etc., and not only topics in the genre of supernatural horror. This reviewer finds that he shares many predilections with Klein, not just favorite authors like Machen but (big surprise!) poetry above all. In addition to manifesting himself as a quite knowledgeable poetry connoisseur, or poetry consumer (his phrase), he is also a remarkable poet himself, as witness "Lament of an Aging English Instructor," but especially "The Book of Hieronymus Bosch"—an exceptional sestina on the grand scale laid out on two adjoining pages almost at the exact center of the collection. This is a masterpiece wherein Klein expresses something essential about Bosch and the human (or inhuman) condition. This sestina results in something as important as any or all the prose in *Providence After Dark.*

How much have I learned from this compilation! Not just about literature and its creators (mostly nineteenth and twentieth centuries), films and their makers, but so much that I did not myself see during the 1970s, 1980s, and 1990s, when I preoccupied myself with workaday jobs or just plain existing. I cannot even begin to broach miscellanea as contained in *Providence After Dark.* Klein speaks out forthrightly against the abuse and murder of animals as literally perpetrated by the new breed of movie-makers, signalized in two essays at the start of section IV. I also learn that, according to modern physicist Lawrence M. Krauss, the cosmos possesses some 100 billion galaxies at large, and that each galaxy contains about 100 billion stars. No speculation or discussion in this estimate concerning about how many planets major or minor may or may not exist relative to all these galaxies and stars!

For me the single most entertaining section is the extended "Sci-Fi Entertainment," as amazing, unprecedented, instructive, and, on occasion, hilarious as any other section or article. The mention of Portmeirion in western Wales (anent the British television series *The Prisoner*) with its rhododendron plantation caught me by real surprise. Machen would have known and cherished this extremely picturesque town and ambiance. Many people came to know of this place only because its use as the locale for a television series.

Whatever Klein uses as his topic or subject, he writes very well and entertainingly. We heartily recommend this collection by one Ted Klein, journaliste extraordinaire.

A concluding aside, lest we forget.

We wish to speak out on something, a verbal usage, easily observable in Klein's abundant compilation, and in many other books and articles dealing with supernatural horror. It lies in the word or term of horror, as aligned with that of terror.

Whether writers or readers of horror fiction, or spectators of horror movies, such people are obviously aficionados of modern fantasy, science fiction, science fantasy, however we define these terms. They all form part of speculative literature.

Such aficionados do not generally confuse such stories with tales of pure physical grue, as in a story or history of murder or wanton or systematic killing. We refer here to the clandestine and willful extermination by the Nazis of Jews, Gypsies, and other minorities in the death camps located mostly in Poland. In these death camps the Nazis murdered some six million people, an awesome total.

However, when we think of all these millions as individuals, we contemplate an infinite number of real horror stories. Those victims who, until the last moment, naked in the gas chambers, still held on to their innocent belief in the Nazi promise of their being resettled in some other location, would have known that last moment as one of total horror and terror combined, when the doors to the gas chambers closed and could not be opened from the inside. These are all tales of horror that we should not forget, albeit different in kind from the tales of supernatural horror.

The story of supernatural horror, as both directly and implicitly defined by him in many of the essays gathered in *Providence After Dark,* Klein beautifully exemplifies in his own fiction, *The Ceremonies* and *Dark Gods.* Machen himself exemplifies it in the novel *The Terror* about the animal kingdom rising up and attacking humans because of their abandonment of spiritual or supernatural beliefs and values, especially as provided by many of the organized religions. The Welsh author also beautifully exemplified it in a story of the radiant and numinous, above all in the novelette "The Great Return," about the return of the Holy Grail, the Sangraal. Thus in a sense the tale of supernatural horror might be interpreted not just as the desire of writers and readers to give themselves a good scare, a great fright, but as a desire toward religion, not necessarily organized religion (no disrespect to the institution), but as an universal need vis-à-vis the physical cosmos.

Despite what Lovecraft states in "Supernatural Horror in Literature," we have never found Machen to be that echt-cosmic in his fiction as displayed at least in some blatant manner. George Sterling, Ashton Smith, or Lovecraft himself are more demonstrably cosmic-minded, or cosmic-astronomic-minded. Nonetheless, however manifested, Machen remains a Titan of the Supernatural.

In the Footsteps of the Masters

HENRY J. VESTER III. *Of Mist and Crystal: Selected Poetry.* Fungoid Press/VirtualBookworm.com Press, 2015. 74 pp. $16.96 hc.

It is obvious that poet Henry J. Vester III is at least a literary connoisseur, as his hardcover book of poetry reveals the lore and appreciation of the modern masters of prose and poetry in the genre(s) of literature involving a general fantasy and science-fiction perspective, as the poet himself reveals in his "Author's Forward" [*sic*]: H. P. Lovecraft, Robert E. Howard, George Sterling, Joseph Payne Brennan, Stanley McNail, Ambrose Bierce, Richard L. Tierney, Ann K. Schwader, and (above all) Clark Ashton Smith, otherwise Klarkash-Ton. The author himself bears witness that he nourished his first tastes in poetry (apart from, but including, E. A. Poe) on the following volumes: *Dark of the Moon,* the anthology of weird and macabre poetry edited by August Derleth (1947); the later and similar volume *Fire and Sleet and Candlelight,* also edited by Derleth (1961); and the *Collected Poems* of H. P. Lovecraft, likewise edited by Derleth (1963). The anthologist-editor published all three volumes through his publishing firm Arkham House (Sauk City, Wisconsin). The present volume has two appreciative and exceptional introductions, the first by W. H. Pugmire, the second by Gregorio Montejo. Henry Vester well deserves the praise and elucidation, the lore and learning, imparted by these introductions.

This first book of poetry, and also the author's first solo volume of any type, is a small handsome hardcover, a little gem of production (5.25 × 8.25″), with a handsome cover by Allen Koszowski, a practiced artist of the weird and fantastic. In addition to the three prefaces, the volume contains twenty-four poems in verse and ends with a poem in prose, as well as with "Some Notes on the Poems" (these are helpful) assembled by the poet himself—explaining and identifying people and places in a playful manner. The back cover gives us basic information "About the Author," now a retired social worker who has worked as a family therapist near or at Santa Rosa, California, but most recently in a large community mental health center at Klamath Falls, Oregon.

Mr. Vester writes in variety of styles and forms whether traditional or non-traditional, clearly and straightforwardly. As noted by Gregorio Montejo, he commands "a dark yet sinuous line," no less than a broad range of imagery and allusion, both of which come to the fore in the tributes to various poetic masters. Chilling moments abound in the poems themselves, but succinctly, as in the poetry of Ambrose Bierce and Leah Bodine Drake. (Relative to some hunters who go exploring where they should not, "In the tower was horrible laughter.")

The poet first strikes the note of lonely and macabre reflection in the opening morceau, "Medicine Wind," and sustains it throughout all nine stanzas:

> I sat this eve alone
> In an unfrequented place,
> Disdaining solace or companion
> In the hour of my reflection.

He has also mastered a subtle allusiveness as presented in the poem's second stanza, where he refers to the sun and the moon respectively:

> And as the desert's master
> Drowned himself again in bloodied sands,
> Its mistress arose in haste,
> As a lover tardy to a secret tryst.

The final two stanzas resume the poem's metaphysical depths in an expert way:

> All through the night the song went on,
> Oblivious of any ear.
> And all the threads of my spirit
> It untangled, reweaving in its own image.
>
> And as the master rose again,
> I suddenly remembered, and
> The spirit wind flew, laughing, away,
> Salting again my bones with sandy tears.

Mixed in with all the macabre reflections, often with startling surprise endings, Mr. Vester reveals a very nice sense of humor, as in one of the tributes to H. P. Lovecraft, "An Old Gentleman Seeks Professional Help." The tribute to pictorial artist Gervasio Gallardo, "Visionary," is no less notable in its precise and serious register of the covers that Gallardo painted for Ballantine's Adult Fantasy series. The poet proves again his sense of humor in "A Yuletide Encounter," where he does an adroit and clever take-off of "A Visit from St. Nicholas," otherwise "The Night Before Christmas," and to hilarious effect. Other tributes to Lovecraft appear in "The Bells of R'lyeh," "Dagon's Halls," and "The Scroll of Alhazred." Mr. Vester strikes perhaps his deepest notes or tones in the tributes to Clark Ashton Smith, "To the Shade of Klarkash-Ton" and "Klarkash-Ton Walks at Midnight." In the first cited poem Vester's use of the true second person singular seems especially appropriate and moving. The second piece of homage turns out just as lovely and serious, a touching *jeu d'esprit.*

We can point to other titles and tributes, notably the one to "Ray" (the master fantaisiste Ray Bradbury), but rather than that, and further quotations from Mr. Vester's poetry, we would urge the serious reader to obtain a copy of *Of Mist and Crystal* and con the poems' individual morceaux. Altogether then, we can heartily recommend this book, this unequivocally delectable book, to the literary connoisseur and lover of imaginary poetry. And we have almost forgotten to add that the concluding prose-poem, "Of Ancient Glory" (4.5 pp.), is a rare and profoundly moving work of art worthy of Lord Dunsany and Ashton Smith!

One final note. The author in his preface lists various poets and other writers who have influenced and liberated his poetic vision, his inner landscape of dream and revery. We repeat them here: Edgar Allen Poe, H. P. Lovecraft, Robert E. Howard, George Sterling, Joseph Payne Brennan, Stanley McNail, Ambrose Bierce, Richard L. Tierney, Ann K. Schwader, and Clark Ashton Smith (shades of Poe and Sterling intensified!), and probably others as well (but unregistered). This quality is something that he shares with C. Ashton Smith. It relates to something fundamental to style (or subject), and that remains the *tone* of the language carefully sifted and selected by the poet

(Vester), a quality as impeccable as Ashton Smith's own, or (in French) that of Baudelaire. On those grounds alone Henry Vester finds himself among the modern elect as registered by himself.

We cannot resist quoting in full one more poem, or so.

Echoes

Echoes of a winter wind
Whisper within an ancient skull—

Stir memories of loves long lost,
The more hungered for because
They never were.

Awake

Who treads so softly 'round
That none but ghosts of bats in attic dark
Discern the steps which scarcely tramp the snow?
I lie awake by single candle's glow,
And dare not sleep for fear of that
Which unprotected dreams may show.

Man as a Mystery

ARTHUR MACHEN. *Collected Fiction.* Edited by S. T. Joshi. New York: Hippocampus Press, 2019. Volume 1: 1888–1895, 546 pp. ISBN 978-1-61498-248-7. Volume 2: 1896–1910, 540 pp. ISBN 978-1-61498-249-4. Volume 3: 1911–1937, 558 pp. ISBN 978-1-61498-250-0. MARK VALENTINE and TIMOTHY J. JARVIS, ed. *The Secret Ceremonies: Critical Essays on Arthur Machen.* New York: Hippocampus Press, 2019. 412 pp. ISBN 978-1-61498-245-6.

There can be no doubt that S. T. Joshi has long since become the outstanding scholar of modern imaginative fiction and related materials, the very different kind of fantasy and science fiction, or science fantasy, involving horror and the supernatural, as purveyed by H. P. Lovecraft, Clark Ashton Smith, Algernon Blackwood, and many others, including other British writers, and thus not all associated with *Weird Tales,* the "Unique Magazine" that flourished from 1923 on into 1954, as primarily edited by Farnsworth Wright.

Not only has Joshi, with exemplary care, prepared the corrected texts of any given author, correlating them with first printings and/or with the original manuscripts when and wherever available, but he has also sought out discarded or alternate versions, going far beyond mere professionalism or ordinary devotion to literature. His work is thorough and as impeccable as possible. Joshi himself remains the complete professional and more than that, a creative scholar, a status not at all common or commonplace. Nonetheless, he has his own blind spots, as do all critics and scholars, but he works fantastically well within his limits or limitations. With such an editor we can have complete faith as to the integrity of any given text that he has handled, especially pertinent when it comes to an author as idiosyncratic as Machen.

In assessing the overall register of all that Joshi has edited, we must not overlook the complete collected poetry (including his many translations) by Clark Ashton Smith in three volumes (Hippocampus Press, 2007–08), nor must we overlook the complete collected poetry (including his poetic dramas) by Smith's mentor George Sterling (Hippocampus Press, 2013). And this limited enumeration represents but a fraction of S. T. Joshi's overall labor to date, mirabile dictu!

Joshi's best virtues as a creative scholar are on display in one of the latest and most important productions from Hippocampus Press premiered at the latest Lovecraft gathering in Providence, Rhode Island, the NecronomiCon IV, in August 2019. These are the three volumes of the collected fiction of Arthur Machen. These volumes represent a consummation piously to be wished—and now terminated. All possible kudos to editor S. T. Joshi, the typesetter David E. Schultz, and the owner-publisher of Hippocampus, Derrick Hussey—a formidable triumvirate, indeed!

Before we consider the fiction by Machen and the volume of essays on Machen by other writers, let us consider selected aspects of Machen's life as they relate to his oeuvre, no less than something of the background of that life and career. Let us look at the British royal background against which his life played out. Victoria, born in 1819, died in 1901: queen of Great Britain, and sovereign over the entire

British Empire, reigned from 1837 to 1901 during a period when that same empire encircled the entire globe and attained its apogée, a period of unparalleled prosperity and social reform for that commonality.

The same dynasty, the House of Windsor, continues to reign since Victoria: Edward VII (1841-1910) reigned 1901-10. George V (1865-1936) reigned 1910-36. George VI (1895-1952) reigned 1936-52. Daughter to George VI, Elizabeth II (born 1926) has reigned since 1952. All during the period from 1819 on into the present a series of remarkable prime ministers have actually ruled, and run the country and the empire.

We mention this royal background for the benefit of the Americans in the U.S., many of whom are not Anglophiles, and who do not know the importance of the British royal family as part of the overall British tradition. The British sovereign, whoever it might be, abides somewhere in the historical or current background. Thus Machen was born in 1863, twenty-six years after Victoria's accession, about one-third through her unparalleled reign, excepting that (so far) of Elizabeth II, who has reigned now sixty-seven years, as compared to Victoria's sixty-four.

Machen was born, educated, and grew up at Caerleon-on-Usk during a very different period from that in which he died in 1947 after World War II. Apparently he was eighteen or so when he emigrated from southeast Wales to try his luck (employment) in the British capital at a time when tradition in various ways probably loomed larger than what it does today. Although he left his hometown, it never left Machen, with all its Roman and Arthurian associations. The Roman ones included not just the very solid Roman walls and other remains of the legionary fortress itself, but also the many items on display in the little Roman museum that contains legionary and other Roman artifacts found in the little town itself and the immediate area.

Sometime before World War I, but obviously after 1912 the following episode took place in Ashton Smith's life as well as in Machen's. As told to the present writer by Genevieve Sully and/or her daughters Helen and Marion, few other Auburnites knew this fact. Somehow a copy of *The Star-Treader* came to the attention of Arthur Machen through the agency of one of Timeus Gaylord's family in England. Machen read it, or at least part of it, and was impressed.

The same family member duly reported this favorable reaction back to Smith and his family in California. It must have proven gratifying and encouraging. It also confirmed his mentor Sterling's own high opinion. Collateral approbation from afar is always welcome, especially as emanating from a writer like Machen.

Mark Valentine has argued that Machen, with "The Great God Pan," unintentionally transformed Pan from a "rustic, bucolic image" into one of "illicit sex and cosmopolitan decadence." We cannot avoid contrasting the negative aspects about Pan in the writings by Machen and other English Symbolists with the more positive ones in the writings of the French Parnassian poets and other writers, which tend to be the radiant and numinous ones of Leconte de Lisle and José-Maria de Heredia. Witness in the latter's unique collection *Les Trophées* the poems devoted to Pan and Priapus. How different is this treatment from that of the English Decadents or Symbolists!—like the difference between day and night!

Finally, but finally, let us now turn our attention to Machen and the works at hand. With the Machen copyrights now legally expired, any enterprising publisher can reprint Machen's texts in any way that he sees fit. Derrick Hussey has taken advantage of this expiration to make available the books on review here, impeccably presented, an overall 1644 pages. Earnest readers and students of Machen receive a great amount of literature for their money. Thus Hippocampus Press has furnished an entire new generation or audience of readers with newly minted materials. This exceptional accomplishment deserves recognition and genuine celebration. For me, especially at eighty-five, reading and rereading these texts has proven an overwhelming experience! I have remained a fervent admirer of Machen and his writings ever since I discovered them as gathered in *Tales of Horror and the Supernatural* (Knopf, 1948). Appositely, this book appeared right after Machen's death.

By the time of my Arthurian research trip with close friend Jack Hesketh (during the early 1970s) in the west and southwest of Great Britain (largely Wales, Somerset, Dorset, Devon, and Cornwall), Jack and I had both become veteran Machenites, and thus we perceived the ever-changing landscape as under Machen's own spiritual sponsorship. Our daylong visit somewhere east or northeast of Caerleon to the Temple of Nodens (a very large temple complex) at Lydney turned into the single most remarkable highlight of our trip in Jack's automobile.

At least one-third or one-half of the fiction collected into the three Hippocampus volumes is completely new to me, above all the short stories, although I recognize "Out of the Picture," "Out of the Earth," and "N," always a special favorite. Here are such memorable works as *The Terror,* "The Great Return," *The Hill of Dreams,* and others, not to mention such unified collections as *The Chronicle of Clemendy* and *The Three Impostors,* as especial in its manner as *The Hill of Dreams.* Altogether then, the set of three volumes represents as rich a feast of unique and erudite fiction as any aficionado could hope to read.

Rather than galloping through all the material new to us for this review, we reserve all this unread stuff to experience at leisure sometime the coming winter of 2019–20. For those readers hungry for intelligent and informed critical commentary on Machen and his literary output, we can surely recommend *The Secret Ceremonies,* as edited by Messieurs Valentine and Jarvis, and as written by some two dozen writers (including Machen himself discussing his own books). In closing these remarks or thoughts on Machen, we would very much enjoy seeing a reprinted and expanded version of Machen's ironic gathering *Precious Balms,* which would include all the reviews of Machen's books (in the British press) as of up to his retirement from writing circa 1937. We would also enjoy seeing his three autobiographical volumes, *Far Off Things, Things Near and Far,* and *The London Adventure,* all gathered into one big tome, and with photos of Machen, his family, and his friends. We must alert the reader that in Volume II, right after *The Hill of Dreams,* he will find Machen's collection of exquisite prose-poems, *Ornaments in Jade.*

Despite all the clever and smart-ass people who pronounced against Machen and his writings during his lifetime, from start to finish, he has indeed survived. These four volumes bear ample witness to that fact of survival. (Oh that marvelous lyrical prose!)

(Clandestine afterthought! Another point of interest between Machen [with his sacramentalism] and the critic redacting this review. Writings about Machen inform us that he was Anglican, High

Churchman, Anglo-Catholic. This reviewer was raised as a [Roman] Catholic—a faith long since renounced—but which allows him to understand in depth Machen's own ceremonialism.)

An aside, or postscriptum, please note well. I did not mention in the main body of this review several obvious particulars about Machen and his writing, whether fiction or nonfiction. This non-mention is intentional, and so I shall discuss them here in this concluding aside. Whatever he writes, Machen almost invariably seems discursive, which puts the reader at his ease. This works as an adroit ploy for his fiction. The one exception, or one of the few such, is "The Bowmen," the short story that reads almost like a news report from the battlefield: the miraculous intervention (during World War I) of St. George with his Agincourt Bowmen, or "the Angels of Mons," whereby the English briefly found salvation, and 10,000 German soldiers died. The news media picked this up as something genuine.

Another major point, about Machen's typically indirect mode of narration in his fiction. The narrative itself is clear and suave as the author tells the story, revealing his little surprises as he goes along. In general this functions well for him, if not exemplarily for what it is. Why did Machen adopt or innovate this narrative mode, say, in contradistinction to a bald news report? It creates at once the sense of an interesting and enigmatic puzzle, thus emphasizing one of Machen's major tenets as a "spiritual" writer: that man, or any human being, is a mystery made for mysteries and surrounded by mysteries.

We must add, lest we forget: The covers by Matthew Jaffe and Nicholas Day, and cover designs by Daniel V. Sauer, are both distinctive and original for all four volumes. The frontispiece photos, by E. O. Hoppe and John Gawsworth illustrate and illuminate the physical Machen.

Mencken the Poet

H. L. Mencken. *Collected Poems.* Edited by S. T. Joshi. New York: Hippocampus Press, 2009. 145 pp. $15.00 tpb. ISBN 978-0-9824296-3-1.

It is obvious that Mencken early in his life studied poetry with care and intelligence, most likely in school and on his own. This keen interest

shows up in his cultivation of the forms from French poetry, as trans-
ported into English by poets like Austin Dobson, A. C. Swinburne, and
other poets of the later 1800s and early 1900s. No one need feel con-
descending toward Mencken's young adult poems. S. T. Joshi sensibly
makes no outrageous claims for them, but they do deserve publication
or republication; they demonstrate an aspect of Mencken's writing and
personality that few suspect, or have suspected. Taking them for they
are—adroit, sincere, and unpretentious—they stand up rather well to
casual scrutiny, that is, with few or no gaffes. Welcome, H.L.M., to
Derrick Hussey's modern school of traditional poets!

So now the supple Muse of H. L. Mencken presents itself to our
absorbed perusal. By what mysterious thaumaturgy or manoeuvres
behind the scenes does this volume come forth into physical reality?
The editor reveals himself as none other than the amazing and prolif-
ic editor and author S. T. Joshi, who is (as it turns out) a leading ex-
pert on Mencken and his enormous output—a fact that we had not
known until reading this on the back cover. On what writers or body
of literature is Joshi not an authority?

What a contrast this unexpected but well-met little volume makes
to the usual book of poetry from Hippocampus Press!—poetry that is
almost always dark and grim and forbidding, albeit well conceived
and crafted. Most, if not all, of the poets thus published work in tradi-
tional forms or modes, where technical gaffes manifest all too readily.
Versifier, watch your back! The hounds or demons of criticism are
looking over your shoulder like specters at the feast, prepared to
pounce whenever you might slip up or nod.

Mencken's own poetry makes a significant and agreeable surprise,
above all in his mastery of rather involved verse forms from the
French like the ballade, the ode, the sonnet, the rondeau, the roundel,
and the triolet. And he writes happily and largely out of his own young
adulthood, with exuberance, with a sense of laughter and fun. This is not
your typical youthful bard, melancholy, weeping and sighing over lost
loves, or yet about the dire problems of the day. As when has there not
been grim problems and issues at any time in the history of humanity?

Mencken's poetry is uniformly well factured. Here are several exam-
ples of his craft and ingenious wit. They spread over a wide range of tone
and subject matter. We choose them almost at random.

A Ballad of Looking

He looked into her eyes, and there he saw
    No trace of that bright gleam which poets say
    Comes from the faery orb of love's sweet day,
No blushing coyness causes her to withdraw
Her gaze from his. He looked and yet he knew
    No joy, no whirling numbness of the brain,
    No quickening heart-beat. Then he looked again,
And once again, unblushing, she looked too.

He looked into her eyes—with interest he
    Stared at them through a magnifying prism.
    For he was but an oculist, and she
Was being treated for astigmatism.

A Sonnet to a Wienerwurst

Cylindricality is grace, and thou,
    The acme of the form cylindrical,
    Art graceful as a springtime madrigal,
Or the fair curves of Dian's snowy brow;
And also, as the few who love thee vow,
    Thou hast the charm that haunts the mystical.
    Besides, thy toothsomeness is capital—
Far greater than ambrosia's, I trow!
O, fairest flower of Hohenzollern-land!
    Thrice blest thou art, with flavor, charm and grace,
Though cavaliers with stigma would thee brand,
    Yet hast thou fed a sturdy, warlike race;
Their dog-like courage maketh them command,
    And thou!—Tut! tut!—what need to hide thy face?

Within the City Gates

    We can but dream of murmuring rills
      Mad racing down the wooded hills,

Of meadow flowers and balmy days
When robin sings his amorous lays;
    And lost among the city's ways,
    To us it is not given to gaze
In wonder as the morning haze
    Lifts from the sea of daffodils,—
    Of all but those on window-sills
    We can but dream.

On Passing the Island of San Salvador

(The first land sighted by Columbus)

Low lies the puny ride of glistening sand,
    Flecked, like a long-lost path, with tufts of green,
    Helpless it seems against the waves, and lean—
Yea, like forgotten offal of the land:
Few watchers pace the measure of its strand,
    Few gleaners in its surge-plowed gardens glean;
    Silent it sleeps, the mocking seas between,
That on the Day the world's great chasm spanned.

Yet, where the fretful breakers battle there
    Time was the Dreamer saw the palms and knew
The victor's joy! To him the land was fair,
    And doubly fair to all his weary crew:
So holds it now the charm of all most rare—
    The deathless beauty of a dream come true!

We first encountered Mencken on his own ground when we were conducting the research for our bio-bibliography of Clark Ashton Smith. Smith along with Sterling contributed several poems in verse and prose to the *Smart Set,* coedited at the time by Mencken. This rather took us by surprise (during the 1960s) because we had not then known of Mencken's predilection for romantic poetry, nor his acute appreciation of poetic technique and craft, such as this little volume copiously demonstrates. All in all, this little book comes as a welcome and refreshing change of pace from the doom and gloom purveyed too abundantly and ubiquitously for our taste, that is, as of nowadays and/or nowanights. Those acquainted with Ambrose Bierce's pungent wit and satire, whether in verse or prose, will find echoes here, but without Bierce's nastiness.

Some Lichen-Encrusted Ladies and Other Horrors

Wade German. *The Ladies of the Everlasting Lichen and Other Relics.* Bucharest, Romania: Mount Abraxas Press, 2019. 76 pp. Frontispiece by Jean Delville. Illustrated with woodblock artwork from 1825. (Photo-pictured end papers, black and grey.) 120 euros hc. Limited to 88 copies.

A new book by Wade German, and from Europe, the Old World in fact! A new volume of poetry, and his second one, is cause for a party, for a celebration, even if a caveat emptor seems apt. It is indeed strong stuff. Among the bona fide poets in the genre of supernatural horror, the current scene boasts quite a few notable figures: the veteran master of sonnets Richard L. Tierney; the equally veteran master of sonnets and other forms traditional and innovative Frank Coffman, only recently arrived and recognized as a major voice; and the two younger and extraordinary poets, coadjutors, in Southern California, Ashley Dioses and K. A. Opperman. To which of these four should we reward the *Palme d'Or,* the Golden Palm? We could not decide the issue. Let more adroit and better informed heads discern, and judge the matter. We cannot.

Before we deal with the contents, all poetry of horror or of existential unease, we must say that this tome is possibly the most sumptuous, slender, but substantial volume of poetry that we have ever examined, cogently illuminated with older art, including the frontispiece by the French Symbolist painter Jean Delville of the later 1800s. The interior illustrations appear in the lower left-hand or right-hand corners of the given pages. This is a true deluxe edition, enshrining some very dark offerings to a very dark Muse in all truth.

As to the contents, the collection has three sections: "Nightscapes," with 16 poems; "Prophecies and Dooms," with 15; and "The Monstrous Voice," with 3 extended pieces: "Scylla and Charybdis," at 4 full pages; "Eurynomos," at 3 full pages plus; and "Gargonum Chaos," at 5 full pages plus. At 34 or 35 lines per page, these last pieces amount to a sizeable something, particularly since most of the other poems (with a few notable exceptions) are comparatively shorter. Thus overall the tome contains 34 poems.

The four "Nightmares" that open the second section could pass for very supple translations from Leconte de Lisle, even if he did not write much poetry of supernatural horror, but rather mythological. Not quite halfway through the first section we meet the ladies featured in the book's title, enclosed in the "Ecclesiastical Triptych" to notable effect: "Relics," "Black Robes," and "Ladies of the Everlasting Lichen," whom we would not care to encounter outside the pages devoted to them! Lichen-encrusted skin, indeed!

The third section, "The Monstrous Voice" (truly monstrous), limns a triptych of quite horrible, if not ghastly, and super-ugly prodigies. The first is a dialogue between Scylla and Charybdis, and which of these two is the more disgusting is a moot question. They themselves find each other no less repugnant. The second is a monologue featuring the blue-black ghoul entity who devours corpses, but not the bones. The third is a dialogue between Stheno and Euryale, just after the hero Perseus has killed their sister Medusa, and with her head has left the scene on the flying horse Pegasus.

These three final selections read like episodes from some recently discovered Elizabethan or Jacobean drama, say, by John Webster, and worthy of that same author who created *The Duchess of Malfi.* The final section of this volume is definitely not for the squeamish. It did give the present critic a real sense of horror, but not so much supernatural and rather more of physical disgust, of genuine revulsion—not at all dissimilar to coming upon a pile of dead, rotting bodies being consumed by myriad maggots and other insects, and with foul stench. Connoisseur, beware!

We shall not quote from these last three horror-orgies, but rather some of the briefer and less demanding lyrics, that is, less repulsive, but still strong in their own way. From the first section we quote in full "Oracle," and from the second, "Naotalba's Dream Song," followed by the beautiful tribute to a recently deceased fictioneer, well known in our genre, "The Tomb of Wilum Hopfrog Pugmire." Yes, the second poem cited is yet another excerpt from the play by Robert W. Chambers, *The King in Yellow.*

Oracle

What were the things you meant to say
Before you left for other lands,
Those distant regions, dim and grey,
To dwell amid eternal sands
That know not night, nor break of day
That twilight realm without a sun,
The kingdom of oblivion?

Hear you, that we would here receive
The mysteries that you can tell
Of worlds beyond, but few believe?
Hither to us and doubt dispel,
If only for awhile to leave
Your house in Hell ..untenanted
Come whisper us wisdom of the dead.

Naotalba's Dream Song

(From "The King in Yellow")

The yellow fungus thrives and thrives
Like upon our lips and hair,
A pallid shroud upon our lives
And souls that breathe the haunted air

Beneath black stars, where we revive
The shadow of our old affair,
Where yellow fungus thrives and thrives
Like dust upon our lips and hair.

No prophet spoke of what survives

The evil wonders waiting here—
This land of wakeful corpses where
Our love would moulder if alive,
Where yellow fungus thrives and thrives.

The Tomb of Wilum Hopfrog Pugmire

In some strange hollow fearful minds defame,
The sentinels of Sesqua keep the path;
One reaches it through circles of black math
To find the obelisk that bears his name.

Here, in the hour twilight creatures dwell
The mossy mound that is their master's tomb,
The rosy shadows blend with purple gloom
And moan before the Night's black magic spell.

Even as he explores dark gulfs of sleep,
Weird spirits conjured out of unknown space,
Like lovely horrors, at his grave increase;

They hear the wisdom of the worms that creep;
And ever watchful, ward his resting place
From those who would profane his dreamful peace.

Quite apart from the number of pages and the overall size between the two volumes, we could not imagine a greater contrast between two books than that between Wade German and the Collected Writings (mostly poems but some well-chosen prose) of Leah Bodine Drake (forthcoming from Hippocampus Press). When he reviewed her first book (and of poetry), *A Hornbook for Witches* (Arkham House, 1950), for the *New York Times Book Review,* Orville Prescott considered it to be rather fun but in a grisly way (and repugnant). However, what a difference between Wade German's grim and uncompromising tone and vision on the one hand and on the other L. B. Drake's whimsical tone and perspective on things. In the final analysis we might prefer Leah to Wade, but art is a democracy, and we can accommodate both of these artists, and many others besides.

The Sun Sings Loud and Clear

LEAH BODINE DRAKE. *The Song of the Sun: Collected Writings.*
Edited by David E. Schultz and S. T. Joshi. Illustrations by Jason C.
Eckhardt. New York: Hippocampus Press, 2020. 767 pp. $60.00 hc.
ISBN 978-1-61498-266-1; $30.00 pb. ISBN 978-1-61498-26.

Let us announce at once that this book represents a magnificent
achievement on the part of all who worked on it, directly or on its be-
half. With such energy and strength and critical acumen as I still pos-
sess at eighty-four, let me proclaim and acclaim the physical fact of
this volume or, I should say, tome. First, the poet herself, Leah Bod-
ine Drake (1904–1964), even if long deceased. Second, the owner-
editor of Hippocampus Press, Derrick Hussey, who has accom-
plished more than any other publisher we know (including August
Derleth of Arkham House) to bring out quite a sizable library of col-
lections by poets old and new. Third, David E. Schultz, the chief tex-
tual researcher, editor, bibliographer, and indexer, who put the
volume together literally as an objective artifact, searching through the
requisite libraries in the Midwest (Drake's own terrain), and S. T.
Joshi, who helped establish the texts and bibliography. Fourth, the
able and painstaking research coadjutor, Jordan Smith, who quested
through the periodical resources of the New York Public Library to
locate many published poems and other materials that might other-
wise have lain unheralded and unknown. BRAVO, IF NOT BRAVISSIMO,
TO THEM ALL!

The big book itself, 6 × 9 × 1½, is the usual handsome item to
which Hippocampus has accustomed us, the readers and connois-
seurs of the house's publications. It is as complete a collected poems,
plus miscellanea, as we could hope to have for long-term delectation
and study. It has quite an able and substantial introduction full of bio-
graphical and bibliographical data put together by David E. Schultz.
This is indeed an unparalleled collection of imaginative poetry (plus
much else) comparable to the output of George Sterling and Clark
Ashton Smith. This tome reveals a long life and career fulfilled, a ma-
jor poet, especially a major woman poet, of which genus we can rarely
have enough. Drake achieved wide publication during her lifetime

both in the little magazines as well as in the fancier big-time ones. She won a good number of prestigious prizes, but had only two books of her own poetry published in her lifetime, the first, *A Hornbook for Witches* (Arkham House, 1950), now much sought by collectors, and at exorbitant prices.

Drake engaged in and sustained friendships with such remarkable authors as Manly Wade Wellman and C. S. Lewis, both of whom admired her poetry, but she had many other admirers as well. Early in her life and career she performed as a dancer and a model—yes, she was a handsome woman—and enjoyed her life and career very much, as well as the benefits accruing from her physical beauty. Lest we overlook it, we must mention here the striking cover (design by Dan Sauer), which incorporates an exotic drawing by Leah's mother, Cornelia B. Drake, depicting some beautiful Far Asian woman wearing an exotic Chinese-appearing robe, with a beloved peacock on a little swing in the upper left-hand corner. This art adds a lovely touch indeed!

In case we have not made it explicit enough, David E. Schultz in his usual role of typesetter for Hippocampus Press has beautifully laid out and typeset the entire tome. Jason C. Eckhardt as usual has provided some exceptional drawings, fifteen in all. We would assume that it is David who accomplished the section or subsection of alternate readings and unfinished poems. The introduction more than adequately details Drake's life and career. Because of her father's occupation of petroleum-seeker, her parents traveled around a great deal, finally settling down for an extended period in Evansville, Indiana (Schultz nicely supplies a little map on p. 27 to show the many cities where the family resided across the U.S.), where Leah primarily worked as a journalist, contributing an enormous amount of material to the *Evansville Courier,* reviewing among much else a staggering number of feature films from the major Hollywood studios. She complains about almost going blind from all the movies her job compelled her to witness and review.

She was married briefly, about a year, and then divorced; she did not care for married life, as appears obvious. She primarily lived with her parents as an adult and took care of them in their decline. She acted as a person of strong character and a certain distinct nobility. From her poetry and other materials Drake was evidently very well educated, well read, and intellectually sophisticated. But the interested reader can con all that in the introduction. There is evidently enough material still extant for a full-fledged biography, above all literary.

Just what exactly does this big book contain? Let us list the contents: the introduction, an extensive group of some fifty photographs, a list of drawings by Eckhardt, the collected poems (the largest section by far), alternate readings and unfinished poems, fiction (four short stories), nonfiction (a representative selection), published letters, unpublished letters, an appendix (of miscellanea by and about Drake), bibliography, indexes of titles and first lines of poems. The collected poems include the following sections or subsections: A Dream of Samarkand, Descent of Angels, Fantasy in a Forest, Honey from the Lion, Precarious Ground, We Move on Turning Stone, and The Face in the Water. The section titles derive from the titles of representative individual poems. What a wealth, what a plethora, what a treasure trove of wit, invention, whimsy, pure fantasy, and sheer imagination do we have here in this collection of collections! Even in those manifold poems presumably depicting the everyday or the commonplace, Drake retains an edge, an awareness of the Otherworldly, the Unseen, and the Other Side, constantly displays this extra sense as if it formed part of the five or six traditional senses, but somehow lying beyond them, as if within easy reach or summoning for those fortunate enough to invoke this outré sense through word, phrase, imagery, and pictorial or sculptural art.

Like Ashton Smith, Drake happened to live and practice her craft during what turned out to be a very barren period for traditional poetry and romanticism, from the 1920s through the 1960s, until the romantic renaissance that began with *The Lord of the Rings* by J. R. R. Tolkien and then Ballantine Books' Adult Fantasy Series under the editorial guidance of Lin Carter. (The Hollywood movies of the 1930s and 1940s furnish the one paramount exception to this dearth of serious romanticism in an intellectual or aesthetic sense.) Drake's own *Hornbook for Witches* appearing in 1950 stands at the virtual midpoint of those four or five barren decades.

Drake saw the beginning of the "big thaw" but Smith did not, even if he may have sensed that in a cyclic *manner* it was returning. In a way it forced such lone poetic exemplars back in upon themselves, and made what they still managed to create stronger and more vivid: Smith in the 1940s with his love poems inspired by Madelynne Greene, and Drake in the 1950s with her free-wheeling whimsy and somewhat gentler fantasy. They were less likely to compromise with the temper of a harsh and alien timescape. We can only be grateful that they persevered. Smith in the 1950s had at least the not inconsiderable comfort of a warm and loving wife and the home that she provided for him in an area—Monterey, Carmel, Pacific Grove—that he had first come to know at length during June 1912 under the aegis of his mentor, George Sterling. In consonance with that gentler time, let me quote some of Leah's lovely and unconventional lyrics, even if stemming from a somewhat later period. We quote the title poem "The Song of the Sun" from pp. 294; "Unlikely Story" from pp. 429-30; "To Certain Poetry Critics" from pp. 310; and last, marking a perfect poetic summit, "The Black Peacock" from p. 259-60.

Song of the Sun

Set in the streaming void
By the Hands that made the night,
The sun with a mighty voice
Shouts for his own delight.

With body and breath of fire,
Hung beyond hope or blame,
Nothing is his desire
But to roar with a living flame.

Ere the first planet spun
Tilt-wise around his throne
He sang the song of the sun
For the sake of the song alone.

An earth or two may bask
In his warmth—he does not care,
He is conscious of no task
Burdened upon him there.

And let who will employ
His powers for wrong or right:
He sings in his boundless joy
And the song of the sun is light.

And worlds may totter and fall
And all man's grief be done
Before the rapture fails
In the huge heart of the sun.

Unlikely Story

Down to the dragon's house of stone
The young knight came.
The dragon, sleeping on his throne,
Blazed like a flame

With coil on coil of body scaled
And pavonine,
Crested with gold and turquoise, mailed
With tourmaline.

And must he slay this bane of kings,—
This mosaic'd wonder,—
Robber of princesses,—whose wings
Were folded thunder?

A beast so perilous and bright
Gave earth a glory:
It seemed a counteract of right
To end its story.

More ancient than the mountained land
Or primal wood.
The great worm slept. With sword in hand
The young knight stood

Irresolute. The kings he knew
Were cruel, and all

The princesses were dull. He'd rue
Beyond recall

This deed! And yet he knew he had
High precedent . . . .
"The devil take tradition!" said
The knight, and went.

To Certain Poetry Critics

They say we shouldn't praise the violet
Purpling the secret hollows of the Spring,
Avoid the plough, the seasons ancient ring!
As for the moon—she mustn't rise or set
For any poet now! We must forget
Archaic words like beauty when we sing,
Deny the rose, and out to limbo fling
All that pre-dates the dynamo or jet!

But Nature still refuses to suppress
One ripening apple or one harvest-row
To please a critic! In a trite re-birth
Each year they come again, and men will bless
Hackneyed creation, and his songs will show
And love as old as Adam for the earth!

The Black Peacock

When the peaks of Kâf receive the dawn,
And the doe seeks water with her fawn,
Down in the gardens of the Khan
            Wakes the one black peacock.

An alien in the feathered herd
Of peacocks indigo and verde,
He is the sole obsidian bird,
            The proud black peacock.

In what strange jungle did he nest?
Beneath what peri's burning breast?—
This darkling prince shunned by the rest,—
    The lone black peacock?

Beside the marble-prisoned lakes
He cries his grief. His screaming wakes
The close, night-drenched acacia-brakes,
    The sad black peacock.

And humbler birds, grown silent there,
Thrill to the anger and despair
Of one too splendid and too rare:
    The proud lone sad black peacock.

It is instructive and rather sobering to perceive Drake vis-à-vis Nora May French (1881–1907). Nora was born into the generation just before Leah's. She did not enjoy a fulfilled life as a person, nor a fulfilled career as a poet. Unhappy in love and life, she committed suicide at twenty-six, cutting everything short. Leah evidently did not need an ordinary romantic relationship in her life. She worked as a journalist, and in spite of difficulties (especially toward the end) she led a fulfilled life as a person and completed her career as a poet. This big book engineered for Hippocampus Press represents the vindication and fulfillment of Drake as a creative artist, even as *The Outer Gate* (Hippocampus Press, 2009) does the same for Nora May French, albeit in a much more limited compass. I have always felt a powerful affinity with Drake, even more so than with French. Following in the generation just after Drake's, I was born in 1934 but did not begin writing poetry seriously until much later. (I do not take into account here my earliest poems, my juvenilia, created when I was eleven and twelve during the winter of 1945–46, and then during that of 1946–47; these pieces amount to no more than ten poems.) I may note here some genuine resemblances between Drake and myself. Both Drake and I have written little fiction, that is, in prose. (Poetry, after all, is or can be a form of fiction.) Four of Drake's short stories exist. I have written a single novel and several prose-poems that could count as compact and concentrated short stories. (That does not rule out the possibility that I might not write fiction in the future.)

Drake as a journalist wrote an enormous amount of material in the form of reviews—concerts, all manner of books, literally thousands of movies. But she dedicated her real creative life to poetry. On the other hand, I as a freelance writer have written manifold essays mostly about books (poetry above all); some of these factor as reviews major and minor; this roughly connotes (but not in quantity) with the huge mass of Drake's journalistic writings. Like Drake, I have devoted much of my life to creating poetry, much of it in short forms with meter and rime, and a sizable amount of blank verse.

In my youth and adolescence during the latter 1930s and most of the 1940s and continuing on into the first half of the 1950s, thanks to both parents who worked in two different movie houses, I also witnessed thousands of movies produced by the leading Hollywood studios. Thus movies in the case of both poets may have honed our sense of the visual in their poetry, above all in regard to conscious imagery. In terms of the quantity of our poems it is a pure coincidence that, whereas Drake has written more than 360 pieces, I have composed some 370 pieces, or 380, counting juvenilia. Affinities can exist on many different levels among poets working in traditional forms, as this little accounting demonstrates, from Sterling and French and Smith to Drake and Sidney-Fryer. In this case the affinities are fairly tight and close-knit. Smith himself had become quite an admirer of Drake's work and acquired several copies of her first book of poems, the *Hornbook.*

A big sustained tide of applause for everyone involved: the original poet-journalist; the owner-editor of Hippocampus Press; the chief textual researcher-compiler-editor (and his editorial coadjutor, as if that worthy person did not already have such a very large amount of editing to his credit!); and the painstaking research coadjutor: all of whom have come up with a huge and astonishing volume, and not to leave out the more than able artist responsible for the fifteen drawings (as listed on pp. 17–18). They have all done themselves proud in what they have achieved for dear and very gifted poet-painter-in-words: Leah Bodine Drake. No better homage to her memory could have come into existence than this compilation, the result of the assiduous labor by many conscientious persons. It stands as much a tribute to them as to the original poet-imagist. This tome remains as a sustained act of piety on behalf of a remarkable creative individual. As an elder poet I salute everyone who busied themselves in this pious and echt-protean enterprise. For me personally *The Song of the Sun* represents a crown jewel, or (rather) a jeweled crown, among the many recent productions by Hippocampus Press!

Interviews with Donald Sidney-Fryer

Frederick J. Mayer

To interview Donald Sidney-Fryer is in itself an immersion within the world of Fantasy-Romance. One cannot avoid bringing in that world as it is as much a part of his being as was the person I know who bears the name of Sidney-Fryer. And so it was the afternoon and the conversation/interview I had with Donald at his current address in Sacramento.

When did you start writing and why?

When I was 27 I started to work on a number of sonnets and consciously tried to put together some vague and recorded dreams. Spending months on these first few poems most of which I did not retain but there was one or two I did with further changes.

I started writing because of the various pressures from within and 1 could no longer resist. My muse has always been a reluctant one. Then, when I was 35 I started to do public performances which I wanted to do for a variety of reasons.

You talk about dreams. Do you get a lot of ideas from dreams?

I use dreams in a symbolic sense, not just dreams one has nocturnally, but conscious daydreams, conscious dreams that you create—as Machen created—really present tense, he creates because it is always happening—it is always there.

About your public performances, how did you get into doing one man theatre-like readings?

I became fed up with all the negative criticisms of Spenser, really maligning reactions as how I see Spenser. 1 just had to demonstrate how I really feel about him and to convey that. I give some poetic justice literally rendered to Spenser. I enjoy his work tremendously.

Do you have any personal future plans dealing with Spenser?

As a matter of fact. right now I am putting it together. We really need financial aid badly. Though, we may do it all ourselves. Make our own costumes, etc. The readings are fantastic. Spenser as an entertainment—readings that have never been done before. Charming, intimate—they (the readings) can even be enjoyed by firelight.

You hinted at other present plans dealing with your one-man theatre. What are they?

I intend to do one-man theatre of my own works. Getting into my own Atlantean Saga. It will be an attemptable vehicle. I'm really excited about it. The program can even be done like samplers. Each performance can be what I wish to stress at the time. With samplers it doesn't have to be rigidly planned. Have a skeletal structure and stress different parts. I'm tired of doing structured programs and the like. And, I'm working on some long fiction about Atlantis, though I hesitate to call it a novel. Its idea is simply to tell it all together on one level—very simply, telling a story. Certain events will have certain significance because it is impossible to avoid, especially how you structure and sort the events and the characters.

Why select Atlantis as your Romance-Fantasy vehicle?

First, it was a substitute, a replacement for that of writing about my home, old New Bedford, Massachusetts, where I was born. You have the two dialogues featuring Atlantis by Plato, who is sublime. This tradition endures through Roman times up into Renaissance. It's all involved to keep alive the flame of imagination and wonder. For me, Atlantis was a metaphor of that. It is an emotional poetic allegory. I would equate it like searching for a guru. That is why it (Atlantis) still intrigues me. To me [Clark Ashton] Smith was like a poet from ancient Atlantis.

What you can say then is that you in one sense are equating your home to Atlantis?

Yes, both Arthur Machen and I luckily had former great areas where we were born upon which to draw from. At the turn of the century. New Bedford was the center of whaling. They were Princes of the Sea. Oh, what a world to draw upon! I adore Victorian things.

You mentioned Smith. did you know him? What are your ideas about him?

Yes. I met him twice. I came up from Southern California to Monterey where he and Carol were. The second time. I needed a place to stay and they invited me to stay at their place. He was generous to young people. He considered this in almost a 'holy' aspect to do what he could for young people. A great guy. He read some of George Sterling's poetry for me. That was a great treat. He turned me on to Sterling. He made me appreciate Sterling strongly. To me Sterling was the epitome of Romanticism which strongly influenced my style of Romanticism.

I know you are just finishing up a piece of work which will list many of the areas of information on Smith and that it took quite a bit of work. Did Smith have any influence on you in the creative sense?

Smith was an impetus. He most definitely was a 'Master' for me. and I felt no reason to resist this force. I knew I would have to be a disciple in a way of him. But specifically Spenser caused me to do my creative writing. He spurred the fantasy. Smith spurred me into doing more scholarly writing. I would like to add also that there is a person still living today who had a great influence on me. Fritz Leiber. I have a tremendous respect for him. He helped on the technical aspects of writing and giving me more of a balance as a writer. I find that I appreciate more of his own writings the older I get.

In the many years in the field of Fantasy Literature, do you see anything happening for the good/bad for this area today?

Of course, now a lot of 'old timers' in the field are getting the recognition they so deserve and are coming into their own. Really fine people, fine writers who have struggled in the salt mines. I am very encouraged because a lot more people are reading fantasy and getting more of an identity with it. Instead of the old concepts needed for security. It seems we are a 'How To' species that cannot operate without prior instruction. I really enjoy reading today's fanzines. There are so many good ones that I cannot tell them from the pro magazines. I have more sympathies for those who put together fanzines. I put more energy into those when I write for them. I would like to say there are a lot of real geniuses around such as Richard Tierney. Most of his sonnets are unpublished except for a few in some publications such as *Nyctalops*. He continues with real depth Lovecraft's style or tradition.

During the past summer you did some readings for a program called Arkham House Theatre on the radio station KERS and plan on doing more this Fall. It had tremendous acceptance. Most of the readings were from Clark Ashton Smith's works. Was any certain one your favorite and why?

I enjoyed certain readings. Some I enjoyed over others because it is where my head is at. I would say 'Xeethra,' Xeethra is really sublime. I have read 'Xeethra' myself several times. 1 find that I can always read it and get something from it. Many of my young friends across the nation today can relate with him [Xeethra] and pick up on him.

Why do you think the young people of today can still relate with that tale?

They are stirred by the emotion. Smith shows some transcendent vision of some kind. Of course. I do have a personal attachment to it as well. Smith read it for me the second time I was with him. But, I too relate to Xeethra and his tale.

How would you describe Donald Sidney-Fryer, the Romanticist?

Romanticism goes way back. It begins in the modern sense in the high Middle Ages and the songs of the troubadours. I have done a considerable amount of research as well as also studying their physical practices. I relate to being one of those troubadours in a sense. Wouldn't it be thrilling to find out what was considered 'romantic' by those people in that period? And, try to get into their frame of reference. It can be a magical experience.

As always, time passed too quickly, and the interview ended. There is a fine line between the performer/artist and the everyday man. But, there is no "everyday" man. Donald stated that the late George Sterling was the epitome of Romanticism. Well, Donald Sidney-Fryer is the living epitome of Romantic Fantasy today, a fine person, and a man I can call a friend.

Rick Kleffel

When did you become interested in the literature of the fantastic?

I've always been interested in fantastic stories, but it wasn't until I was in the service and thanks to the well-provisioned library—this was in the U.S. Marine Air Base in Opa-Loka, Florida—and the library there, some librarian had purchased a number of titles from Arkham House and also [August] Derleth's anthologies of science fiction and his anthologies of supernatural horror. To me, they were all fantastic stories. This was in the mid-fifties in the middle of the Cold War, and these stories provided another dimension, to which I could find an alternate reality, or escape. Especially, first discovering [H. P.] Lovecraft, then [Clark Ashton] Smith, and then [Robert E.] Howard, sort of altered my life in a positive way.

I was in the service, and thanks to the wonderful Acres of Books that used to exist in Long Beach, you could still get a good number of Arkham house titles—of course, this was back then—for not much more than they were originally sold for. So I got copies of *Genius Loci The Dark Chateau, Dark of the Moon,* which was a Derleth anthology of the poetry of the fantastic, *Lost Worlds,* and *Out of Space and Time.* Strangely enough, I liked the stuff a lot, but I didn't read it at once, I just dipped into it.

It wasn't until the spring of 1958 when I got copies of [Clark Ashton] Smith's earliest poetry collections, 1912, 1922, and 1925, *The Star Treader, Ebony and Crystal,* and *Sandalwood.* Of course, I was no stranger to poetry, but Smith's stuff is unique. It isn't just fantastic, but he is always concerned with the larger question, in this case of course following in the footsteps of Sterling, very much concerned with the cosmos, and what I call "the cosmic astronomic." I just sent out a want list to The Antiquarian Booksellers' Association of America in the Bay Area, and I managed to pick up copies of his early collection for very little. It wasn't until 1960 that I memorized somewhere between one-third and one-half of *Ebony and Crystal,* which rather changed my consciousness. That spring of 1960 I had decided to compile a major bibliography of his work.

When did you meet Clark Ashton Smith?

I met him twice, in August of 1958 and September of 1959. When I first went to Auburn, I wanted to look Smith up . . . when I showed up on his doorstep in Pacific Grove, he was quite gracious and invited me in. I visited him several days in a row and then I came back that following September. It was Labor Day Weekend, there was no place to be found, so Clark and his wife Carol invited me to stay with them. I cleaned his kitchen ceiling with a bucket of warm water and vinegar. Meanwhile, Clark and I were having literary discussions. He was a man, by the way, of profound erudition. Quite frankly, I don't think I would have written had I not met Smith's writings and then met him.

He was born in the late 1800s, at the end of the so-called Romantic Century, so of course Smith is a Romanticist in that narrow sense. Of course he's much more than that. I think that had for me, a potent charm. At that time, I presumably knew very little of the major revolution caused by, first of all Walt Whitman, then T. S. Eliot and Ezra Pound and Harriet Monroe of *Poetry* magazine in Chicago. However, as you know, we are not all locked into the same step, the same march, some of us do march to a slightly different drummer. The more I got to know Smith and his work, the more I respected him for being a survival from another period. But his thought was always so amazing and futuristic.

Could you talk about Ambrose Bierce? You edited some collections of his work.

I'm less interested in his satiric stuff and more interested in his fantastic stuff. His style as a storyteller has been very well presented and summed up by Lovecraft in his *Supernatural Horror in Literature.* He uses a very simple plain style. Bierce himself loved an elaborate style, even though he did not write that way. Evidently, *The Arabian Nights* was some of his favorite fiction. When I did an anthology of his hundred best poems, I was guided somewhat by what Sterling said of his serious stuff, so ended up cutting the volume down, from a hundred to fifty. The volume succeeded and it correlates with some of his better fiction. There is a quality in Bierce, that Fritz Leiber, who was a very good critic, summed up very effectively when he said, "Bierce—the man with a phallus of ice." In other words he's going to fuck you over in some way. When I first discovered Bierce, in the service, it was so potent that was all I read for two weeks and then I just had to stop reading him. He's certainly an original figure.

The reason he wrote the way he did, was he was in the Civil War, and took part in some of the worst battles. There's hardly a major battle that he missed, and he rose to be a major from being an enlisted man. After going through that, he had no illusions about humanity.

He strikes me as being a precursor of Rod Serling's *The Twilight Zone.*

Oh yes, *An Occurrence at Owl Creek Bridge.* That was made for Serling's format. It captures Bierce, he goes through all this and it's only in his mind. He's going to be hanged which is not a very nice death.

Talk about Smith's enduring legacy for the fantastic, in both his prose and poetry.

Well, I cover all this in *The Sorcerer Departs.* Fortunately, I came off of eight years of French language and literature, so I knew in terms of form that Smith had far more in common with European writers, the Symbolists, the Romantics, but at the same time, he's very different from them. The tone is very different. Smith, because of his fascination with the cosmos, is always trying to evoke for the reader, the sense of the absolute. He shares this with Bierce; there is this stark quality, uncompromising, and that certainly shows up in much of his poetry and also in his stories. It seems like you're surrounded by this world of great beauty; maybe it's an illusion, and the next thing you know, it's like a film that's been edited and all of a sudden you're in a desert and all alone . . . maybe lonely.

About your performances: how do you choose the material and how it inspires your own work?

I started performing during the "hippie" period, which seems strange because in one way some of the stuff I was doing seemed to be the essence of that which is academic. I perform whole parts from *The Faerie Queene;* not that much because each canto takes about an hour if you read it or recite it aloud. I'm not trying to become well-known. I'm trying to use my energy to make other poets, such as Smith, better known. The academics I came to know were wonderfully open. Spenser was a classic, but I wasn't presenting him that way, I was presenting him as something alive. And there's a lot of very humorous things in Spenser and by performing them I brought them out. Spenser made me a poet; Smith was too perfect. After reading Spenser, I was able to create some new forms, which had never existed. Smith says somewhere that, "the forms and themes of poetry do not become outworn or exhausted; the exhaustion is in the individual poets." I basically agree with that, except at the same time, all poets have a right to experiment and to innovate.

Could you tell us about the instrument you play?

It's a bass lute of a special design. For that reason I usually use a little amp with it so I can make the lute at least as loud as my voice. We use guitar strings, apart from the bass strings, which I get from Germany: they're specially made. The overall case is about four feet. It has a very large body. What's remarkable about it, because it has a rounded back, it has peculiarities of tone, so even though I don't have an electric axe, there's a great variety of tone I can evoke, by playing at the bridge, which is a harder sound, so-called metallic, and playing it in different places. However, if I'm using it to accompany the poetry, the music is there to support the poetry, not the poetry supporting the music.

What is your place in the world of fantasy fiction, and the place of poetry in the world of fantasy fiction?

I'm trying to give voice to those people who aren't here, who did not have the benefit, for a variety of reasons, of access to an audience in the way that I do. Especially Smith, Smith was unfortunately a rather retiring person, but his poetry demands that you be vehement at times. Even though there are parts of Smith that seem relatively easy to read, it's tricky, especially with the polysyllabics. You have to be very careful. *The Hashish-Eater* is a very difficult poem to project, because it is so strong a poem in places, the temptation is to shout it. I tried that once and I ended up with no voice. I discovered parts of my vocal apparatus that I had not ever known to exist because I needed to use them. It is an exhausting poem to perform; it's exhilarating, but then one of the reasons I wanted to record it was that I wanted to hear it without having to read it aloud.

We speak the language, the words of dead people. Without the dead people, we aren't here. Most people don't look at it like that. We're all brand-new, and we've got these nifty new automobiles and nifty new computers, and in one sense, it's frosting on the cake. There's not one piece of technology out there that wasn't already in use in some way, somewhere else, long ago.

Darrell Schweitzer

[The three volumes of Donald Sidney-Fryer's *Songs and Sonnets Atlantean* have recently been reprinted by Hippocampus Press as *The Atlantis Fragments*. This interview was conducted at the World Fantasy Convention, San Jose, California, October 31, 2009.]

You're one of the few people in our field to be, basically, a professional poet. Is this what you started out to do, or just how things worked out?

I have written some fiction. I never liked it. My poetry grew out of a background I extrapolated from Plato's Atlantis, those two dialogues, the *Critias* and the *Timaeus*. But I never wrote the novel until 2008-09, starting February 2008 and finishing February 2009. So I finally did it, and I am glad I waited, because, quite frankly, had I written it earlier, I would have made it too long, too elaborate, and ponderous. But I did manage to do it. I was just concentrating on the story with enough texture to make it seem real. Now I am subjecting it to a variety of readers, highly selected, to get their reaction. I'm pleased with it as the author. But does it communicate anything of significance to others?

I also wonder how much you consciously placed yourself in the tradition of northern California romantic poetry, of the sort for which you have been a lifelong advocate. Did you discover this school later, like discovering a root to what you were doing, or were you always aware of it?

I discovered Clark Ashton Smith's poetry in the spring of 1958, when I quit UCLA for a semester. I had the leisure and the money to find his collections, among others, thinking I was going to be collecting these early poetry collections by a bunch of Arkham House authors, but none of them came up to his high standards. But it wasn't until the summer of 1960, when I memorized about a third to one-half of Ashton Smith's *Ebony and Crystal,* that I suddenly gained a much better appreciation of his depth and range. Then the Leibers, Fritz and Jonquil, urged me to read Spenser's epic, *The Faerie Queene.* Another friend in Auburn had also urged me. He said that it reads better than Scripture. This all took place during 1960–61.

It was probably that reading of Spenser, that experience, that made me into a poet. It also alerted me to forms that I thought would be useful. So I get my forms from Spenser, and I have created a new sonnet form from one of Spenser's own. As you know, the Shakespearean has three quatrains and a final couplet. In Spenser's form, they interlink by rhyme. I noticed, because I was using the form, that the first nine lines of what I was creating became a stanza, a Spenserian stanza. Then the next three lines, the tercet, naturally detached itself and then came the couplet. I had already considered separating the couplet from the rest of it and treating it like a separate verse-paragraph. Many people today think that the discussion of form is arcane. In the Middle Ages, however, discovering a new form would have excited French poets everywhere, whether the troubadours in the south of France or the *trouvères* in the north.

It seems to me that we just live in a less poetic age now. Most people don't seem to read poetry. Would you agree?

Yes and no. I think people find it in other places. A lot of the early rock lyrics are full of poetry, the way they interact with the music. Jefferson Airplane, Quicksilver Messenger Service, or the Grateful Dead, certainly. People get it from popular song, and now from rap, which *is* a kind of poetry, willy-nilly. Also, they get it from such wonderfully written prose works by Peter Matthiessen, which are very evocative. Or Rachel Carson, who wrote very simply but very beautifully. I think that people find poetry where they find it, without it necessarily being formal poetry, however you define it, whether traditional form or free verse or free form. As you know, because you've done all sorts of poetry yourself in various styles, none of it is free. [Laughs.]

Do you think that English language poetry jumped the rails some-
where in the twentieth century and lost its audience?

No. Let me say something. This is very important. It is true that
we are probably the leading nation on the planet right now. We're
king of the mountain. There are something like over 300 million
Americans. However, the British Commonwealth comprises some-
thing over one billion people, and most of them speak English. Tradi-
tional poetry written in traditional form is not regarded in that world
as unmodern. For example, John Betjeman, not so long ago, was a
very popular poet. There's A. D. Hope down in Australia, who writes
with meter and rhyme, and very well, I must say. So this business that,
just because you don't write like Walt Whitman, you're not modern
is complete nonsense.

As you know because you've done both, using meter and rhyme is
not easy, to make it work, because unlike free verse or free form
sometimes, it's glaring if it is imperfect.

What I am noticing is that poetry is a hard sell. You long for the days
in which someone like Longfellow would really be read by the public.

There are comparable people. You know Dana Gioia did an awful
lot, probably the best thing of the eight years under Bush and Chen-
ey. He is the leading New Formalist. The New Formalists are this
group of poets who write directly out of their lives, contemporary
events, but they use meter and rhyme, and they use blank verse, and
they do it very well. Gioia has often said that poetry that sells two or
three thousand copies, that's a fairly big sale. He was not referring to a
phenomenon like Rod McKuen, whose poetry is more like lyrics—but
by itself it seems lacking. That's my own opinion. I don't envy Rod
McKuen. I don't want to be like him. [Laughs.]

Why does fantasy work so well in poetry?

That's interesting, that term "fantastic poetry." Most poetry until
very recently has always been highly imaginative. It is often a form of
fiction. Even if it depicts something that is supposed to have hap-
pened, it's been; *shaped.* So, where does the fantasy come in, and

where doesn't it? There is a lot of poetry that, without being overly fantastic, is very imaginative. I mean, *Paradise Lost* ... Ignore the theology. It's a huge fantasy. Most of Shakespeare's plays are historical *fantasies*. Yet they have become our concept of Julius Caesar, Macbeth, King Lear—the subject given doesn't exist for us, really, before Shakespeare.

Getting back to writers closer to us in time—did you ever meet Clark Ashton Smith?

I met him twice, toward the end of the summer of '58 and the summer of '59. I had already met some of his friends in Auburn, and it was through their auspices that I got to meet him.

What do you remember about him?

By that time he had rather aptly become a Buddhist.

L. Sprague de Camp visited him once, and de Camp was reminded of an extinct volcano. But Smith was ... I don't know if I want to use the word shy. Diffident? He didn't particularly like appearing in public. He had lived most of his life in the countryside. He was a retiring person. Bur if you look at some of his poetry, it demands to be shouted out. He wasn't going to shout. Some of his friends mentioned it to him, that he should be more vehement in reciting his poetry to friends. To do his poetry justice, I have performed and recorded a number of times "The Hashish-Eater." That is an absolutely exhausting poem to project because you have to get into the emotion that is projected in those verses. It's tricky, besides, what with the polysyllabic adjectives. You have to really watch what you're doing. Actually I think it should be done by a whole team of people with voices like James Earl Jones!

Thar might make him more popular. The conventional poetry world, as far as I can tell, has not yet discovered Smith. Certainly when I was in college, the professors had never heard of him.

I've discussed this problem with Dr. William Farmer, who now lives in Corpus Christi, but he grew up in Auburn and got to be particularly close to Smith in the last three or four years of Smith's life. His attitude is that the people who discover Smith deserve to do so.

That's an interesting way of looking at it, but I think there are many people who would enjoy his work, even though, philosophically, Smith is very much against the grain: he is very much the specter at the feast. He reminds you of unpleasant truths, that we are a tiny species living on a tiny planet in a tiny solar system, and the cosmos is unlimited and not necessarily that friendly toward us. That doesn't bother me, but it might bother some people.

We can give Smith credit for one thing. He is now well-known enough to make writers he associated with better known. I have to admit that I would never have heard of George Sterling without Clark Ashton Smith. Probably a couple generations ago it would be the other way around, but nor now.

Ambrose Bierce was a mentor to Sterling. Sterling was a mentor to Smith. Now Nora May French was not influenced by them. Her main models were Tennyson and Housman. But there were others in this group. For example, Herman Scheffauer. It depends on how wide you want to make the group or how large. Bierce, of course, is known. That's not a problem. By the way, in their dedication to what they perceive as the truth, Bierce and Smith have a lot in common. They don't compromise. They're going to give you the unpleasant news whether you want it or not. But I do think that eventually Smith's going to carry the whole group.

How much to you think your work is influenced by Smith?

My work is influenced a great deal in a way, but, had I not read *The Faerie Queene,* I would not have become a poet. And I'm not the first of those many poets who have been influenced by Spenser. It begins with his own time. There was "The Shepherd's Calendar," about 1580. That was a very experimental work, but it took the work of his maturity, *The Faerie Queene,* to have even greater influence on everybody, technically. Marlowe got Spenser's sense of melody into blank verse, and Shakespeare in turn was influenced by Marlowe, and of course he certainly would have read Spenser, who was universally considered the great poet of the day, that is, in Britain. But there's hardly a great poet in English since who has not been influenced by Spenser. Milton was very much influenced. If that's not so true in our own times, it's neither here nor there; bur Archibald MacLeish in the preface to one of his collections says that in rereading poets, he preferred to reread Spenser because of his exceptional depth and variety.

Also I realized that I had to do something original in regard to form, because if you're going to spend all that time using meter and rhyme, you'd better make sure you have a good theoretical model. Otherwise you're wasting your time. One great thing about the abandonment of traditional form among many American poets is that at least they are not repeating all the tired use of the same phrases, the same limited rhymes—you know: *love, above,* and *of.*

Or *moon, spoon, and June.*

Yes. Right. The beauty of strict form at its best is that it makes the language more incisive. Also, in my case, when I rediscovered English through Spenser, I had just finished eight years of study in French language and literature. Actually, I studied the extant literature from Charlemagne onward, although the language of his time wasn't really French quite yet. But by the time of the jongleur Rutebeuf, the 1200s, and then, of course, of François Villon, the 1400s, poetry that we can call modern in certain respects is in full flower. My favorite of this period, the late Middle Ages, is Charles d'Orleans, the one who lived in captivity for 25 years in England. Then come the great poets of the French Renaissance, Clément Marot, Louise Labé, and then, above all, the Pléiade, Ronsard, du Bellay, and all the rest. Next come the great poets of the 1800s, not only Victor Hugo, the greatest of them all, but Théophile Gautier and the Parnassians headed by Leconte de Lisle and José-Maria de Heredia. Thus all of that had an influence on me. It is through these poets that I approach poetics in English, poetics influenced by the long tradition of French prosody. Also, I can read poetry and literature in other languages besides French.

Is the effect of that to make you aware of the particular way that English works?

Yes, it did, because it made me more conscious in a way I might not have been. It gave me critical tools I might not have had. I don't want to be restricted just to English language poetry, as marvelous as it is. I can read Heine, somewhat, in German. I can read Goethe, a limited amount. I've studied Italian. I can read with relative facility Spanish, which has some of the greatest poetry. I can read stuff in Portuguese, though I don't know it in the same way as I do French. Also, I am part French.

Have you ever actually composed poetry in French?

Just a little bit. Smith did it very well, and he also wrote very well in Spanish. These languages don't all work the same way. For example, blank verse in Italian does not have the same effect as blank verse in English. In Italian, it's "blind verses," they call them. *Versi sciolti.*

Is it—?

There's no rhyme.

Like in Latin where all the words have the same endings anyway?

Not quite, but close. I was just reminded today. A beautiful woman was speaking to me. She was a poet who had come over here from Paris, and she was quoting me some beautiful stuff from the *Aeneid.* I had four years of Latin in high school and we read Caesar, Cicero, and Virgil. We had to translate the first six books of the *Aeneid.* She recited her selection beautifully, with; real feeling for the meter, a feeling that I had forgotten. It's been something like 50 years since l read Latin in any amount or depth.

One doesn't like to predict one's own legacy, but inevitably we think about it, so do you think Smith will carry you along too? Will you be seen as a follower of the school of Smith?

Yes, it's possible. Who knows what the future will hold. I don't know. I am glad that I woke up to his value long before anybody else seemed to have done. But the value was there all along. It wasn't until Jack Chalker edited the *In Memoriam* that I wrote something. I made it too long and had to cut it down—Jack was very dubious about some aspects of it, but he printed it and later said that my essay caused the biggest surprise. So many people just don't have the background to appreciate what Smith was doing.

What background does one need to really appreciate Smith?

You have to have a fairly large vocabulary. I had no problem with his vocabulary, but I saw words being used that I'd never seen before being used the way he used them. Obvious examples, although not fashionable now: magisterial, supernal, ineffable . . . but I knew all those words from Latin, ineffabilus, ineffable. I had no problem. But, again, it was thrilling to me to see him using these kinds of words, and he was using them exactly, dead-center on, in terms of meaning. If you don't know the word, then you look it up. It resonates in the given space. And I don't know anybody but Smith who uses a word like "burglarious" referring to a burglar, or to jars as "abdominous."

In Smith's case, the man of genius is at the mercy of people who don't have his knowledge. So they don't understand either the depth or the range.

What do you think about deliberately using rare words in poetry, as opposed to writing simply?

Some rare words are the only words to use. By the way, they aren't so difficult. In other European languages they tend to be almost the same word, unless it's an Anglo-Saxon word or a Celtic one. But they exist in a variety of languages. Anything from Greek or Latin, you're not going to have any real problem. In the Romantic languages, as you know, Latin grammarians were borrowing wholesale from Greek literature and language.

I find that the problem I have with some Smith poems is that if I have to stop and look up a word, then it's like reading a translation. It loses spontaneity.

I never have had that problem.

I find that if I just read it through, there are in effect lacunae in the text. If I stop and look everything up, then I have to reconstruct the poem mentally, and work up to an understanding of it. Possibly a lot of readers lack that kind of patience.

I've never had that problem. For example, this is very simple. He uses words deliberately in certain versions for emphasis:

Colours, and gleams, and glamours unrecalled,
Richly thy petals intricate revive:
Blossom, whose roots are in Eternity,
The faithful soul, the sentience darkly thralled,

> In dream and wonder, evermore shall strive
> At Edens lost of time and memory.

That's pretty clear for poetry of some substance.

Also, this business about inversions, which most careful poets avoid today. Inversions are native to the Germanic languages. Sometimes you want an indirect mode. Look how, in *Paradise Lost,* at the very beginning, Milton doesn't directly launch into what he's doing. He has sort of a negative catalogue and then he finally says *Sing, heavenly muse.* Sometimes one does use an inversion. You want that, for emphasis. Does everything always have to be *Cat sees rat; rat sees cat?*

However, yes, a real imperfection in something written in traditional form does show up very easily.

Have you made a deliberate attempt to pass on the tradition by inspiring other poets?

I am in a position to encourage many writers of different types. If they seem to know what they are doing, I'll say, "Hey, you're doing it okay. Just continue." But unless you really know what you're doing, don't try using meter, rhyme, and all that stuff. Just write something in free verse and see how that comes out. Or if they want to write something formal, I say, okay, write a Shakespearean or Elizabethan sonnet, because you have three quatrains, not linked by rhyme among them, and a couplet. There are a lot of good examples of that sonnet form.

It's like people who try to convert other people to their religion and then do just the opposite of what they preach. Thus it's the same way with poetry. Unless you are really called to doing it, don't do it.

If we're going to have something on the level of pleasant jingles, intended for children, *A Child's Garden of Verses* is an exquisite thing. That's done very well. Or the Mother Goose rhymes, as you know, mostly oblique political satires.

It may be a change in the culture, but our present-day political slogans are not going to survive for hundreds of years as nursery rhymes.

No, I don't think so. That's another thing. It is true that poetry can concern itself with anything it wishes to handle. At the same time, the last thing I want to read about in poetry is politics. We can't seem to escape from it, and the politicians.

I'm thinking specifically of the "Rock-a-Bye-Baby" rhyme having to do with Charles II in a tree.

I didn't know that.

A few years after his father was executed he tried to reclaim the throne and invaded England with an army. There was a battle, the Royalists were routed, and Charles spent a night in a tree, so the story goes, hiding from the Puritans. That's what they're making fun of in the song, with the cradle rocking, falling, etc. It's about the king and his supposedly imminent downfall.

You know the *Little Jack Horner sat in his corner,* etc. That refers to Henry VIII taking over the monasteries, because they were loaded with wealth. Otherwise these rhymes are given to children, aptly, it would seem, until you check the background. But why would I want to lay waste to my powers writing an epic about Cheney and Bush Jr.?

Short of mockery, maybe.

Yes, that.

This leads us to a serious question. Remember that Lovecraft wrote an essay called "What Belongs in Verse." What do you think belongs in verse?

Anything that can be made to fit, if the poet has the skill. I met a poet here [at the convention] on a panel. Her name is Rain Graves. Her book is called *Barfodder.* She's writing in bars, about seeming ne'er-do-wells, people who hang out in pubs and bars. It's great fun. There is a lot of nominally nasty stuff, but it's presented in such a way that it's not unpleasant. It makes you laugh. I feel like I've been there too, in those taverns.

Who are some of your other current favorites?.

Some of my favorite poets, hmm . . . I am always rereading the French poets of the Renaissance and also the Parnassians. They are technically just about perfect. Leconte de Lisle was head of that group. Although some of these poets I had read in school; but also I read them on my own, which is a totally different matter. They're all worth reading. Leconte de Lisle reminds me in some respects of Smith. Smith is only a more imaginative Parnassian.

Are you done with Atlantis now that the big omnibus from Hippo-campus Press has appeared?

Apart from trying to find a publisher for the related Atlantis novel, more or less.

The novel is an Atlantis novel?

Yes, it is. The poetry grew out of the background I had created for the novel, but I didn't write the novel until within the last few years. Obviously Atlantis is a metaphor for me. People ask, "Do you believe in Atlantis?" I do believe in it. I respond, "At least metaphorically." It has real emotions attached to it.

After that, maybe I will be doing something else. Maybe I will concern myself with census returns. [Laughs]

But will they rhyme? Thank you, Don.

An Addendum by Donald Sidney-Fryer

If the powers that be should permit a humble codicil to Darrell Schweitzer's amicable and astute interview, I would like to add a few more words about my writing output than what emerged in the consultation between interviewer and interviewee. First, before going back to *The Atlantis Fragments,* I should mention the companion piece to my magnum opus in poetry and fantastic imagination. Albeit not yet published, my magnum opus in prose remains my most considerable and sustained piece of work, a monumental history of theatrical dance (mostly concerned with the typical narrative ballets of the 1800s, whether in the Italian or French style), constructed around the long and rather amazing career of the Italian composer Cesare Pugni (1802–1870), who wrote or adapted music to order for an unprecedented number of dance productions from about 1820 until his death in 1870. He collaborated with some of the best ballet-masters of his time during his active professional career. But the story continues after his death up through the first season or so of Diaghilev's Ballets Russes and concerns itself with the critical issues from the mid-1800s to the present.

Comprising more than 5,000 regular double-spaced typescript pages, divided into four main parts, and gathered into two massive tomes, this opus is *The Case of the Light Fantastic Toe* (otherwise *The Romantic Ballet and Signor Maestro Cesare Pugni, as well as their survival by means of Tsarist Russia: a Chronicle and source book*). The aficionado of science fiction or fantasy might well ask how such a monograph connects with developments in the tradition of science fiction or fantasy. It connects directly. The ballet theatre of the 1800s became the chief provider of often sensational fantasy on the stage, as was realized through flesh-and-blood performers dancing and miming their way before opera-house audiences throughout Europe. Luigi Manziotti concocted lavish spectacles in Milan that might pass as a species of science fiction, and one in particular, *Excelsior* (1881), as "a kind of Jules Verne ballet" (in Cyril Beaumont's accurate phrase).

The monograph supplies, in one form or fashion, the plots of most of the dance dramas under discussion from the early 1820s in Italy up through the early career of Michel Fokine (1905–08) in St. Petersburg. With Pugni's career and its aftermath providing the overall narrative frame, the ballet plots furnish the lesser narratives, often of bewildering variety, and seldom other than fantastic in subject matter, given the Romantic Ballet that began in 1831–32 and that found rebirth of a kind in Diaghilev's Ballets Russes. The structure of the monograph rather resembles that of *The Arabian Nights,* that of stories within stories but arranged within the unifying narrative frame afforded by Scheherazade as the storyteller.

The monograph's compiler or composer presents this history in both depth and in detail, richly supported by contemporary reviews, later historical texts but of the same period, and other sources. Constructed on a scale comparable to Edward Gibbon's masterpiece *The Decline and Fall of the Roman Empire,* the history forms overall an extraordinary assemblage of material, much of it translated from Italian, French, German, and Russian, even if the compiler had to rehandle the English to bring it into accord with formal nineteenth-century language. The compiler put it all together from Autumn 1980 through Autumn 1999—yes, twenty years in all—but the earliest research conducted for it goes back to the mid-1950s. The young ballet-dance-historian Adam Lopez (Tulsa, Oklahoma) is currently editing and supplementing the overall ms., transferring it to electronic files.

All together then, this opus constitutes one grand and unique aesthetic adventure.

But now let me turn back to *The Atlantis Fragments*—from one type of fantasy to another! Even if I remain quite grateful to the general approval in the field of fantasy and science fiction that has greeted the three successive series of *Songs and Sonnets Atlantean* (1971, 2003, 2005)—whether warm personal reactions or generous published reviews—it would seem that only a very few people, above all the late Professor Charles Wolfe of Middle Tennessee State University outside Nashville, understood what I was trying to achieve with my synergistic method, my novel mixture of poetic text and concluding body of notes both factual and fictional, as revealed in each successive installment.

Using the innovative apparatus of what appears in each case as no more than a miscellaneous collection, the overall project unfurled as a kind of allegory about nature, a kind of extended ecological metaphor of our planet Earth. More narrowly, it is also a myth about poetry, traditional and nontraditional, but above all else it is a myth of and for our present world. In this triple myth (allegory is nothing if not mythopoeic), we as the dominant species equate with both Atlantis and the Great Cataclysm all rolled into one, given our ever-expanding human population, the succeeding destruction or transformation of the planet, and the destruction of at least half of the other species, going forward at the present moment.

However, when the first series appeared in June 1971, while I knew that I had accomplished something unique, it required Professor Wolfe (as one of the original subscribers, that is, as one who ordered a copy from Arkham House in advance) to give me a clearer concept of what I had actually done. He wrote to tell me just what shape that something unique had assumed, to wit, a kind of synergism. According to the late, great professor, this was the projection of ancient myth through a series of short lyrics with accompanying notes to explain and extend various points and issues recondite and otherwise.

In general terms, only without the apparatus of notes, this also equates with what Spenser, although different in kind, achieves with *The Faerie Queene* (1590, 1596, 1609) in overall structural terms or what Clark Ashton Smith does in *Ebony and Crystal* (1922). Again, this is the projection of epic myth (or epic vision, for the most part) by means of a series of lyrics, with the major difference in Spenser's case being that *The Faerie Queene* represents a highly organized opus in strict formal presentation, divided into books, cantos, and stanzas, each Spenserian stanza being thus a brief but sufficient lyric.

In this way, I went from Ashton Smith, as the fount of inexhaustible fantasy at the end of a great poetic tradition, all the way back to Spenser, not just as the same (the end of both English medieval and English Renaissance) but as the original source of poetry and imagination during the Elizabethan Age, the apogee of the belated English Renaissance. Furthermore, as part of that largely fictional projection, I took on the task of reviving the Spenserian stanza, but mostly by itself (that is, in terms of a solitary lyric) as a vehicle for lyric expression, something rarely attempted before.

I also took on the task of expressly creating or inventing a new "triplicate" sonnet form, based equally upon the Spenserian stanza and the Spenserian sonnet, consisting of three parts, a Spenserian stanza, an intervening tercet, and a final couplet (or in some instances, a final quatrain). Because of the interlocking rhymes the Spenserian sonnet is not the easiest form to negotiate. I made this choice to invent and use this new sonnet form, not just for its novelty, to impart a certain freshness, but as a conscious gesture of poetic style, both in terms of what was appropriate to the subject matter and in terms of old-fashioned aesthetics. Thus this apparent restatement of nominally Ashton-Smith poetic substance, as combined with Spenserian form and sensibility, does in fact result in something new, something original, all of it in order to give the subject matter, the "message" (if you will), a much-needed pristineliness.

For Lin Carter

(In memoriam.)

To you who viewed so much with pristine vision,
Who also called attention and acclaim,
Who saved them from neglect and from derision,
To many names out from forgotten fame,
And rescued all of them from any blame,
To you we give our heartfelt thanks in turn,
And seek to save your name in turn from shame,
To bring it back like ashes from an urn,
To make it with a deeper flame a little while to burn.

Your constant and more brilliant light has long since lit our route,
And thanks to your clairvoyance how much more can we discern
As we go down our path as if with trumpet, drum, and flute.

You leave a gate, a beacon, and an open sesame,
A key for unknown land, for unknown sky, for unknown sea.

Have we already forgotten so soon Lin Carter, and how much we
devotees shall always owe him, shall be in fact indebted to him, for all
that he has done (and continues to do posthumously) for our field of
fantasy and science fiction, for science fantasy? I, Donald Sidney-
Fryer, as one poet, author, aficionado, and critic, have not forgotten.
Nor the many astute and fascinating discussions I had with the late
great Fritz Leiber, that doyen of fantasy and science-fiction writers, as
the successive paperbacks in the Adult Fantasy Series (with the little
logo of the unicorn's head tucked away in one corner of the covers)
began to appear from Ballantine Books, and continued to appear, for
quite some little time (a decade or more), starting in the early 1970s
(or maybe a little earlier), if memory serves, and helping to lead to the
first three World Fantasy Conventions (initially fomented and bank-
rolled by literary agent and connoisseur Kirby McCauley), which took
place in Providence, New York City, and Los Angeles, a significant

threesome of cities, indeed: the magic number three: during 1976, 1977, and 1978, respectively.

When the first title in the series appeared, I was working in some public baths on 21st Street in the Mission District of San Francisco (where I resided c. 1965–1975)—the said baths aptly called the 21st Street Baths—that first title was *The Three Imposters* by Arthur Machen (a name already sacred for me). How thrilled I was when I walked east a very short distance from the baths to the northeast corner of the intersection at 21st and Mission Streets, where the local cigar store sold variegated merchandise, not only tobacco products but also sundries, including paperbacks on tall revolving circular display racks. The store carried the current paperbacks or pocket books (pocket pool, anyone?), and voilà! There it was that I discovered that first title and all those following. What a delectable find!

I had already met Lin Carter in person at one or more f. and s.f. conventions in Northern California, and had become just as impressed with him in person as I already had in print, that is, as a writer and editor. Lin was a trim, handsome, and medium-sized gentleman with a small trim beard and moustache such as I have worn myself lo these many years. As I recall, we had a number of significant conversations, during which inter alia I reminded Lin that modern fantasy went back in time at least no later than the renaissance, no later than the latter 1500s to the reign of Elizabeth I of England, no less than to her poet laureate Edmund Spenser and his unfinished epic poem *The Faerie Queene* (1590, 1596, 1609).

Lin conceded my point but established his own, that what he meant was the most recent efflorescence of modern imaginative fiction (of course, in prose) that went back no further than the latter 1800s, to such notable authors as William Morris, Arthur Machen, Violet Paget, A. Conan Doyle, and so forth. I realized his point, and concurred, no problem, amen!

The huge, mass-market success of the paperback edition, as furbished by Ballantine Books, of *The Lord of the Rings* by J. R. R. Tolkien, had led as directly as possible to Lin Carter pitching the idea of the Adult Fantasy Series to Ian and Betty Ballantine. It soon became a physical reality, as capably edited and introduced by Carter himself in the case of each volume. The series lasted quite a long time, and even if not quite as much of a success (speaking of sales) as the Tolkien trilogy, it led to the greater promulgation of many hitherto unknown or little known books and authors, not just the pivotal figure of H. P. Lovecraft but in particular of one C. Ashton Smith. During the early 1970s (aided by some striking art covers) three paperbacks as notably edited by Lin Carter appeared under Smith's name: *Zothique*, *Hyperborea*, and *Xiccarph*; it almost included *Averoigne* until Ballantine pulled the plug on the series overall, alas! But the fantasy series had served its original purpose very well. It brought renewed attention to many books and authors that had slipped into undeserved oblivion.

For me the success of the series, above all in regard to C. Ashton Smith, meant more, meant much more, than to most other aficionados. I had been waging a one-man crusade on behalf of C.A.S. and his *oeuvre* since the mid-1960s, since I had compiled a bibliography of his poetry and prose in the early part of that same decade, ready for publication during 1965. Don Grant in Rhode Island accepted it but waited until the latter 1970s to publish it, until C.A.S. had become somewhat better known. Finally Grant brought it out as *Emperor of Dreams: A Clark Ashton Smith Bibliography* in 1978. Meanwhile Arkham House (by this time Smith's regular publisher) had issued at long last Smith's poetry omnibus of *Selected Poems* in late 1971, the MS. of which the publisher had received in December 1949, but had also waited to publish it for some of the same reasons that Don Grant did anent my bibliography, not to mention monetary ones.

In response to the publication of the *Selected Poems*, plus the encouragement from the appearance and success of the three Ballantine paperbacks by C.A.S. in the early 1970s, I wrote a major article-review, quite an extended essay, about the poetry omnibus almost concomitantly with the paperbacks. Harry Morris accepted the essay, and published it under the aegis of his Silver Scarab Press as *The Last of the Great Romantic Poets* in 1973, and thus as a proper book or booklet. The book had an added importance inasmuch as it presented a major exposition of the Romance or Romantic tradition from the Middle Ages through the Renaissance, and then through the so-called Romantic Century of the 1800s, ending up with Ashton Smith, born in 1893, but also paying considerable respect to such associated figures like his poet-mentor George Sterling (1869–1926) and poet Nora May French (1881–1907), not to mention Sterling's own poet-mentor Ambrose Bierce (1842–1914).

For what Lin Carter achieved for Ashton Smith, not to forget the other authors and books—never mind the overall Romantic tradition (and that of modern f. and s.f.)—via the Adult Fantasy Series; I proffer this humble tribute. Quite apart from Lin Carter's own achievement as a very well informed editor, and general man of letters, he was an accomplished fictioneer, poet, critic, and literary historian. The field of fantasy and science fiction (and/or science fantasy) owes Lin Carter an enormous debt. Not only did Ballantine Books distribute the Adult Fantasy Series throughout the U.S., but the volumes also went out of the country and overseas (even if not promulgated that way by Ballantine directly). Thus the volumes also percolated into Canada, and in a sense throughout the commonality of the Anglophone world whether known as the British Empire or the British Commonwealth, even if not intentionally so by the original publisher. That is all a large order of achievement, which we owe to both Ballantine and to Lin Carter.

RANDOM LINES

Poems in Verse and Prose

To Rah Hoffman,
in memoriam.

Contents

RANDOM LINES

To S. T. Joshi

In honor of the occasion
of his sixtieth birthday.

A holy man of letters, and much more,
A scholar, a critic, a novelist,
A connoisseur and master of strange lore,
A genie bearing treasures in a cyst,
A pouch, as gathered by a dactylist,
A guru pointing out a wonderwork,
So much more than adroit, a daedalist,
A teacher pointing out with sword or dirk
A source of dazzling light amid the general mire and mirk:

And even more: a scribe, a scrivener, a scrivenist,
A monk in some scriptorium, a cleric, clark, or clerk,

Divine amanuensis, or amanuensisist!
Uncloistered monk, a copyist, who hath preserved the text,
Oh S. T., "St." or Saint Joshi: tell us what might come next!

To an Alchemist of Dreams

(For Michael Fantina.)

To you who are the wizard-bard of all,
Master of covert spells and incantations,
I say: you should have sung in some great hall.
Better than any ale or wine oblations,
Your cunning verses with their fascinations
Build more on art and insight than mere skill.
They serve in place of sacred revelations,
Or like your blooms of Nithon, they fulfill
Better by far than someone else's blossomings of ill:

Better or best by far than some poetic schemes,
Your song of songs, your songs of Solomon, distill
Our hunger for some cosmic alchemy of dreams:

Keen alchemist of reverie, dream on and on—
On past the realms of sunset . . . and on past the realms of dawn. . . .

Encomium

(For Gail Fryer Scannell,
on Mother's Day, Sunday, 13 May 2018.)

Today we have assembled here to hail
One who has given of herself to others
As artist and as person without fail,
Since we agree to celebrate our mothers,
We have become like sisters and like brothers,
United thus as one big family.
Whether as relatives, or alien others,
We must at least get on in amity,
So she our friend might hear some praise, beyond my homily.

Our mothers urge us to behave as kind and generous,
To live in brotherhood, or even yet, sorority—
Our lives would otherwise become too harsh and onerous.

So let us act like great good kids, and follow their advice,
And we perhaps might edge somewhat more near to paradise.

Supremely Difficult

During a federal investigation
A senator instructs: an answer need
Not be "a talismanic incantation."
That such a phrase on record should succeed
Astonishes! We would prefer to read
Not the record, but more, the talisman!
Much less the give and take of legal screed,
We would much rather con E. M. Cioran,
Than study any holy book, or Bible or Koran. . . .

He is in human form the antithesis of God,
His most insistent critic; but we must not ban
The Skeptic All Divine, the universal prod.

From such a mind or consciousness there can be no escape—
From such a smug, smart-ass, impossible, contrary ape!

Durn it all!

Enquiry

(as made from planet Moon)

For Dean Franklin Coffman II,
on going around the Sun seventy times.

How many times have all of us not been recycled
On planet Earth, or back again to Otherwhere,
As well as to the Other Side no less recycled?
When in so many forms and shapes, yet unaware
Of them as we might be—but then, why should we care?—
Except past lives or not, they all accumulate:
They all pile up to make us opt which way to fare,
To forge ahead, before we might think it too late,
As if in answer to some prompting that might seem like fate?

We ask this of you as the dean of sonneteers
The same way as we might perhaps interrogate
That other poet-bard, the dean of balladeers:

What can we do more than the mere rhetorical,
The existential?—which is our umbilical.

Whim-Wham, Whimsy, Whim

(1500, 1605, 1697)

A psychic residue from former times,
Perhaps a legacy, perhaps a gift,
In expiation of forgotten crimes?
With pen and ink—to sieve, to sift, to shift,
To waste no word or phrase, to use with thrift,
Alerted by some belfry's noontide chimes:
To not permit a pause, a break, a rift,
To write as "iffed," as if hieroglyphed,
To scribe, to shrive, to script, to shrift, to scriven swift!

Enticed by rose, by violet, by butterfly,
My Muse remains, it seems, eternally adrift
Beyond Parnassus—on some castles in the sky:

Castles with towers and battlements, fashioned of shade and cloud,
With gates and courts and corridors—where fiends and phantoms crowd.

On Visiting Edward Gorey's House

(Latter July 2018)

In Barnstable, on picturesque Cape Cod,
An artist lived by name of Edward Gorey,
A guy that some would think was rather odd.
Inside his house of one and one-half story,
His art was black and white, but seldom gory,
The simplest means remained his medium.
His art bestowed on him wealth, fame, and glory,
His gallows humor yet made no one glum—
Unless that one at worst were comatose, or ill, or numb.

His art made people laugh, reflect, and then relax,
Made them guffaw, or sing or dance, or om or hum—
It made them flexible, or tractable, and lax.

Such art of making laughter forms the greatest amphigory,
A miracle, a boon, conferred by Master Edward Gorey.

"A Talismanic Incantation"

"What if Kant had preferred the art of invocation
Over philosophy, the love of wisdom, that had held his awe?"

—Random enquiry.

Like any self-respecting bard,
When in mode incantaneous,
He would intone clear, clean, and hard.
Whether as miscellaneous,
Or yet as instantaneous,
He must in style discriminate.
He would not wax extraneous,
But rather differentiate,
With nicety, from one condition to another state.

With such "a talismanic incantation," oh!—
As poet laureate might I pontificate?—
With that kind of descanting, of enchaunting, ho?

Abjure philosophy as gibberish or cant,
And what is more, but worse, as fustian or as rant.

Wanderlust, Wonderlust, Wonderlost

On past the seacoast, out upon the main,
Let us fare one more time, but under sail,
To find some island-realm, yes once again!
A place of delectation or of dwale,
A site of sunshine and of swale,
A field of pasture, of calm pasturage:—
A fine expanse where gentle winds prevail,
A harbor-haven of safe anchorage,
A nest of lush and lavish verdancy, of greenest foliage:

A port of call for those adrift and lost in wonderment,
An island like Theleme of unassuming privilege,
A springboard to a vaster isle, a vaster continent:

Do we need Charon to traverse that main?
    What waterage, what water-rage?—
For people or for goods: yet once again
    Is death the only water-wage?

A Lone Complaint

(July–August 2018.)

So hot and humid, it would rudely try
The patience of a sinner, of a saint,
Of any ordinary gal or guy!
It makes me as an elder nearly faint,
As if I suffered underneath restraint,
Or feel as if at times I cannot breathe.
So, pardon me if I make due complaint,
One of the things I still can do with eathe,
While in my heart contrary feelings fight and seethe.

What tumult and what conflict still can rage here in my breast!
This ghastly, all-pervasive moisture does not help bequeathe
A greater calm inside this old and agitated chest.

Sometimes there is no other choice, thus no alternative,
To violent emotions, which is where sometimes we live.

Random Lines

As managers we think we are the best?
Can we see past a thing's own quiddity?
Are we still nothing further than a pest?
Vehicular exhaust, plus high humidity,
Impede our breath, no less the air's lucidity,
This carbon dioxide released upon our sphere.
What price then, this vehicular mobility?—
As we look out, on through the window bleak and bare!—
Is the end of our air, of us, how close is it, how near?

While we ride roughshod on our carefree, careless way,
For all the noxious gases in the atmosphere,
We as a foolish species, we have yet to pay!

Will this whole planet turn into our species' bier?—
We act not out of love, but only out of fear.

The Bird of Fire

He came upon the glade, the young muzhik,
Dazed by the flock of those bright birds of fire,
His ears caressed by some unknown musique:
Beyond the praise of bard or harp or lyre,
As if at risk from something dim or dire,
But irresistible, and multi-hued:
Like incense flames out from a funeral pyre,
As if with frankincense and myrrh endued,
As if with purple, silver, gold, and orichalch imbued.

Such blazing colors did those firebirds' gorgeous tails reveal,
And more splendiferous than any peacock's dazzling brood
In spite of their kaleidoscope, how loud they scream and squeal!

The muzhik, unobserved, yet stood both cool and calm,
Then bowed away, as if he had received a special balm.

Nightmare

Still on the edge of sleepy consciousness,
She had not yet plunged on into her dream,
Despite that threat not any more the less.
What was the threat? A nightmare quite extreme,
Where only gruesome panic ruled supreme,
And prisoners met death by spear and sword.
Unable to complain except by scream,
Their unresisting flesh stabbed, slashed, and gored,
The pitiful and harmless victims of some Golden Horde.

She fell asleep, she dreamed her dream, she woke up with a scream:
It would be better by bucolic vision to be bored,
Than to be struck with panic, by some nightmare all supreme.

She did not have that dream again, for quite a little while,
Unless her thoughts turned negative, contemptuous, or vile.

Turn On, Tune In, Drop Out

(A mantra for the dispossessed and those estranged.)

What could be more exotic than the lyre
With wooden or with ivory frame, and played
With plectrum on its heptachord of wire?
Except the lyrebird with its brave cockade,
Its lyre-shaped tail, when spread out unafraid,
One of the wonders of the Antipode.
A lordly male who makes no vain parade,
Surely this bird is worthy of an ode,
In solemn tones of rhapsody, in arch-poetic mode.

What would I not give to behold this thrice-resplendent bird—
Ensconced within, at freedom in, its nativist abode—
Perhaps a year out of my life, to see his feathered herd?

Is it a miracle, is it coincidence,
    that man and nature duplicate—
A sign of deity, a sign of providence,
    that things distinct can mix and mate?

High Altitude

(In homage to Daniel Merriam's painting
of the same name, 2005,
depicting a large-scale tree house.)

Far better still, up in an ivory tower,
And lodged amid the branches of some tree,
Built when Victoria waxed in amplest flower,
Squired by Prince Albert as her honeybee:
A kiosk-mansion raised as by decree,
Impeccable, exuberant, a bower—
A spot wherein to loiter, to be free,
A place to sojourn for a special hour
With turrets and with finials firm upon the central tower:

Please let me roam there at my will, with turrets underneath,
A place to linger and to rest, while free from any power,
A space for refuge, like some forest glade, some distant heath:

All hail in reverence to this tree house deluxe,
A fitting residence for humans and/or spooks.

Aislantis

Per common rumor, Iceland *was* Aislantis,
An ancient Atlantean pied-à-terre,
That formed part of the Empire of Atlantis:
A time and place both fortunate and fair
That might have pleased Rimbaud and Baudelaire,
Given their esoteric preference:
Volcanos, geysers, hot springs, noxious air,
As constant geographic reference,
Inspire a smart response, command a certain deference.

The landscape shapes and nurtures us, our culture's upward thrust,
But in a general sense, and in a not forever sense—
In turn we shape and nourish things, per our own taste or gust.

Might we go back once more to this Atlantis,
And to its giant pied-à-terre, Aislantis?

Apples from Eden

It was most likely the Persians during the Achaemenian dynasty who first formulated the concept of Paradise for us, probably even before the venerable Hebrews in their holy book, as a large protected garden, pristine and primordial, but clearly demarcated within palpable walls. A girdle of far-encircling walls with at least one gate, possibly more, for those who tended and managed the parklike space.

On one occasion my great and good friend had parked his medium-sized and four-door automobile next to an apple orchard somewhere within the inland Californian delta, just as we did a few years earlier next to a pear orchard in the same general ambiance. Only now, instead of accessing some sweet and golden pears, we were accosting some almost ripe apples.

We had emerged from the vehicle, and had each claimed a piece of fruit, meanwhile blessing whatever farmer had not forbidden us with a sign not to trespass upon his easily approachable groves of apple trees. Ripe or not quite, no other apples could have tasted more delectable and wine-like, crisp and crunchy. I have no idea as to what modern variety they belonged, and it does not matter in a strict sense. They were apples, and they tasted sublime.

Could any apples from a mythical Eden have tasted this good? Could not these apples emblematize or symbolize, as well as any, those of Paradise? These are but rhetorical questions, incapable of response, and only of expression.

A Modest Prince upon a Plinth

Field Marshal Prince Banurangsi Savangwonse, the Prince Banubandhu Vongsevoradej, a splendid black cast-metal statue on its plinth amid a public square in Bangkok.

A piece of paper with the name above, plus other data—souvenir of our half-dozen sojourns in Thailand with the Thai people! They had slipped from easy memory, the happy times that we spent there, whether in Bangkok, Ayutthaya, or Koh Samui, above all thanks to Stan Gayuski then at the resort that he managed, catering to refugees from the White Man's Universe.

What a handsome and hospitable people. "Welcome the strangers!" per King Mongkut, indeed! A wonderful culture somewhere between India (but without the caste system, luckily) and China, the Thai language is tonal like one of those native to the Chinese.

The name and statue remind us of how long we spent looking, and marvelling, at this facsimile of the prince upon his high plinth, while we stood in the shade out of the hot sunlight. The statue remains as a monument to the earnest program of modernization or Westernization to cope with the Europeans. The program succeeded. The Thai welcomed the strangers, they retained their culture, their language, and their soul, despite the chaos and commotion of that period, the life (1819–1901) and the reign (1837–1901) of Queen Victoria, respectively and respectfully.

That Modest Prince upon His Plinth

The suit (trousers and jacket) do retain a somewhat Victorian quality but, as worn by Prince Banubandhu, clearly adapted to the warm climate, perhaps more chic and elegant compared to French and British fashions. The prince is handsome with regular features, appears hospitable and approachable. With his hair neatly cut and combed, he wears neither cap nor crown. The clothing and the paraphernalia carefully selected for symbolic display emblematize the prince general and the then earnest program of Westernization undertaken by Siam and its rulers.

This above all is true of the telephone on display here—we are reminded that the telephone came into existence in 1876—this is one of those French-style telephones of the latter 1800s (a chic model yet in use in France and elsewhere), its rounded base neatly demarcated, and with the receiver and the speaker fashioned all on the same handle, with the elegant mouthpiece and little hearing horn, very Gallic in mode or model. The telephone on view here captures the utter enchantment cast by the prince on his plinth, and not equestrian for a change.

An Immodest Artist Before His Easel

(Salvador Felipe Jacinto Dalí y Domenich, 1904–1989.)

Dalí, thou master of strange imagery,
Oh Salvador, thou sterling imagist
Of thine own world, of thy ménagerie,
Thou mage, thou poet-painter-alchemist,
Somehow thou hast subsumed the gist, the grist,
Of all art of the present and the past—
With satire and with wit, but with a twist
Of humor worthy of a clown aghast,
And with stupendous fantasy made firm, made fixed, made fast.

Those noses on crutches, each displayed at great length,
And with the other treasures of thy mind amassed,
They flash as icons of unprecedented strength.

Whether surrealistic or surreal,
    It makes a magical reality—
Composed of dream, the fanciful, the ideal,
    In turn it makes its own ideality.

Sadko

(Skazka and opera.)

The tale of one protagonist, Sadko,
His voyages on land and in the water,
Can only stir our jealousy and awe.
He sought the hand of the Ocean Tsar's own daughter,
And if outright he could not so have bought her,
Except by trick or enigmatic thing.
What could he therefore otherwise have brought her?
The song that sirens and their kindred sing?
An echo from the hall, the cavern, of some deep-sea king?

Most heroes after due heroics pause, and settle down;
A few, a very few, in fact continue with their fling—
Adventure in and of itself is target, goal, or crown.

They still excite our jealousy, our passion, and our awe,
The few that do keep on, like merchant-wanderer Sadko.

Sea Mood

Beyond the shoals and sandbars lies the shore,
Itself no more than sand-packed littoral,
With stranded whales, where sea-birds dive and soar:
The steadfast source of things habitual,
Nature dictates that somber ritual,
Her creatures' quest for ready drink and food:
Is it pedantic or too literal,
Is it not unenlightened or too rude,
To emphasize pure need and instinct with exactitude?

Tranquility sometimes deceives, and often gives no clue:
Beneath the surface and the silence, darkling forces brood;
Beneath Earth's inmost crust, the fiery gases are at brew.

But still this peerless quietude exerts a sovereign spell
That signifies a paradise rather than inmost hell.

Barren Harvest

Musing upon the friends of many years,
We are amazed at their beneficence,
From them, but not the further stars and spheres!
We take no heed of gross maleficence,
As if it were the one clandestine sense,
Beyond the five we know, and thus concealed:
We take no heed of blatant wall or fence,
Nor yet of those in evil ways congealed,
Nor those in barren harvest past the hope of any yield:

If art is "useless" in a sense—per expert Oscar Wilde—
To wit, as in a piece of heraldry upon a shield—
Art feeds the mind, the heart, the soul: it feeds the inner child.

To find and reach our common or uncommon goal,
    We must explore or search both near and far afield,
In unknown lands, with some old map, or ancient scroll—
    To find that common weal, perhaps a common weald.

Haphazard Rimes

We are not like the seasons or the tides,
On schedule, but more often off and on—
We plan, but fate or nemesis decides.
Howevermuch the future we might con,
Or yet consult arcane phenomenon,
Mere happenstance can turn our plans amiss.
We need but wait, and things will change anon—
Before the butterfly is it remiss
Of us that we should note the golden-colored chrysalis?

We are not just by protocol constrained, coerced, or bound—
We need but wait to see some change, the metamorphosis,
When circumstance will self-explain, and things might come around.

We are no longer at the beck of any come and go,
We do not any longer bow before hormonal flow.

Queen Elizabeth II: 2018

On witnessing an hour-long documentary on television (Home Box Office) about Elizabeth II and her family—on Tuesday evening, 2 October 2018, first broadcast locally on the Monday evening just before.

> "To the most high, mighty, and magnificent Empress ... Elizabeth ... Queen of England, France and Ireland and of Virginia ...." From the dedication at the start of *The Faerie Queene*, by Edmund Spenser (1590, 1596, 1609).

I

Elizabeth I, Victoria, Elizabeth II. A few parallel sets of dates and figures, reflecting these three reigns, might prove instructive, and reveal unsuspected relationships and resonances. Elizabeth I (1533–1603) reigned 1558–1603 for 45 years. Victoria (1819–1901), Queen of Great Britain, and sovereign of the British Empire, reigned 1837–1901 for 64 years. Elizabeth II (born in 1926) became queen in 1952, and has reigned for 66 years by 2018.

II

So far, at 92, the second Elizabeth has reigned a little longer than Queen Victoria. To date she has thus had one of the longest reigns in recorded history, if not almost the longest one of all, a remarkable achievement in and of itself. For those who can savor historical dates and figures, no less their symbolic resonances, what an exceptional and extraordinary sign of Continuity—Continuity! —something so difficult and unusual to accomplish in human affairs.

III

Even if her immediate imperial congeries of the British Isles have contracted somewhat since Elizabeth I, it endures nominally still. Virginia overseas has long since gone her own way, but yet survives as an English-language territory. The French domains (at one time the dukedom of Normandy) have contracted to the four chief Channel

Islands—Guernsey, Sark, Jersey, and Alderney—lying just west of the large northern projection of *la Normandie*, and still called in French *les Isles normandes*. The dukedom later became part of the French kingdom.

IV

England, Wales, and Scotland still form part of Great Britain and as they have for centuries. The British Crown still claims Northern Ireland, which possession does not make smaller by that much (perhaps not more than one fifth) the overall territory of the large island that Ireland remains, which regained her independence in 1921. Otherwise on the other hand, in spite of these relatively minor losses (not so far removed in space), Elizabeth II has inherited the enormous, but largely overseas, British Empire and/or British Commonwealth.

V

Quite apart from her political significance as head of the Empire—no less than of the Commonwealth of (mostly autonomous) Nations, and of that aspect of the Empire that includes the colonies, dependencies, and protectorates—the Queen of England reigns in a further capacity, that is, as a cultural icon, and in a sense more importantly, although rarely mentioned. She reigns as the Empress of the English Language wherever spoken all over planet Earth.

VI

If the reign of Elizabeth I marked a startling efflorescence in geographical discovery and exploration, as well as development in the arts (including language and literature in particular)—and if Victoria's own reign signalized a similar efflorescence in continuing discovery, science, industry, and the arts as well—then the reign of Elizabeth II (1952-2018, that is, to date) has witnessed in an unprecedented manner an astonishing explosion in all areas of human endeavor all over planet Earth.

VII

This explosion even extends now beyond the planet on into the unplumbed profundities of Outer Space, on into the cosmic-astronomic immensitudes "sublime and without end." Thus the human race, the human species, finds itself poised at the threshold of a marvellous new age—the New Age! —if not in fact already inaugurated by the First Moon Landing in 1969.

APOSTROPHE

O Thou Elizabeth, Avé!

Thou Queen of England and the English everywhere, no less than the Queen of Great Britain, and of Northern Ireland, as well as that remnant of France, the Channel Islands, *les Isles normandes*:

Thou Head, thou Sovereign, of the British Commonwealth of Nations; thou Empress, thou Suzerain, of the British Empire, and of her colonies, dependencies, and protectorates whether past or present:

But above all else, the Empress, the Emperesse, the Impératrice, the Impératrix, of the Commonality of our English Language, O Thou Suprematrice:

All hail, respect, and awe! To Thee, our humble thanks, and mayest Thou fare well! Valé!

The Garden Bench

It was an old cast-iron bench, still sturdy,
Unrusted, painted white, with curlicues—
There nothing perched save the rare vagrant birdie:
As senior editor should I refuse
To take note of the two athletic shoes
That someone left down at the bench's base?
What would I otherwise elect to choose
For celebration but some act of grace,
Of graciousness, for something new, to save one's face?

To save one's face by something odd or new, what's wrong with old?
These thoughts concern the two athletic shoes, at bench's base,
As well as any reference that they perhaps might hold.

A lyric in fixed form, traditional, can prove as wild
As one in non-fixed form, when by tradition not beguiled.

Delphinidae-an

The dolphins had solicited a porpoise
To enter their community, their pod,
And he accepted, to indulge their purpose:
They got along well without rule or rod,
Where each one served as his own demigod,
Leaping and frolicking throughout the waves:
Feeding on schools of fishes like the cod,
Whether in sunlight, or where tempest raves,
They did not fear that Mother Sea might send them to their graves:

They revel out on Mother Ocean, but along the shore,
While weaving in and out of grottos, of whatever caves,
Might a few cetaceans, mayhap, venture to explore?

Unusual, of course, but notwithstanding that withal,
Never let us rule out that seldom individual.

Definition

It was a sullen autumn afternoon,
The leaves had not yet flared or flamed apart,
When death-bright colors made an extra boon.
Straightway that hits the crux, the core, the heart,
Of that event, and thus the better part—
How often beauty is defined by death,
Per Mother Nature in her artless art,
But beauty in herself transcends mere breath,
However she may die, and like the phoenix reincarnateth!

For without death per se there is no lapse, no fall,
And life cannot complete her arc, her depth, her breadth—
Despite the miscellaneous, there *is* the all:

However obvious these evident acknowledgements,
Pray pardon me mine absence of the true magniloquence.

Inconsequentiality

Neither poetics, neither politics,
On this occasion, shall inform our chant,
But rather fleas, or flies, or lice, or ticks.
Yet are these pests unworthy to descant,
Perceiving their real power to disenchant,
And to infect us all with rare disease?
Hello! —what I propose is not just rant,
But something undetected that can seize,
Can grasp, us all, and—suppliant—can bring us to our knees.

These little creatures can reduce the bulk of us
At any time of youth or age to taste the lees,
The dregs, of human life, as with a blunderbuss.

Inconsequentiality? And is it then but seeming,
Until disease-possessed, and overwhelmed, we are not dreaming?

Consequentiality

Not much less than the Pyramids,
Giza's Great Pyramids in truth,
Both Karnak and Louqsor impress.
Those ancient people were less than astute?
The scale of their big temples there
Astonishes as man-made edifice,
As palace-temple-house establishment.
Nor films nor photos can convey
The impact of their size at large
When seen in person right up close.
All adjectives cannot but fail
At such a task to represent
Or otherwise delineate
Their mammoth scale in quarried stone.

Some of the columns have the width,
The thickness, of an elephant
As measured strictly all around.
If you look upward from the midst
Of those supports to the clerestory,
It might cause you a tad of vertigo.
One notes the still fresh, vivid colors
Upon the underside of those the highest stones,
The giant lintels that extend across the aisles,
The space between the colonnades.

Ponder the size of any sphinx itself
As placed up high, each on its plinth,
Proportionate just to each sphinx.
Ponder the avenue of all the sphinxes
From Karnak at the north to Louqsor at the south
Over a track, a line, about a mile in length.

This Thebes, Thebae, Diospolis,
What a great city-space extended here!

What a great village-town once flourished—
The hundred-gated Thebes, the hundred-pyloned Thebes!
From temple-site upon the north
To temple-site upon the south,
It lifted up east of the Nile itself.
The old Egyptians called it Waset:
Amazing, that parts of it have so long survived!

In their own way these temples are
as potent, and impressive, as
New York City's sky-tall towers.

An Autumn Promenade

To walk along a sunlight-dappled road
Before the autumn's turning of the leaves,
It is to taste the green, its last abode.
As pressed against the house's lower eaves,
Are they not like the harvest's higher sheaves,
As gathered from the summer's lavish growth?
Or is it Nature in herself that grieves?—
How can we grasp this autumn's extra slowth?—
Should we not otherwise address it with a sacred oath?

Let us enjoy while yet we can this genial heat,
And let us share this warmth with nothing wrong nor wroth,
So we can walk with even pace, with steady beat.

This gentle warmth seems like a dream within a dream,
Enclosed within the autumn's glamour and her gleam.

The Seasons with Their Charms

The seasons now supply me with my needs—
The substance of my dreams and poetry—
With autumn leaves, with springtime buds and beads.
The autumn with her flaming goety,
The springtime with but half the moiety
Of glamour that the dying autumn holds
Still manages the status-quo-etry,
The peacock spectacle of greens and golds,
The subtle blues and reds and whites that ever the spring unfolds.

The hottest summer, could it shun, could it forbear?—
A little bud that yet unfurls as it unfolds
From inside of itself, that winter cannot spare.

Each season has a status quo
                              to which all things adhere,
An ideal pattern and a pulse
                              from which they cannot veer.

Happenstance

The sky once more was overcast but calm—
The lack of offshore breeze, par for the course—
The early-morning twilight proved a balm.
For Cape and Islands there is no one source
Of weather forecast, nor is there recourse
When that prediction haply turns out wrong.
You cannot sue the weather or the source,
The weather seer, throughout the whole day long,
When it can change beyond the force of any speech or song.

Human proposes, but kismet decides, is more than true:
To whom or to what does the weather with the rest belong?—
To Mother Nature in herself, to part of me and you.

Methinks, this topic of the weather is a paradox,
Neither quite orthodox, not yet, in truth, unorthodox.

A Mistress of Minor Spells

I

Let us consider the case of Atalantossa, the elder enchantress, no longer as dexterous in her art or trade as formerly. Let us look in on her during one overcast and rain-abundant morning, ensconced inside her semi-tropical abode. At least she had remained a beautiful woman of great charm (quite apart from her spells and philtres), with her long and now silver-tinged hair: a consolation to her when she needed to look into her mirror, but not for magical or cabalistic reasons. She had laid her head over her left arm, while she sat at her conjuring desk or table. She felt exhausted and at odds, if not in truth defeated. Should she give up, or should she keep on?

Her major spells no longer proved efficacious, her epochal and epic-making spells that had guaranteed prosperity and happiness to her many satisfied clients—spells that often involved love affairs, whether with young or older lovers—spells that had occasioned happy resolutions, happily ever after. At least her minor spells appeared to turn out well, implicating little things and creatures, little events and even insects. She should perhaps concentrate on her minor spells. They might continue to attract clients, credits, and coins, even when the very last seemed no more than minimal.

II

Covertly, coming up from under the table, from its left and lateral underside, a very large arachnid came into sight, a giant (and rather furry) bird spider that Atalantoss had imported long since from the tropical wetlands, the tropical rain forest. When he spread his eight legs outward, he could easily cover a large dinner or banqueting plate. Atalantossa did not seem in the least afraid, but smiled him a welcome. With his five pairs of eyes he could notice this, or feel her friendly vibrations close at hand, even without touching. All at once a new mood and a new energy infused her being, her very self.

Atalantossa lifted her head and sat upright, refreshed from her moment of repose. She ever so lightly caressed her pet, her favorite, her familiar. He responded by coming near her, by rearing up on his hind legs, and gently touching with one or more of his front legs the left-hand or sinistral cheek of her still beautiful face. She knew the spider's gesture as affection, approbation, and encouragement. Again she lightly caressed him; and he slowly edged away, and moved back down under the table. Their little exchange or interview had gone well, or very well. The enchantress felt herself renewed.

Heorte and Heorth

"Just as the heart is the hearth of the body, thus in the same way is the hearth the heart of the home." *An old saying.*

Just as the heart serves as the body's hearth,
So does the hearth serve as the home's own heart,
Beyond the kitchen garden, sink, or garth.
To handle them requires both skill and art,
Imagination, fantasy in part,
Plus intuition, prophecy, and more.
One might need guidelines, recipe, or chart,
To navigate, manoeuvre aft-and-fore,
Up high, from chimney flue, from ceiling clear down to the floor.

To look up in a chimney flue, tell what it might be like?
Like looking up inside a giant cannon's giant bore:
Do not look long!— the wind might cause a piece of soot to strike.

We have strayed far from heart and hearth:
Heorth and heorte—how clear like Eorthe!

Manhattan Towers

Thursday evening, 25 October 2018,
in honor of Clark Ashton Smith.

Aloft, Manhattan's empyrean towers
Could not have stood out more than what they did,
Like stone, glass, chrome, steel, brick, and concrete flowers.
Is it for me to check by grid, by quid,
With blueprint, or with blue-lined ozalid,
Away from indoor space by going out?
For who shall tell us no, shall us forbid,
Just as things happen, or they come about,
Whether announced by whisper, or by graduated shout?

The hotel lobby seems a calm and civilized oasis—
Look at the tides of traffic and pedestrians without!—
But still the deeps between the towers attain a kind of stasis.

The rituals of art proceed inside a sheltered room—
Remote from prophecies of death, destruction, or of doom.

The Glass Elevator

The Biltmore Hotel, Providence, Rhode Island.

How many curiosities of elder time manage somehow to abide within our big modern cities constructed within the older walls or on the older foundations! The modern City of London, that primordial square mile from Roman times, that Londinium edified under the first central Roman administration and then under that of the Western Empire, contains how many vestiges, how many fragments, deep down below! Or perhaps even from the far or nearby future? And thus it is with Boston (Massachusetts), or New York City, or Providence, Rhode Island, inside the Biltmore Hotel.

Built in 1978, approached by its own central and rather fancy staircase, located within the hotel's lobby (say, 60 by 60 feet, but three stories tall), the glass elevator stands erect and extant, but not employed since 2000 A.D., according to the placard (or placards) mounted on easels near the staircase. Per one placard, "Once used for time travel only ... / ... but the future called / and they want it back." However, first let the hotel get it running again, so that the guests themselves can enjoy the elevator before the hotel sends it back to the future.

The lobby's high ceiling allows plenty of room for the magnitudinous mechanism banded with bars and posts of some gold mimicking metal, the large cage still holds together where different levels demarcate. A shrine perhaps to some incognate god?—and could that be the Elevator Deity?—perhaps named Excelsior, ever upward, ever higher?

There it stands tall and proud, a marvel of metal, glass, and machinery, an enginery of awe from the future, or so the placard on one easel proclaims. It goes from the first floor to the eighteenth (just above the seventeenth, the grand level containing the ample ballroom), less of metal but more of special glass. Note that the elevator does not go down to the basement, to the floor with the furnace, down to the hotel's Avernus.

(The doors to the regular, smooth, and self-operating elevators continue to stand in place in the hallway beyond the immediate lobby.)

The next occasion when I might attend some convention at this truly grand Providence Biltmore Hotel, I pray that I might find the elevator-marvel running again as it once did in those days of yore, of deep antiquity, from 1978 to 2000! We scriven this hope on 12 November 2018.

Hallowed Evening

(All Hallows Evening, 31 October 2018.)

The gates had opened to the Other Side—
The outer, inner, and the midmost gate—
Their double valves, or leaves, had opened wide.
On this one night and evening, on this date,
The living can reserve, can dedicate,
Some time and reverence unto the dead.
Is it not then quite apt to consecrate,
To honor, those who somehow left, or fled,
This world, and for the Other Side, a somewhere free of dread?

Where could this somewhere be, a space inside another space?—
An island, an asylum, an abode, just for the dead?—
Enclosed inside a different set of laws, an unknown place?

Who knows just where a Hallowed Evening might not end, or lead?—
Where stranger entities than ours might not reside, and feed?

Autumn the Painter

Autumn the painter with her full-blown palette
Arrives but rather late, post-Halloween,
With colors hammered home as with a mallet.
Amid the leafy trees their farewell green,
No less the verdancy of evergreen,
Yet linger here and there: but now the spread
Of yellow, russet, orange, lend their sheen
No less than to this red, this dazzling red,
As well as to this dynamo, of dying and the dead.

And is it not a favor, and the rarest privilege,
To wait on Autumn through her death, upon her dying bed?
Does it not grant advantage, nay, but more, a certain edge?

The colors flash and range and spread, from brightest down to somber,
From purple, gold, and pale flame-gold, down to the lightest umber.

Transience

No longer orange, yellow, red, or green,
The autumn leaves have turned to brown, and fall
In random piles, wherever leaves convene.
How suitable that leaves and needles fall
In season, in the autumn, or the fall,
But still somehow the evergreens outlast.
As circumstantial of a greater fall,
The year declines, has now declined, has passed,
The planet shifts or tilts, alone against the vast.

Against the stars we cannot hide, exposed are we, and nude;
Alone with moon or sun, our year has passed, has overpassed;
The planet moves as ever through unknown immensitude.

Are we as transient as the flea, the fly, the tick, the ant?
Has not our species gained a special edge, a special grant?

THE LITTLE CAMEL-BEAST WHO COULD

(A fable.)

The Little Camel-Beast Who Could

(With all due apologies to Pyotr Pavlovich Yershoff
and his *Konyok-Gorbunok*, created 1834, published 1835.)

Fresh out of school, American, Smith-Jones by name,
Employed on his first big-time dig, or excavation,
The young and novice archaeologist had paused
Again before that odd, unknown hieroglyph.
Once more he thanked his lucky stars that his first season
Was taking place in winter rather than in summer.

And also fortunate, inside its grove of palms,
The temple stood alone inside its little vale;
It had survived intact, even the solid roof.
It was an unassuming fane of no great size,
But otherwise exquisite in its make and style,
As dedicated to both Isis and Amoun.

Ancient and Modern Egypt, how supreme in age!
Why was Amoun, the god of Thebes, here so far north?
The other archaeologists were also puzzled.
Constructed by P-tolemy, the second of that name,
Why did it stand plumb in the heart, plumb in the south,
Deep in the barren desert land amid the Sinai?

Not far from Mount Sinai, otherwise Mount Horeb,
The high peak of the Gebel Musa mountain group,
At not less than eight thousand six hundred fifty-two feet,
How had it come about, that folk had overlooked
This locale for so long, or so it would appear?—
Despite its nearness to the monasterium,
St. Catherine's Monastery, amid the sterile waste,
Full well established by Justinian the First,
Five Hundred Sixty-Five, but well and firmly built
Five Hundred Forty-Eighlt on through Five Hundred Sixty-Five.

Or could it be the monks had purposely neglected it?—
Thus leaving it alone, not even changing it
Into a church or chapel of the Virgin Mary,
Since Isis had prefigured her as archetype?
As these thoughts once more swarmed inside the young man's head,
He kept on looking at that odd hieroglyph:

The little one-humped camel, seemingly a dwarf,
The unknown cypher, but the key, as only one detail,
Inside that country scene, beside the river Nile,
Achieved in bas-relief, the colors vivid still: .
A picture of domesticated animals,
With people—farmers and officials—interspersed
With quadrupeds of diverse kinds, all shapes and sizes,
With horses, oxen, asses, and with cows and goats and sheep.

The little beast stood out, contrasted with the other camels,
Full-grown, full-sized adults, and larger by two thirds
Than him, the little camel-beast, erect and tough and proud.
The young man suddenly recalled how P-tolemy the Second
Had introduced the one-humped camel from the Middle East,
From the Levant, and had popularized its use—
Camelus dromedarius—here was the evidence!

He mused unto himself, "P-tolemy the Second,"
And then he said aloud, "P-tolemaeus Philadelphus,
Who lived for over sixty years, and reigned for almost forty,
A long life and a long reign for a P-tolemy,
Considering their murderous, back-stabbing ways:
He finished up the Lighthouse on the isle of Pharos,
No less the Library of Alexandria,
The Biblioteca Alexandrina, now renewed."

He noticed something he had not remarked before:
Someone had written long agone, in ancient Greek,
Beneath that country scene, and painted it in black,
Now near illegible, a note about the little beast:
He had been brought to court at Alexandria,

Where he resided as a pet, where he lived a long life;
They designated him P-dyllion, P-dyll for short.

When not at court, he loved the Sinai as his stomping ground,
Whither they let him go, whenever he so wished,
Whereby they named him, dignified him all the more,
The protector or the patron or the guardian of the Sinai.
Nor did they fear for him when he had gone from court,
For he could course fast as the wind, and even stomp a lion:
Adroit, alert, and tough, he had great force and speed.

However, young Smith-Jones had spent way too much time,
On this hieroglyph, on this peculiar cypher;
He had some other temple parts to scrutinize
Related to the current job or task at hand:
He would continue to consider and to con the symbol.
He mused, "P-dyllion, the little camel-beast who could,"—
It sounded like a fable, or a children's tale;
So, after one more look, he smiled as he walked on.

Sometimes the present serves as prologue to the past,
As well as to the future tense, its ordinary role.
Laid out much longer east and west than south and north,
The town of Alexandria was quartered by
Its two chief colonnaded streets into four sections
Exactly parallel, but with the northeast separate,
The royal quarter with its proper royal harbor,
With temples, palaces, and shrines: splendiferous display:
Plenty of room for all those daft P-tolemies!

Near where the two main streets meet up, and intersect,
The Soma stood, the tomb of Alexander Magnus,
Alexándros Megálos, and/or Alexander the Great!
Hereat the gates or gate stood open night or day,
Permitting access to the hero's crystal coffin,
Where he lay, incorruptible, eternally a youth,
Clean-shaven, beautiful, and handsomely accoutered,
Protected by the pillared, stone-made shrine and canopy.

And this was where the royal guards would let him out,
The little camel-beast, P-dyll, whenever he so wished:
Sometimes all that he wished was just to roam the town.
One middle morn he exited, and bowed before the tomb,
As was his wont, which warmed the heartstrings of the citizens.
Thus having paid his due respects, he wandered off,
Protected by the royal coronet around his neck,
On into that metropolis, unending, vast.
When he came to the opened eastern gate, he paused,
And noticed once again the little beggar boy,
Forlorn, unparented, but with a valiant smile;
He was besides a tough and handsome little guy.
The camel's heart was touched, he neared him, and he spoke.

"My noble sir, would you not like to be my mascot,
To help me when I need: please note I have no hands.
If you agree, then put your arms around my neck,
And get up in between my long neck and my hump."

Aghast, amazed, the kid jumped up, and did as he was told.
He grinned, and spoke, "If you are *the* P-dyll, then I am Pan.
Your offer I accept," and then he mounted up,
As he had been advised, between the hump and neck.
The citizens? They stood amazed as those two trotted off,
Out through that opened eastern gate. The guards all wore big smiles.

Look at a map of Egypt, and please note how far to-west
It lies inside the delta of the river Nile,
Does Alexandria, the Graeco-Roman capital,
Just inland of the sea, of that great inland ocean,
Which ancient Egypt knew, and named, the Great Green [Sea].
The delta of the Nile, how far it spreads to-north!
From west to east athwart the land to Israel,
That is, from Egypt at Pelusium, it takes less time
Than to traverse the delta's width there at its widest
The route the most direct while using all the bridges
That span the many streams, and not less the canals,
To reach the western regions of Sinai's peninsula.

There was no need to rush, P-dyll and Pan could take their time,
The little camel-beast proceeded at a gentle trot.

How lush and fertile lay the land, the crops rose everywhere,
Wherever they could grow! The grains had precedence.
As P-dyll pointed out, the little boy took note,
And was astonished or amazed, as things demanded:
This voyage represented his first voyage anywhere,
His eyes grew big and wide with wonderment and awe.

Although Pan knew the capital like the back of his hand,
Her temples, palaces, and shrines, her many marketplaces,
This trip aboard P-dyll became a revelation,
A genuine apocalypse, and all the more a marvel.
If the camel does duty as the ship of the desert,
Then P-dyll would take rank as but the merest skiff,
As no more than a little boat, but oh my, such a skiff!

Now, after several days and nights, while sojourning
At diverse inns and farmers' homes, they reached at last the Sinai,
Once they had passed Pelusium, but still on Egypt's land.
That royal coronet around P-dyll's long neck
Had guaranteed a royal welcome everywhere they went.
Meanwhile the diverse people whom they met, they gave
Young Master Pan some new and novel clothes that fit him fine:
New tunics and new kilts, new buskins of good make,
But nothing overmuch, just good and elegant.
And now before their plunge into the furthermost Sinai,
They had supplied themselves with needed tools and food.

P-dyll would eat whatever herbs and grasses he could find;
They would find water at whatever wells they chanced upon;
They would not then depend upon the nomad tribes
Who wandered from one waterhole to yet another.
They would sleep out beneath the stars and nightly skies;
Also they would bring water in small sealed ceramic jars.

At first Pan found the barren landscape dour and daunting;
Then slowly he began to find it beautiful

With colored rocks and mounded earth that cheered their steadfast way.
Sometimes they chanced upon an older house abandoned
Because the well no longer could supply sufficient water.
P-dyll explained that they were heading down to Mount Horeb
That overlooked the Sinai's southernmost expanse;
There they would join the working crew constructing a new temple.

There King P-tolemy had sent by ship an expedition
To build a temple to both Isis and Amoun,
In expiation of a vow that he had made
Resulting from a dream, from some nocturnal vision that
He had whereby both Isis and Amoun commanded him
To build a temple to them both amid the trackless waste
Inside a little vale not far from Mount Horeb.

Once they, P-dyll and Pan, connected with the building crew
And visited with them awhile, then they would take a ship,
A royal ship, returning them to Egypt's littoral
Across the Suez Gulf that stretched west of the Sinai.
From there a caravan across another desert
Would bring them to the Nile, where they could take another ship,
Another royal ship, back down to Alexandria.
Such was the general plan and route as laid out by P-dyll—
Meanwhile reality and circumstances might yet
Intervene to modify or change both plan and route:
Wind, sand, simoom, and scorpions might have a part to play.

Whenas the two of them would speak, one to the other,
Young Pan did not expect P-dyll to turn around,
To look at him; impossible at any rate,
Pan held on to P-dyll, his arms around his neck.
"Hey, P-dyll! / "Yes, I wish I had some. / What? / Hay! / What?"

"I thought that you were happy with the plants that you could find
By the side of the road, or only here and there. No?"
"Well, overall I am okay, but I do miss my manger.
I'm spoiled, I'm civilized. I can't say, just like you,
Given your marginal condition, there, by the eastern gate,
That is, until it was that I adopted you."

He paused, and then spoke on, "I hope at least that you are happy now."
Pan could not speak, but suddenly burst into tears.
He spoke, and merely said, "There, that's my gratitude!"—
He wiped, he dried his eyes upon the camel's coat.
Pan was quite comf'ably ensconced between the neck and hump,
Where he sat on the folded woolen blanket that
Did duty as a saddle, and at night he used for cover.

And so the long trek going south went on and on and on. . . .
P-dyll and Pan between themselves, they had agreed
That Pan would be the one to talk whenever they would meet
Those of the nomad folk, several or a group.
Then Pan would speak as wisely counselled by P-dyll;
No need for other folk to learn, to be aware,
That in all truth the camel talked, a magic beast.

Pan's spiel had thus been set, and always went the same:
"I am that Pan, the servant of P-tolemy, the king at Alexandria;
I ride and guide this royal beast, as per command,
Until the precinct sacrosanct to holy Mount Horeb,
To meet with those who build a temple-shrine for Pharaoh."
Or if and when they met with trouble or with threat,
P-dyll with Pan would take off like the wind;
No chance that anyone or anything could overtake them then.

One late afternoon, before the fall of night,
P-dyll and Pan had stopped for their nocturnal rest.
P-dyll with his capacious mouth was helping little Pan
To pick up any odd pieces of anything that he could use
For a fire, botanic burnable materials,
When suddenly the wind came up, then ever stronger,
A simoom! Looking for shelter, they espied not far away
A cavern mouth that opened up inside a mountain.
Carrying then their gear, they wandered deep inside to stay the night;
Meanwhile the desert storm would pass, would overblow.

The cave was empty, and so it seemed okay to use.
Then Pan set up his fire, while the storm blew like hell outside.

They could sleep safe and sound, as they hoped, all that night.
It must have chanced at midnight that they heard a muted growl,
As from a major carnivore; it could be nothing less.
They both woke wide awake at once, and by the lingering fire
They saw a desert lion searching for a lair.

The storm had overblown. P-dyll told Pan to stay,
And all at once he changed into a creature
Such as Pan never saw before. He seemed to grow
At least two times his size, and maybe even larger;
His eyes now blazed with fury and with fire, and then
He launched himself before the lion could recover,
And with full force titanical he hit the carnivore
With his four hooves, with all his power, and killed him just like that.

P-dyll next cautioned Pan, to have no fear, that all was well.
They could sleep now both safe and sound, as they had hoped,
All the rest of that night, and then go on their way;
But it did take a while for both of them to settle down,
And finally to fall asleep, even if somewhat fitfully,
The lion's corpse to serve as barrier and warning.

The next morning P-dyll and Pan enjoyed the moving-on,
Leaving behind the dead *leon* as carrion for others.
Another day, another trek, another night,
Another camping-out, and underneath the stars.
And on this other night they slept a perfect sleep,
And so the long trek going south went on, to end at last
Within that precinct sacrosanct to holy Mount Horeb.
Thereat they met up with the crew that was constructing
The temple dedicated still to Isis and Amoun,
In expiation of that vow made by P-tolemy.
Of no great size it was a temple of exquisite make,
No less than style, beneath the care of master craftsmen,
Where some were still incising in and on the walls
Tableaux and other pictures with hieroglyphs.

How good it felt to find themselves amid Egyptians!—
Whereat they found an honored place, or thus it seemed,

In such a royal-most encampment per king P-tolemy.
P-dyll? He found sufficient hay. Pan? He shared the meals
Provided by the crew that waited on the building crew.
One sculptor took a fancy to P-dyllion,
And in a riverside tableau he carved a pictograph
Depicting, so it seemed, our dear P-dyllion.

How long did they spend there, P-dyllion and Pan?
A half month, maybe more, they revelled in the campsite
With its flamboyant tents, and elegant pavilions:
P-tolemy was wont to treat his craftsmen very well!
Although the work gangs there, and of whatever sort,
Did not perceive P-dyllion quite as a magic beast,
They recognized him as at least in fact exceptional.

One day P-dyll took Pan up to the top of Mount Horeb,
Which overlooked the landscape near and far, thus all of it,
A panorama that quite took away the breath:
With mouth agape, young Pan appeared both awestruck and amazed.
Other than that ascent, together they explored
All of the southern part of that peninsula,
And there was much to see, no less than to discover.

When they returned to camp, the workmen would request
To learn what they had seen, what prodigies and wonders.
"Hey, Master Pan, where did you go, what did you see?"
How few the animals, the people, or the verdancy!—
And he would hold forth in discourse: "Deep canyons and wide valleys,
Great mounds and hills of sand, with very little green,
Except the palms and plants that grow near waterholes,
That grow by happenstance: there is no irrigation.
Oh how I miss that greenery, oh how I miss the Nile!"
Thus very few became inspired to go off on their own.
They, all of them, missed the Nile, they missed the verdancy,
With pangs of homesickness, and with high-flown nostalgia.

One night, before the dawn, Pan entertained a visitor,
Where he lay wrapped and warm within his woolen blanket.

It was a big black Afric scorpion, which crept
Inside of Pan's cocoon, drawn by his youthful warmth.
There prone and sound asleep, Pan rolled upon his side,
And inadvertently disturbed the scorpion,
Which only could react, at best, instinctively:
At once he moved his tail, and stuck his sting on into Pan.
It hurt like hell, and woke him up at once. He screamed,
And jumped out of his blanket, where he lay next to P-dyll,
The scorpion? He also moved from that cocoon,
Scuttling away but not before P-dyll had stomped on him.

Pan's scream awoke the camp. The workmen all came running
Into the little tent where lodged Pan and P-dyll.
P-dyll stood next to Pan, protectively it seemed:
Pan held his forearm where the scorpion had stung,
Moaning and groaning and whimpering in pain.
He pointed at the stomped-on, mashed-up scorpion.

Whereat a foreman counselled Pan to lay him down,
And taking out a small but sharpened knife, he cut
A tiny X across the sting, and stuck his mouth
Upon the wound, and sucked the venom out, and then
He wrapped a clean rag all around the forearm with its wound.

There, it was done! The foreman spoke, "Stay down, and rest.
Keep the wound clean, but otherwise do not touch it.
The pain should lessen presently, without undue delay.
Don't be afraid. You shall not die. You shall survive.
We'll watch by you till dawn, and on into the day;
We'll take turns to make sure you have no more like visitors."
Due to the shock, now Pan felt little pain, and he lay quiet;
And all this while P-dyll also lay quiet by Pan's side.

Pan stayed abed for several days, with a slight fever,
But that soon passed. Wisely he did not eat or drink,
Except a little wine made from the king's own grapes.
The fourth day he was well. P-dyll and Pan could then go on.

Pan packed his gear upon P-dyll, there was not much.
He bade the working crews farewell, and thanked them for their
    kindness,
No less their hospitality, dispensed in Pharaoh's name.
Mounting P-dyll again, Pan headed for the port to-west.
There they embarked on some Egyptian merchant ship:
But for P-dyll as royal beast with groom, the trip was free.

The trip across the gulf to Egypt's western shore
Went fast and smooth—good wind, good sail—calm sky, calm sea.
The corresponding port lay not quite opposite
The Sinai port they left behind, more to the north.
At this new port they disembarked to find a caravan
To cross the desert land, to take them to the Nile.

Again the coronet around the camel's neck
Obtained for Pan and for P-dyll another gratis trip
As honored guests for several days and several nights.
The leader of the caravan assured the both of them,
"We have great honor and great pleasure in your company."
After the several days and nights, they reached the Nile;
How dear, that river and that land reached out to them!—
The steady stream, the lush and fertile verdancy!

Thereat they had a big surprise awaiting them:
The agents of the king, the Pharaoh as it were,
The Pharaoh in all truth, were standing near the shore,
Beside a royal barge with ready crew on board;
The word of their arrival had preceded them,
And once the agents viewed our two, they sought them out at once.

"Avé! P-tolemy is anxious for his pet's return,
He has been gone far longer than he had foreseen.
We know that you," nodding at Pan, "are now his groom.
We come to take you back to Alexandria by boat,"
And here he pointed to the gorgeous watercraft.
The agents guided them aboard the royal barge,
Which cast off at the shore, while heading down the stream.

In hardly more than several days, they reached the capital:
How joyed they felt, P-dyll and Pan, to have reached home at last!

Pan felt a little nervous even if P-dyll felt calm.
Out of sheer circumstance the camel had withdrawn;
Pan had perforce come to the fore, as tutored by P-dyll.
Nevertheless, P-dyll would soon regain his stride,
Once in the presence of P-tolemy the king,
Wherein the camel-beast felt free to charm at will.

Pharaoh did not hold court that day, but had retired
Inside his private suite for counsel and for peace,
So he could think and plan both for and by himself.
The minister of the court escorted P-dyll and Pan
To where the handsome king, arrayed in simple robes,
Sat at his table-desk, surrounded by his many scrolls.

P-dyll had precedence, and friskily did he approach
P-tolemy; he genuflected, and he bowed his head:
The little beast had charmed the king yet once again.
P-tolemy was overjoyed, and got up from his desk;
Then bending down a little, he embraced his errant pet.
"My little friend," he said, "unless you curb your errant ways,
We must curtail your exits from our court. We wish
To have your company much more, while yet we may;
And you, Pan, may continue as his private groom."

Pan blushed, and bowed on bended knee as deeply as he could.
The king came up to Pan, told him to rise, and next
He shook his hand, while Pan inclined his head yet once again.
He could retire to his new home within the stables;
Meanwhile P-dyll enjoyed the full range of the royal quarter;
But soon Pan and P-dyll resumed their hanging-out together,
Though Pan, unlike P-dyll, did not go into private rooms,
Except by open invitation from the royalty.

The king and court accepted this, their hanging-out together;
Most people found the teen-aged boy a winsome chap:
He had a lot of charm, and also spoke quite well.

Pan might grow somewhat more, but would remain a little guy,
No more than medium height, while tough and muscular;
But never underestimate street kids or beggar boys.

Alas, Pan seemed to have a destiny with scorpions,
And once again with a big black African one,
Which crawled inside his stable bed, and stung him on the arm,
The other forearm, but this time *he* sucked the venom out,
And felt but little pain. Perhaps he had immunity?!
Quickly the sting-wound went away, and all seemed well,
Apparently with none or little ill aftereffects,
The sting-wound healing fast, no blemish left behind.

The king had summoned Pan, together with P-dyll,
To visit him again inside his private suite,
Where he sat at his table-desk, to hear once more,
Young Pan's succinct report about their recent odyssey.
Now Pan had garbed himself in sandals, tunic, kilt;
And that was all, deferring to the summer's heat.

So Pan relived again the scorpion's attack,
No less than that most recent one, a night or two agone.
At which the king suggested that young Pan should find
A berth or bed outside the royal stables and their like.
Pan bowed with grace, and thanked his royal majesty,
Noted already for his kind and gracious ways.

Now, suddenly, he who was Pan cried out in pain,
Clutching at his forehead, and no less his crotch:
His body seemed to passage through some transformation,
Enduring agony, a metamorphosis:
His legs had altered to the hind legs of a goat,
With cloven hooves, with shaggy hair below the knees.
The genitals had changed to those of some studhorse
Contained, or snuggled, in a cup or orifice,
Thus in the manner of the larger quadrupeds.
Out of Pan's upper forehead two large horns had grown,
Two large recurved, or retrorse, horns transversely ridged in front.

Pan had exploded, he had burst, out of his clothes,
His tunic, kilt, and sandals, now replaced by shaggy hair.

His body had become more muscular than ever,
While changing on into a satyr or a faun,
A son of Pan begot upon some errant nymph.

All at once a vast surge of energy coursed throughout the faun:
The shock of metamorphosis, the rest of it, had passed.
The camel and the king had witnessed this in wonder.
This awesome transformation that had changed their friend:
The second scorpion's attack and sting and venom
Somehow had triggered, and released Pan's metamorphosis.

Their friend, the faun, then felt his ears for the first time,
His pointed ears, and gently fingered them with awe.
And like the goat he had a tail, but not so long and thin;
Unlike the goat he had a short and bushy tail.
Pan spoke, but in a deeper voice, and said, "I still can speak,"
A voice urbane, agreeable, suave, and mellifluous.

The king spoke next, "We had begun to doubt the older gods,
The old religion, but not now, you have dispelled our doubts!
If you continue in the shape into which you have changed,
We could return you to your father's home in Arcady.
You are now one with Faunus, deity of animals,
The god of crops and prophecy, whom we, the Greeks, call Pan.
But if you stay, it might prove gauche, when someone asks
If you are genuine, a real faun or a satyr.
And then you might retort that, 'No, this is a masquerade!'
P-dyllion and you could roam the streets together:
You two should make an awesome pair, parading wheresoever."

The king then chuckled as he smiled at both Pan and P-dyll:
Pan had reached over to caress P-dyll's pale yellow coat.
The king began to talk again as if he just recalled
A topic he had wanted to discuss but had forgot.
"A subject of great pertinence in terms of certain needs!"
Here he directly stared at Pan's box there between his legs:

"It might be easier for you to have access
To females here in our own megalopolis.
Or else a servitor of ours could procure them for you.
There might be more than just a few that might want to get close,
Who definitely might want to engage with you!"

He paused, and then began again. "As for P-dyll,
Let us look to see if we cannot get for him
An apt and willing female, and of his own type
And kind, a female midget camel of his own:
Perhaps they might conceive between them a new breed!"
My, such a kind, benevolent friend and monarch!
Pan and P-dyll looked at the king in sheerest gratitude.

NOTES

by Dlanod Yendis

"The Little Camel-Beast Who Could."

Ptolemy II, or Ptolemaeus Philadelphus, lived 309-246 B.C., for 63 years, and reigned 285-246 B.C., for forty years: considering the period and the dynasty, a rather long life and reign. Ptolemy, usually pronounced in English as "tol-e-mi," and accented on the first syllable, is here in this narrative in verse pronounced with the "p" as well as in Greek. The "p" is quietly, not explosively, sounded like a "puh" (as in "pun," no pun intended) with no vowel sound, or as little as possible.

". . . his first season / . . . in winter than in summer."

Egypt's winters can be cool at night, her summers can be very hot, indeed.

"Why was Amoun . . . here so far north?"

Isis and Amoun, an odd coupling, but not unknown to each other.

"Despite the nearness to the monasterium"

St. Catherine's Monastery covers a large area, and has high walls, all quite stoutly constructed.

"The town of Alexandria"

Until Rome first, and then Constantinople second, Alexandria long remained the largest metropolis on or around the Mediterranean Sea, really an inland ocean.

"Alexándros Megálos . . . Alexander the Great!"

Alexander III of Macedon lived 356-323 B.C. He ruled as king 336-323. His father Philip II lived 383-336. He ruled as king 359-336.

"Protected by the royal coronet around his neck [i.e., P-dyll's]"

The royal coronet around his neck commanded special protection and privilege, as well as free services and free goods, food, etc.

"The camel's heart was touched . . . and he spoke."

Whenever P-dyll speaks to the boy in public, he does it sotto voce, so people will not suspect him as a magic beast.

"Or if . . . they met with trouble or with threat"

One time before meeting some strangers, P-dyll advised Pan, "I don't like the way these look. Feet, move on!

"The cave was empty, and so it seemed okay to use"

Pan: Maybe some desert lion uses this cave for his lair? P-dyll: Don't worry. If a lion shows up, I'll deal with him.

"They recognized him as . . . exceptional."

Apart from chewing his cud, P-dyll impresses the workmen more like a big dog than anything else.

"Except a little wine made from the king's own grapes."

Some royal vineyards lay outside Alexandria, but most of them were dispersed throughout the kingdom.

"But for P-dyll . . . with groom, the trip was free."

P-dyll to Pan: The king, our Pharaoh, will want a good and full report.

". . . the camel-beast felt free to charm at will."

Like all intelligent and intuitive non-humans, P-dyll knows perfectly well when and how to charm people, and no less with whom to score.

"The second scorpion's attack . . . / . . . released Pan's metamorphosis."

Pan's metamorphosis from human youth to young faun or satyr is no less remarkable than anything in Ovid's *Metamorphoses.*

". . . they might conceive . . . a new breed."

Might Ptolemy want to create a new species of midget camel by matching P-dyll with a suitable female camel?

"Cultus Poeticus." (Concerning Caer Leon on Usk, utilized by Tennyson as a chief locale in his *Idylls of the King.*)

Lord Tennyson, Alfred, first Baron, 1809–1892. English poet; and poet laureate, 1850–1892. Despite all the fluctuations attendant on his reputation and his *oeuvre* after his death, especially during the first half of the 1900s, Tennyson still remains quite a great poet.

Caer Leon on Usk: The Britanno-Roman (i.e., Keltic) chieftain, or *dux bellorum*, later known as King Arthur, evidently made Caer Leon on Usk one of his chief headquarters, or capitals, along with Cadbury Castle, identified with the legendary Camelot. Arthur, or Artorius, utilized the Roman Amphitheatre for meetings and manoeuvres. The amphitheatre stands right next to the southwest corner (a true bastion) of the stout wall still surrounding the former legionary fortress. The rounded shape (an oval) of the structure apparently gave rise to the later Round Table of legend that became linked with King Arthur and his knights, himself the leading *cataphractarius*, or mobile and armored horseman, thus the chief knight among his own knights.

POSTSCRIPTUM

Ambivalence

"Thank Goddess for iamb-iambus!
That metric does not spark this line:
Try both, try ambo, or try ambus,
It is only a symbol, a sign."
—*Random rime by unknown poet.*

Confronted by an awkward choice of two,
Unless one choice is obviously deadly,
Apart from that which is no more than due—
Far harder to select than from a medley,
Unless without a guide we choose misledly,
We have no choice, it seems, except to choose!
We do not speak of it, foreheadly,
A good point or precept: better to lose
The argument or dispute than the focus or the fuse.

What we state here, let us confirm, we mean forthrightly—
Better it is to face the choice, than to refuse—
We do not speak in jest, nor do we take it lightly.

Ambivalence! Is it a curse, is it a benefit?
Or do we count it as one more exotic perquisite?

Sometimes Lofty Towers

(For David C. Smith.)

Sometimes I see, far-off, some lofty towers,
Which lift above a massive pile of stone,
A space where we could sit and watch for hours.
Unless fate forces us to grasp this koan—
We do not always reap what we have sown—
Why should we yearn for sometimes lofty spires?
And there would we still find ourselves alone?
Spires, circles, towers—what is it that so fires
Our dazed imagination, but—far more than that—inspires?

The circles, towers, and spires contrive to set our minds aflame!
How could the stars and planets work without unending gyres?
The circle, symbol of perfection, everywhere the same.

An archetype inside a mental spider web is caught,
And so those lofty towers exist beyond all conscious thought.

Helsingor, or Elsinore

One dank and melancholy morning
Out from his towers of Elsinore
Some young prince peered as if in mourning.
Elsinore!

Languishing for his Helenore,
Or could she have been Elinor,
And not Ophelia cast aside?
Elsinore!

Might she have been his lost Lenore?—
Who died too young, a suicide,
To whom, herself, she felt that life had grossly lied.
Elsinore!

Mere disillusionment? It might exact a lofty price.
No problem on the outside? Maybe some on the inside?
Do not disparage someone else's pain: give kindness or advice.
Elsinore!

My watchword? When by circumstance too much oppressed,
Let Hamlet be Hamlet, let sleeping Hamlets rest.
Elsinore!

Winter Solstice

(Polonius speaks on the weather and on human mood.)

Despite the solstice, winter has not yet
Arrived with her full arsenal of cold,
Remember how much colder it will get.
Go back to bed, I say to young and old,
Under the covers put all else on hold,
Or work for others in a heated room—
Or for yourself, remember to be bold,
Keep sunshine in your heart, a vernal bloom,
Unless you might succumb to mood of glum or gloom.

Remember, keep in mind: know that a crumb of light,
A candle, can suffice to lighten up a tomb,
A line of torches can illuminate the night.

Pray pardon us our homilies, our platitudes—
If they work out, plray give us back a range of gratitudes.

Eyepiece

When in the muted vigils of the morn,
Before the rising of the sun per se,
Always a little twilight is aborn—
The fading phantoms of the night give way
To those more solid phantoms of the day,
Chaotic and confused kaleidoscope:
As light and shadow fence and spar at play,
As if in answer to some horoscope,
We search out the beyond, far-off, with monstrous telescope.

In order to perceive, and then to grasp, we need and use
Goggles and spectacles, or telescope and microscope:
There is no ocular device that we shall not disuse.

In order to perceive and grasp, we do need some assist—
Eyesight, insight, outsight, and all of this as eucharist.

Cultus Poeticus

(To whom therefore belongs the glory?)

When in the further corridors of dusk
We chance across this odd phenomenon—
We find ourselves in Caer Leon on Usk.
And there on Arthur Machen's turf we con
The Roman objects in the *mouseion,*
And amble from one to another thing.
While in one quest we blindly stumble on
Another, that of the *Idylls of the King,*
Of high king, one Arthurius, whom bards today still sing.

But thanks to one great bard, the long-term poet laureate,
One Alfred, Baron Tennyson, these laurels that we bring,
To him, to Machen, to Arthurius, we consecrate.

We honor those firm values that we somehow still hold dear,
Howevermuch chimaerical such honors might appear.

Finis Coronat Opus

Well, at long last I have come to the end—
No poetry—let me embrace this fate—
Let me not fight it, but let me befriend:
Between these hubs I now shall navigate,
Shall improvise, and shall administrate,
As if in parliament, as if at court.
So what price then is this my chosen fate?—
Mine absence at some harbor, or some port,
Or at some seat of power, a palace, castle, and/or fort?

For not in politics, nor in the status-quo-etry,
Nor in the bank, or market place, nor in judicial court,
I find the latchkey on a string in prayer or poetry:

Lest the key on a string might float away, and thus disappear,
In this way I shall realize my best hope, or my worst fear.

(Oblivion.)

APPENDIX: Juvenilia

Herewith is the Saga of *The Monthly Chronicle* and the juvenile poetry by Donald Sidney-Fryer, or D. S. F., Junior. During the years 1946-1947 (the winters of 1945-1946 and 1946-1947) the two brothers Ronald Jean Fryer and D. S. F., Junior, wrote and edited on their own initiative a modest (mimeographed) newspaper *The Monthly Chronicle*. Then in their early teens, the brothers (Ron at 12 and Don at 11) created the paper for the housing development Presidential Heights (opened to renters of limited means around 1940) under the administration of Franklin D. Roosevelt in the north end of New Bedford, Massachusetts, the former chief whaling port.

The brothers lived with their mother Annette Teilliere Fryer, and still attended Mount Pleasant Grammar School almost adjacent to the housing development. (Their parents had separated and divorced.) At that time their father D. S. F., Senior, owned and operated Clarke's Lettershop, a mimeographing business in an office on Purchase Street in downtown New Bedford, at (Room) 432 Masonic Building. The father took the business over from another relative, Marjorie Clarke Fryer, married to one of the father's brothers, one Kenneth Fryer. Donald Senior encouraged and allowed the brothers to use the equipment (typewriters, stencils, mimeographing machine, etc.) on Saturdays to create and manufacture the sheets for their little newspaper.

Ron became the editor-publisher, while Don filled the role of reporter, associate editor or publisher, and poetry editor. But both typed or "cut" the stencils (the chief part of the physical work, apart from the preliminary writing). They did this with great care to avoid typos and other errors, which they could still correct with the special correction fluid. Then their father would run off the copies of the sheets from the completed stencils on the mimeographing machine. The boys gathered the neighborhood news from the tenants living in the housing development, and would then write it up in proper style. During the entire run of the newspaper—each issue has 4 to 6 big pages, but printed on one side only, simpler and easier to do than on both sides the boys themselves delivered the copies to the subscribers, who gave positive response to the succeeding issues, 12 in all.

During summer vacation from school, July and August, they eschewed publishing any issues, but otherwise put out an issue for every month from February 1946 through April 1947. Throughout the active run of the little newspaper (which promoted subscriptions and so forth) Donald Junior contributed a poem to almost all the issues. Technically and chronologically they rate as juvenilia. The poet was only 11 when the paper began, and 12 when it finished. The brothers ceased publication because of the increasing demands made on them by their school work and studies, first in late grammar school, and then in high school.

This appendix forms the only corpus of juvenile poems that the now Donald Sidney-Fryer produced. He stopped writing poetry until he turned 27, and began his mature work in March 1961 with the sonnet "Avalonessys." Nor does the original poet-author claim the right of their inclusion here except on the grounds of completeness. These early poems remain stupid, obvious, and commonplace. However, the young poet improved as time went on for over a year or more. The best poems remain the short ones, because he had less room and opportunity for miscalculation and errors in taste and style. The poems listed here include the following titles per issue of the newspaper.

Winter in Vermont	February 11, 1946
My Little Forest	March 11, 1946
The Tulip	April 10, 1946
A Ruby-Throated Hummingbird	June 25, 1946
My Kitten	September 10, 1946
Autumn in New England	October 10, 1946
Change	November 11, 1946
Winter Fun	January 10, 1947
Anniversary	February 10, 1947
It's Spring	April 14, 1947

Winter in Vermont

There's maple sugar smell in the air
The Trees are leafless, cold and bare
The Fire upon the hearth is eating the timbers
And the fire has ate so much nothing remains but the cinders.

The Snows have come, the Yuletide has gone
And today starts out with a crisp clear dawn
The men are collecting the maple tree sap
A man calls me "Come help me, chap."
It'll be the middle of the day soon
And I have to get home at noon.

When I get home the fire is burning
The butter, my mother she is churning
Mother, I got some apple syrup for dinner sake.
For I know we're having griddle cakes
Son, go sit beside the fire
And soon my cakes you will admire.

The day has fell, the night is almost here
And soon the round faced moon will appear
The wind down the chimney blows
This winter in Vermont all of this shows.

Note: My mother rarely churned butter, and we did not have a real fireplace but a purely decorative one to one side of the living room. We had our dinner at noon, and supper at night.

My Little Forest

I know I will always be
Under these old and different trees
To hear song of birds and buzz of bees.

To see the beautiful sun always shine
To see the trees especially the oak and Pine.
To see the snows melt in the spring
To hear the frogs and crickets sing
In summer, to see the trees fair and strong
I know they can do nothing wrong.

In autumn to see the leaves falling with glee
The trees lay their fruitful boughs for me.

In winter to see them cold and bare
All of this with God I share
All of this is on a little hill
I see it from a nature made windowsill
For God made this nice little forest
and it will always act its best.

The Tulip

1.

Do you know the crib of the fairy?
Well, the pretty dancing Tulip has said
That a mother fairy tucks her child
And rocks her child in this flowery bed.

2.

In southern Europe and Asia Minor
They were first found growing wild.
You know, tulips are grown in Holland
And loved by every Holland child.

3.

In Holland they are grown everywhere,
Don't you pick even a single one
For you'll make some Hollander angry
For in Holland they're loved by everyone.

4.

I will always love these flowers
They are the prettiest ever seen.
They are always rainbow colored—
Red, White, Violet, Black and Bluegreen.

5.

Do you know from what they are grown?
From a bulb, and not a seed,
If you want some good cheer
Then a Tulip you will need.

The Ruby-Throated Hummingbird

A ruby-throated hummingbird
    Was sipping honey from a flower
When suddenly its tiny ears heard
    "Why don't thou sip from yonder bower?"

The words came from a lilac bush
    With delicate flowers, gay and bright,
A breeze came and gave the tree a push
    And dew-drops fell, making a pretty sight.

The hummingbird sipped the honey
    And thanked the tree with its ruby-throat,
Then the hummingbird flew away with glee,
    That's the best drink he'd had, he quote.

My Kitten

My kitten's coat is black and white,
  He doesn't cry, scratch, or bite.
It sometimes acts like a little clown,
  And sometimes so sad it'll even frown.

It has the funniest habits you've ever seen
  And washed up so much, it's immaculately clean.
I think that it has the nicest fur that's ever come to town,
  And I sometimes really think it's imported eider down.

It has the strangest manner that's ever come on earth
  And it's always had that manner since its birth.
By the fireplace that's nesting in the hall
  It even cuddles up so much, I really think, "Is that a ball?"

Sometimes in the breakfast hour, it licks my mother's tea
  And after breakfast it washes up and then it [tries] to wash up me.
It has the nicest name of all the little kittens,
  I thought this name was cute, so I named it Mittens.

Autumn in New England

It's autumn in New England,
 The fields are bare and brown;
The golden cornstalks proudly stand
 And the leaves are coming down;
I see the husker's helping hand,
 And Autumn's golden crown.

Change

Leaves that crumble blow away,
　　Leaves that grumble* still don't stay.

Then the snow comes tumbling down,
　　Cold winds blow around the town.

Then it's winter gay and free,
　　Now a crystal laughs with glee.

*grumble—waste of time

Winter Fun

The leathern straps are tightened,
    The rusting blades are oiled,
The fishes are surely frightened,
    And the children's clothes are soiled.

The ice is braced for braced for vibrations
    Of the skaters, both young and old;
And the one who sees if the ice is strong
    Is a one so brave and bold.

The hill is covered with children,
    Who with their sleds flash by,
They go so far away
    They seem to touch the sky.

But, Alas! Alas! the sun is going down,
    The children can no longer skate;
For they're wanted now at home for supper
    And besides, it's getting late.

Anniversary

We have tried our best to please you,
 We hope you think so, too;
We hope our paper has cheered you,
 When you were feeling blue.

We have worked until midnight
 And sometimes till it was two;
We have worked with all our lasting might,
 To print this paper for you.

We have passed out paper in weather
 That was biting cold;
We have gathered our information together,—
 It was of you the information told.

So now we thank you, our buyers,
 Who have bought what we have sold;
And remember, those who publish this paper,
 Are only thirteen years old.

Note: This was the anniversary poem for the anniversary issue of February 10, 1947.

It's Spring

The pussy willow is in season,
    And the birds have begun to sing.
What's the cause and what's the reason?
    Because Winter's ended and it's Spring.

Have you heard the showers pelting?
    The budding tree is like a king.
And have you seen the snows a-melting?
    Because Winter's gone and here is Spring.

Have you smelled the fragrant jonquil?
    Have you seen the green grass showing?
Have you seen the brooklets swell?
    Because Winter's disappeared and now it's spring.

Now it has come, the bloss'ming season,
    And the holy church bells ring.
What's the cause and what's the reason?
    Because now it's glorious Spring.

About the Poet

Poet, performing artist, critic, and literary historian, Donald Sidney-Fryer is the last in the great line of California Romantics that reaches from Ambrose Bierce to George Sterling, from Sterling to his protégé Clark Ashton Smith, and from Smith to his disciple Sidney-Fryer.

Carrying on the tradition of "pure poetry" begun in early modern English by Edmund Spenser and revivified by the English and American Romantic poets (Samuel Coleridge, William Wordsworth, John Keats, Percy Bysshe Shelley, Alfred, Lord Tennyson, and Edgar Allan Poe), long after the mainstream poetic establishment had abandoned it, the California Romantics created two monuments in verse, Sterling with *A Wine of Wizardry* and Smith with *The Hashish-Eater.*

During his long career Sidney-Fryer has given dramatic readings from these poets and from Edmund Spenser's epic *The Faerie Queene,* across the U.S. and Great Britain. He has written and edited nearly three dozen books and booklets. He has edited four books by Smith for Arkham House, and three pa1perbacks, also by Smith, for Pocket Books, in addition to *A Vision of Doom,* 50 of the best poems by Ambrose Bierce, published by Donald M. Grant, who has also brought out Sidney-Fryer's *Emperor of Dreams: A Clark Ashton Smith Bibliography.*

From 1980 to 2000 Sidney-Fryer assembled *The Case of the Light Fantastic Toe* (published in summer of 2018), his historical monograph on the Romantic ballet. As a poet Sidney-Fryer has crafted *Songs and Sonnets Atlantean* (the first series), the final book to appear from Arkham House under the personal supervision of its founder August Derleth; as well as the Second Series, published by Wildside Press; and the Third Series, brought out by Phosphor Lantern Press; all these are subsumed into an omnibus edition.

Moreover, Sidney-Fryer has accomplished his chief prosodic innovation, the creation of the Spenserian stanza-sonnet, long before the recent and welcome emergence of the group of poets known as the New Formalists, who have restored a much needed and long overdue balance to the ongoing evolution of American poetry and poetics.

Although he resided in California during 1955–2017, the self-styled Last of the Courtly Poets presently lives in East Sandwich, Massachusetts.

CPSIA information can be obtained
at www.ICGtesting.com
Printed in the USA
BVHW040936080621
609001BV00013B/188

9 781614 983385